Our
Legacy
of
Faith

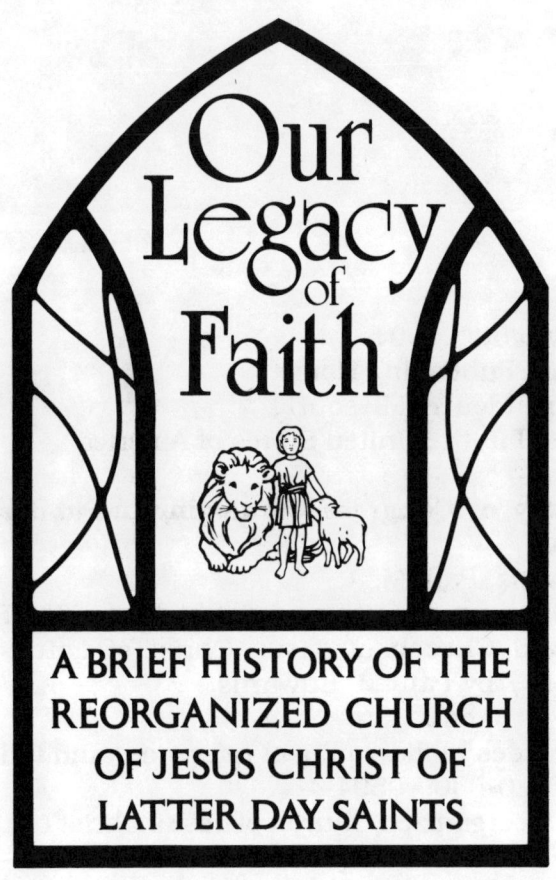

Our Legacy of Faith

A BRIEF HISTORY OF THE REORGANIZED CHURCH OF JESUS CHRIST OF LATTER DAY SAINTS

Paul M. Edwards

Library of Congress Cataloging-in-Publication Data

Edwards, Paul M.

  Our legacy of faith : a brief history of the Reorganized Church of Jesus Christ of Latter Day Saints / by Paul M. Edwards.

      p.   cm.

  Includes bibliographical references and index.

  ISBN 0-8309-0594-4

  1. Reorganized Church of Jesus Christ of Latter Day Saints—History. 2. Mormon Church—History. I. Title.

BX8673.E38   1991

289.3'33—dc20   91-21263
                                                        CIP

95 94 93 92 91   1 2 3 4 5

Table of Contents

Dedicated to Lyman F. Edwards,
older brother and significant friend.

Preface

This short, narrative history of the Reorganized Church of Jesus Christ of Latter Day Saints could not have been written ten years ago. To write a general survey of this kind—a work which must necessarily skim through the activities of many years and include a wide variety of events and experiences—the author depends on hundreds of talks, articles, monographs, biographies, essays, memoirs, and books written by others. The generalist must have available for consultation hundreds of in-depth investigations produced by others from which to draw facts and interpretations. Obviously, if I had found it necessary to do primary research on the many issues dealt with in this historical survey, the job would have taken dozens of years.

Fortunately, since the early 1960s, many scholars of Mormonism have been involved in serious research. They have researched, analyzed, provided interpretations, and made their work available for the use and enlightenment of others. In addition, the expanding interest in history has been responsible for the opening of archives. Many isolated and scattered documents have been located and preserved. Cooperation has developed between scholars of differing convictions, and new areas of understanding have been opened for investigation.

During this period, an unanticipated mass of factual information has been accumulated, and by way of the historical process (presentation, debate, correction), significant new insights have emerged. All were necessary to produce this institutional history.

Many persons have been involved in developing this body of information. In addition to historians (professional and amateur), I would need to acknowledge collectors, librarians, archivists, and even dealers. In a more specific sense, and closer to home, many professional historians and antiquarians in the Reorganization have been a part of this growth.

Just why this happened at this time is hard to define. But it is related to the increasing interest in the cultural side of American history and to the fact that more church members have moved into the field of history as professionals. It was only a matter of time until their general interest in history became more specifically directed toward the history of the movement.

Associated with this new historical interest is a desire to be more objective and to see history more holistically than before; to meet the questions and issues of the past head on; and to do so with faith, but also with integrity. Such persons are aware of the subjective nature of historical interpretation; they acknowledge the influence of background, as well as the prejudices of the author, and seek to pursue their look at a common past with as much objectivity as possible.[1]

Reflecting a drift away from polemics and toward narrative history, this emerging interest is best represented by those currently studying, teaching, and writing.[2] I must acknowledge RLDS Church historian Richard P. Howard whose books, columns, monographs, and reviews have provided vast new resources for the generalists. I owe a particular debt to Dick.

Also among those making important contributions are Professor Alma R. Blair of Graceland College whose insights emerge from a lifetime of study and teaching; Professor Robert Bruce Flanders who set the direction

8

and defined the standards; F. Henry Edwards for his painstaking continuation of factual identification in the "official" histories; Professor Jan Shipps, a Methodist and insightful scholar, who has given us such a good look at ourselves; William D. Russell and C. Robert Mesle of Graceland, careful researchers and splendid critics; Roger D. Launius, one of the more prolific and able of the new breed; W. B. "Pat" Spillman, a colleague who dared to investigate foreign missionary activities. And to Clare D. Vlahos, F. Mark McKiernan, Ronald E. Romig, Wayne A. Ham, Geoffrey F. Spencer, Leonard J. Arrington, Thomas Alexander, A. Bruce Lindgren, Norma Derry Hiles, W. Grant McMurray, James Lancaster, Linda King Newell, L. Madelon Brunson, Richard D. Poll, Steven L. Shields, Valeen Tippets Avery, John H. Siebert, Davis Bitton, Lester E. Bush, Inez Smith Davis, Pearl Wilcox, and Thomas J. Morain just to name some of those who have most influenced this work.

A large majority of their material, however, deals with the pre-assassination church. LDS historians obviously look beyond that date for the development of their own movement, as the RLDS do of the Reorganization. But in both cases the post-assassination period has been less carefully considered. And, as can be expected, the lack of materials becomes more and more obvious the closer our research approaches the present time. Lack of materials about the twentieth century is improving but is still a major concern.

For the reader who wishes to locate more complete accounts of a given period, who seeks a fuller (perhaps better) explanation of events, or some wider or varied interpretations, there are many excellent resources available. This is also true for those interested in further information about theological points of view, doctrinal concepts, customs, church courts, missionary activities, church administration, or biographical materials on church leaders. At the close of each chapter I have included several sources I feel are especially helpful in that subject area. The bibliography contains a somewhat expanded list of materials that could be of great help to those seeking further study.

My indebtedness to all those who have studied and written about the Reorganization is obvious. But special thanks must go to Richard P. Howard, Isleta "Lee" Pement, W. B. "Pat" Spillman, Alma R. Blair, Roger D. Launius, Ruth Ann Wood, Ronald E. Romig, John H. Siebert, Patricia J. Struble, and A. Bruce Lindgren. And to Beverly Spring and the many members of the Temple School Division staff who have been so helpful, I extend my thanks.

The task of writing has been difficult—not simply because of the press of other responsibilities or because of the lack or overabundance of materials. But rather because of the difficulty resident in trying to decide what to include and what to leave out. How can such a complex people be simply presented? How can the vast changes of doctrine and behavior be simplified? Is it possible to represent the traditions as well as expanding historical insights, and to be just to both?

This narrative is designed to make available a short one-volume history of the RLDS Church for the benefit of members and friends who want to know something about us. It is not, nor was it meant to be, a detailed history. It is my hope that the story—interesting, complex, controversial, and now more than 150 years in length—will help us understand something of the power and energy that has motivated the Saints. And that it can be felt without betraying the cautious insights of our own generation.

Paul M. Edwards

Notes

1. See Paul M. Edwards, "The New Mormon History," *Saints Herald* vol. 133, no. 11 (November 1986): 12.
2. For an example of the vast growth in church history, check Roger D. Launius, "The Reorganized Church in the Nineteenth Century: A Bibliographical Review," in Marjorie B. Troeh and Eileen M. Terril, eds., *Restoration Studies IV* (Independence, Missouri: Herald Publishing House, 1988): 171-187; Roger D. Launius, "A New Historiographical Frontier: The Reorganized Church in the Twentieth Century," *John Whitmer Historical Association Journal* 6 (1986): 53-63; Roger D. Launius, "Whither Reorganization Historiography?" *John Whitmer Historical Association Journal* 10 (1990): 24-37.

Introduction

The Reorganized Church of Jesus Christ of Latter Day
Saints has an interesting history. Organized April 6,
1830, the church has grown from six dedicated persons
to a worldwide membership of nearly a quarter-of-a-mil-
lion. The Mormon movement—that larger body of persons
who trace their origins to Joseph Smith, Jr., and that
April day in 1830—number several hundred organizations with a membership in the millions. For those
associated with these movements, the reawakening of
this religious tradition has been called the "Restoration."

The first-generation member of the Restoration was
primarily American and mainly a product of the nineteenth-century search for freedom and meaning. Long
exposed to the Utopian ideal and the promise of a land
of opportunity, the families of these persons risked
everything seeking a more opportune community in the
New World.

Joseph's followers were children and grandchildren
of the revolutionary war generation. As such they had
a passion about freedom and individual rights. These
rights were expressed not only in the unifying principles
of the U.S. Constitution but also in the earlier, and more
radically individualistic, Declaration of Independence.

A series of revolutions fought in America as well as in
Europe left this new nation struggling to identify itself,
its roots, and even its own concept of authority. Anxious
to stand together as a nation of free persons, America
was, nevertheless, immediately involved in maintaining
the difficult balance between freedom and social responsibility.

This generation reflected the early stages of westward expansion, having moved in search of either personal or economic freedom. European characteristics of the tidewater frontier had given way to the rugged individualism of the Ohio Valley as civilization was slowly creeping toward the Mississippi and beyond. These men and women were advocates of the American concepts of destiny, believing this vast westward expansion was God's gift—a cleansed garden—held for so long for a special people. And every event in their lives seemed to reinforce that they were this special people.

Mormonism has always seen the history of America as both preparatory and complementary to their own history. Preparatory in the sense that such a place of openness and religious freedom was necessary for the Restoration to spring forth. And complementary because the path of American growth was the path of their own expansion. They saw themselves as reflectors of the strong social and intellectual currents of the nation and the times.

These early Americans were practical folk who learned most of their necessary knowledge from experience. What book learning they had was learned at their mother's knee using the King James Bible as their reader. They were a practical bunch, wanting their lives filled with activities and beliefs finalized in action. They were building a country, but they were also building a place for themselves.

Like many Americans, the first-generation Restorationists were greatly influenced by their Puritan religious backgrounds. They were at home with the idea of God's providence. But they were, as well, hardheaded frontiersmen and women who were aware of the extent of wickedness in which humans are involved. They were aware of the potential of human sin and the destruction of the world. They demanded that their religion—and whatever theology that encompassed—be an intelligible one. But they also preferred an emotional, even romantic experience.

The story of the Restoration movement is a fascinating one, made even more so by the dedication of those for whom the movement was both a way of life and a promise for the future. Members of the community love to tell this story, often embellishing it with the experiences of the teller. It is a story that has served also as a theology, a story in which tradition's unrelenting voice often speaks more firmly than either memory or scholarship justifies. But it is a story essential to the message.

Americans are a myth-hungry people. Most countries became nations as a result of a long heritage—a mystic past of nations and peoples that came before and who left vast legends upon which they could build. Having deliberately separated themselves from their mother country and considering the Indians as enemies rather than ancestors, Americans have used their history as a substitute for legends, as well as a substitute for political theory. Mormonism is very American in this respect. For our history has provided both our legends and our folk heroes and has served as our explanations for being.

It would be helpful for us to admit to what Carl L. Becker has affirmed, that there are two histories: "the actual series of events that once occurred, and the ideal series we affirm and hold in memory."[1] Thus, when we define history as "the memory of what was said and done," we reduce it to its simplest terms. But we also encompass both histories. The historian's role is often seen as emphasizing the "events that occurred" while

15

discouraging the idealized memories. But, as we can see, what the historian most often does is to identify which memories they will grace with the distinctive title of "fact."

Communities and institutions create memories just as individuals do. And, as with individuals, the past they encompass serves to identify, and on occasion to justify, the present. The present—today—is that moment in time which connects what has been our past with what is the beginning of our future. And, as with persons, it is often helpful for the institution to pause, to reconstitute that memory, to acknowledge the joys and the sorrows (the significant as well as the insignificant), and to reaffirm its aspirations in the light of the memory of what has previously transpired.

I do not have the space—nor perhaps is this the appropriate place—to discuss historical method. Nor is there time to identify the historian's tools for the evaluation of documentation. But both are necessary subjects of consideration for anyone wishing to take history seriously.

The historian's function, along with the priests, bards, and storytellers of previous generations, is to "preserve and perpetuate the social tradition; to harmonize, as well as ignorance and prejudice permits, the actual and remembered series of events; to enlarge and enrich the specious present common to us all to the end that 'society' (the tribe, the nation, or all mankind) may judge what it is doing in the light of what it has done and what it hopes to do."[2]

From the beginning the church has considered it essential to preserve its history. As early as March 1831, while in Kirtland, Ohio, Joseph Smith, Jr., directed John Whitmer to keep a historical record of the movement.[3] Whitmer was baptized in June 1829 and was one of the men listed in the front of the Book of Mormon as a witness. He was the "presiding elder" of the Kirtland congregation, an active missionary, and sometimes secretary to Joseph Smith. He took this responsibility seriously and began his work at once.

> I shall proceed to continue this record, being commanded of the Lord and Savior Jesus Christ, to write the things that transpired in the Church (inasmuch as they come to my knowledge,) in these last days.[4]

One of the first public histories acknowledged the complexity of writing about this "new history," and it described Joseph Smith as "a great imposter, or a great visionary—perhaps both—but in either case one of the most remarkable persons who has appeared on the stage of the world in modern times."[5]

The Reorganization as it first began to gather its people in 1853 felt the need to record its history and chose Jason Briggs, president of the Quorum of Twelve, as church historian. He was never able, however, to publish a history of the movement. When he withdrew, he turned over his material to Heman C. Smith, but most of it was destroyed in the Herald House fire of 1907.

Though our history has always been a significant part of our message, it is not told and retold now as once it was. Therefore, many within the organization discover that they are unaware of anything but the most dramatic highlights. Having grown up with the church, they have a vague knowledge of it but often need more factual information on which to hang the garments of their understandings. Others, outside the community, with whom we work and associate are even less informed but are often interested in having available a short and uncomplicated account.

Thus it seemed important to have a small, compact volume available to those who want a quick, simple reference. The historian within me cries out for more: more pages upon which to develop a better account, more room for longer and more complicated explanations, and more supporting footnotes and dissenting opinions. I am tempted to expound upon information and to provide more subtle interpretations both of our history and about the nature of history itself.

But I understand the merit in having a short history available. Thus I have tried to provide a narrative that tells the story as openly and honestly as possible. At the same time, however, it must not destroy the depth of passion, the sincere commitment, or the sense of mission which is, and has been, so obviously a major part of the story.[6]

Notes

1. Carl L. Becker, "What Is Evidence?" in Robin W. Winks, ed., *The Historian as Detective: Essays on Evidence* (New York: Harper Colophon Books, 1970), 6.
2. Ibid., 17.
3. Doctrine and Covenants 47.
4. John Whitmer, "The Book of John Whitmer Kept by Commandment," published in F. Mark McKiernan and Roger D. Launius, eds., *An Early Latter Day Saint History* (Independence, Missouri: Herald Publishing House, 1980), 25.
5. Charles MacKay, *The Mormons* or *Latter-day Saints* (London: Office of the National Illustrated Library, 1851), 1.
6. For a critical examination of the structures and techniques of writing history, check Savoie Lottinville, *The Rhetoric of History* (Norman, Oklahoma: University of Oklahoma Press, 1976); Marc Ferro, *The Use and Abuse of History* (London: Routledge and Kegan Paul, 1984); Carl G. Gustavson, *The Mansion of History* (New York: McGraw-Hill Company, 1976).

The Scene

As the United States of America celebrated the beginning of the nineteenth century, it was still a young and primitive nation. When the Pilgrims boarded their ships in Plymouth, England, to sail to the New World, they sailed not only into a new space but into a new time as well. They arrived not only on the shores of a brand-new land but also entered an era that was foreign to them, into a time much earlier than they left behind. It is easy to forget that London had gaslights when Manhattan Island was being purchased from the Indians, that Cambridge and St. Andrews universities were celebrating several hundred years of operation as Harvard and Yale were being built.

True, much knowledge and many improvements of the Old World crossed the seas with the settlers, as did many evils of that time and place. They migrated from Europe for religious, economic, and political reasons—leaving a good deal behind as well as expecting a great deal on arrival—trusting that what they found would be better than what they left. And to a surprising degree they found in America a place to begin again. In these terms the citizens of 1800 were primarily children in a world of nations. They had all the advantages and disadvantages of being children: innocence, purity, and unlimited potential. But they were also primitive, naïve, suspicious, and easily duped. It was a time of magic, of metaphysical scares, of buried treasures and awesome places, of extremes of pride and of prejudices; just as it was a time of freedom, newness, dreams and visions, and a place where all those things could well come true.

It would be safe to say that frontier Americans were drunk on their freedoms. Drunk in the sense that the idea of freedom intoxicated their minds, often causing them to see things from a less than realistic perspective. But the reality of unlimited freedom soon began to diminish in the affirmation of America's own imperialism. Manifest Destiny, they called it after a while, had a dark side. This new nation was involved in a series of wars to establish their own freedom from European control, while at the same time they fought the Indians and their neighbor to the north for control of the New World. Certainly the War of 1812 managed to fit into both concerns: fighting what was in effect a "second American revolution" while pushing against neighbors on both the northern and western borders.

This sense of destiny was matched by an increasing disillusionment with the wilderness myth. True, the New World waited for the emigrating European, but it was not as open or free of mystical images as the immigrant wished. The evils of men, like the evils of government, followed them. The dark wilderness they faced was not just opportunity but the home of evil powers, the extremes of human failures, which most immigrants thought they had left behind in the dark forests of Europe.

Expansion was rampant: seen in the maze of invention, in the vast building schemes, and in the unprecedented growth in transportation. It was a time when faith in the future of America exceeded even its vast potential to succeed. Accompanying growth was the disruptive influence of growing pains, of major political, economic, and social upheaval. Slavery, riding to the New World on the back of world trade, was already splitting the nation into armed camps. Missouri, so essential to the growth of the Reorganization, was born in 1820 by a compromise that allowed it to enter the Union as a slave state in return for allowing Maine to enter as a free state.

Early discussions about Mormonism suggested that those who followed Joseph Smith were primarily from New England, that they were more a link with the Puritan past than they were representative of the frontier mind of the new American nation. There is, of course, some truth in this view. But it has become clearer in recent years that the Saints tended to hold generalized views and attitudes more in keeping with the character of nineteenth-century America than with the eighteenth.

This has become clear for two reasons. One is that the images of New England and Puritanism are not as well defined as we might once have believed. A second reason is that the line distinguishing the American frontier from the more solid societies of the eastern seaboard was not nearly as clear as we at first understood.

As with so many things, the answer probably lies somewhere in the midst of these conflicting points of view. In consideration of the meaning of a personal God, in communitarianism, in their view of providential history when concerning last things, most of the Saints came from backgrounds and out of belief systems that were not unlike those of the typical American in the New York or Ohio frontier.

This is true as well when we consider the pessimism long associated with the new Mormon converts' belief in apocalypticism—that is, believing the world was in such a decaying state that only total destruction could save it. We now understand that the optimism of nineteenth-century Americans, living in those places where Mormonism grew, was primarily an optimism about personal accomplishment but that they also harbored fears akin to apocalypticism.

A general realignment of values was occurring: a shift from the Puritan society in which religion dominated social values to the emerging American hierarchy in which society determined the value of religion. In such an age, Mormonism was strangely liberal and clashed with the laissez-faire Jacksonianism of the time.[1]

When we look to what has been called the "origins" of Mormonism—meaning by that the environment in which Joseph's concept took root and shaped the movement—we find that Mormonism rested easily in the nineteenth-century environment. Certainly the beliefs and practices of those persons who called themselves Mormons were different enough to cause fear and envy among their neighbors. But we do not need to add to the burden of understanding by suggesting they represented a historic backlash toward the thinking of the seventeenth century.[2]

The levels of mysticism and magic encountered in American society in the early part of the nineteenth century would seem primitive to us now. We tend to forget the degree to which our sophistication about such things is the result of years of study and an unimaginable expansion of knowledge. The world was still scary for the persons facing the 1820s, a world without much explanation. It was a world that required abstractions—about life and death and the behavior of natural events—in which to place the unexplained events that constantly affected their lives. It was a time when folk religion, with its emphasis on magic and mystical symbols, supported beliefs in supernatural causation to explain those daily events of life that appeared unexplainable. A time when people, things, and rituals all had special powers for both good and bad.

For a pragmatic people desperately in need of answers, the almost total lack of answers in many arenas made it necessary to turn to the supernatural. Old wives' tales, myths, home remedies, herbs, the occult, incantations, and a tendency to personalize inanimate objects all seem quaint to us now. But this was a period in history when the people's language reflected their society and practices and their beliefs in terms of the magical nature of life. These were the means by which people dealt with the difficult, the unexplained, the unbearable, even the intolerable.

This was also a time in which Utopian community building was a vast experiment. The goal was a society where justice and equality were practiced in a manner reflective of religious convictions. Often called communitarian, these experiments were well known and attracted a great deal of interest. Among these were the Oneida community, which held all property in common and practiced a complex marriage system that was often interpreted by nonbelievers as free love; Silkville, the Kansas community where economic equality was to be enhanced by the introduction of Japanese silkworms; the Harmonists, based on vows of celibacy; the Owens Community, perhaps best known, based on control of machinery and the common raising of children; and the Amana Society, a community of common property led by contemporary revelation. What they had in common was their concern for the negative effects of private property, elitism, and any movement that took persons too far from the land which God had given them.

This was also a period of intense democratic feelings. After all, Joseph's mother, Lucy Mack, was born in the same year the American Revolution began in earnest. Andrew Jackson was president when the church was formally organized. Jackson was the epitome of the American myth; a gentleman, a moralist, and an individualist of almost fanatic character. Jacksonian democracy, which followed closely on the heels of the War of 1812 and which was most obviously reflected in the frontier regions where young Joseph grew up, was the governmental philosophy of the citizens of their area.

America was on the move. Having broken through the fabled wilderness and beyond the tidewater, the pioneer spirit was legalized in a whole collection of land acts. In 1830 the Preemption Act allowed anyone who had cultivated public land to buy an additional 160 acres at $1.25 an acre. The population of the United States was not only moving west, it was growing. In 1830 about 13 million people, nine-tenths of whom earned their livelihood from farms, lived in the United States. The population in Ohio, a center for church growth, rose from some 73,000 in 1790 to almost a million in 1830. The nation was expanding internally, expanding its external borders, and intensifying within those borders. Indeed, as Alexis de Tocqueville was to write in his French account, "America was a land where the only consistent thing was change."

The American people were active in religion, and the area in which Joseph resided was one of the most active. Religion, in keeping with residual Calvinistic beliefs in hard work and serious thought, was nearly entertainment. Perry Miller, intellectual historian, identifies the 1820s in New York as a period of revivals of the rankest luxuriance. There was, generally speaking, a reaction against the formal aspects of religion, as well as of science and society and the beginnings of transcendentalism, a belief which taught that human knowledge is not limited either by experience or observation.

In New York one religious revival seemed to follow another, so much so that the area was called the "burned-over district." As the settlers moved through the woods to settle in this new and promising area, they came seeking religious expression and found it in the land they occupied. Certainly aware of—and impressed by—the Indian mounds, they told imaginative stories of early inhabitants and based their prejudices on unsubstantiated events and movement. They were strongly antislavery and as strongly anti-Mason. They were almost hysterical in their belief in the imminent Second Coming of Christ and in the presence of the Holy Spirit in the land and in the events of their lives.

What many churches sought, and what Joseph, Sr., meant by primitive religion, was a restoration of the organization and the theological purity of the early church. They were called Restitutionists. They favored any action that evidenced the first century and were drawn to form Christian communities, often economic in character, of the type Sidney Rigdon was involved in when he encountered the Book of Mormon.

Certainly a point can be made that Joseph's presentations flourished in the mid-frontier period of American history because of an environment friendly to such ideas: an environment of millennialism, restitutionism, denominationalization, and democracy. W. B. "Pat" Spillman makes the point "that the most influential American trait to affect the new church was the very idea that it was possible to create a new church."[3] If one disagreed with the existing church, it was not only possible in the American dream to start one's own, but necessary.[4]

This was the time and the mood in which the Smith family lived. Their ancestors had been migrants, land breakers, citizens of emerging communities, some persons of distinction and power. Father Joseph (1771-1840) was born in Topsfield, Massachusetts, the third child of Asael Smith (1744-1830) and Mary Duty Smith (1743-1836). Joseph, Sr., had ten siblings. The parents lived primarily in Massachusetts, New Hampshire, and Vermont where Asael worked as a barrel maker and part-time farmer. The parents were deeply religious and believed in divine guidance. It was in Vermont that the family fortune began to build and where, in Topsfield, Asael served in elected offices.

Joseph's mother, Lucy Mack (1775-1856), was born in Gilsum, New Hampshire, the youngest of a family of eight, to Solomon Mack (1732-1820) and Lydia Gates Mack (1732-1818). The Mack family was generally known for their nonconformity of thought.

Both Joseph and Lucy were religious people and responded, however differently, to the religious revival where they lived. Joseph, Sr., was a farmer and shopkeeper who, driven by economic disaster, moved his family to Palmyra, New York, in search of new hopes. Working as a hired man, along with his sons, he soon invested in a small farm of a hundred acres or so. The Smiths seemed to have been Universalists, then later Methodists; in every case it was Lucy who was more interested in formal religion than Joseph.

Lucy, along with her daughter Sophronia and son Hyrum, joined the Presbyterian church while Joseph, Sr., and Joseph, Jr., continued to reject the available churches, seeking instead evidence of a more justifiable movement that served their concepts of a primitive church.

Joseph Smith, Jr. (1805-1844), was born on December 23, 1805, in Sharon, Windsor County, Vermont, as the third son and fourth of ten children (one had died at birth). Alvin (1799-1824), Hyrum (1800-1844), and Sophronia (1803-1876) were the older; and Samuel (1808-1844), Ephraim who died as an infant (1810), Katherine who sometimes appears as Catharine (1813-1900), William (1811-1893), Don Carlos (1816-1841), and Lucy (1821-1882) were younger.

We really know very little about Joseph's childhood. What is known seems typical of the times and place. He seems to have been taught primarily by his parents. The entire family was uneducated, some barely literate. Hyrum and Joseph both had limited schooling when in Palmyra, and Joseph probably had some additional education at Bainbridge in 1826. He read easily, belonged to a young man's debating society in Palmyra, and could write though his writing tended to be choppy. His arithmetic skills were quite limited.

He and his family would not have been below average in this regard. Among the poorer people of that time, education was a luxury, and lucky were those who had more than just the barest necessity. Nor should the Smith family be considered either stupid or ignorant—certainly not stupid—and they were more uninformed than ignorant about things of the larger world. There is a tendency to speculate about their early times and, over the years, stories written about this formative period have gained more credibility than they deserve. We are aware Joseph contracted typhus shortly before Katherine's birth, and in time this required some rather significant surgery on his leg. The crudeness of medical treatment meant he undoubtedly suffered a great deal, and we know he walked with a limp for the rest of his life.

There are few descriptions of Joseph, most without benefit of a date, so we are not really sure at what time the description fits. We know he was tall, some reported as much as six-feet, two-inches, and of light complexion. His hair was chestnut, eyes blue, and he was sturdy. His facial hair, when he began one of his beards, was dark, almost black during his middle life. Those who knew him often remarked on his eyes, which seemed to exhibit intelligence and the humor and curiosity that were his characteristics. While most persons described him somewhat differently, they all agreed on his charisma. He was athletic and often bold and impulsive.

He was a complex man about which it was hard to be neutral; he was, in many respects, a private person who found leadership difficult because of its public demands and forced isolation. This isolation is embodied in expressions that have always been identified with Joseph: "No man knows my history," "you never knew my heart." Leadership certainly is, and can be, lonely, but Joseph's melancholy seemed to go beyond that.

30

Perhaps it was because he carried the burden of experiences which he was never really able to communicate as he wanted.

Like all of us, Joseph was a product of his age and environment. He was a child of his times and reflected the moods, desires, beliefs, and methods of his generation. Western New York, like so much of what had been called the "burned-over district," was a hotbed of religious concerns, and it would have been unthinkable to suggest the environment did not have an effect on Joseph as he grew and formulated his beliefs.

During Joseph's early life the family suffered a series of financial reverses and moved often in search of work or more profitable farming areas. The family moved from Lebanon to Norwich, Vermont, then on to the Palmyra/Manchester area in western New York. Here the family found better conditions and set down roots. Here their young son Joseph would have an experience that would alter the religious beliefs of millions.[5]

Notes

1. Klaus J. Hansen, "Mormonism and American Culture: Some Tentative Hypotheses," in F. Mark McKiernan, Alma R. Blair, and Paul M. Edwards, eds., *The Restoration Movement: Essays in Mormon History* (Lawrence, Kansas: Coronado Press, 1973), 1-25.

2. Based on Grant Underwood, "The New England Origins of Mormonism Revisited," *Journal of Mormon History* 15 (1989): 15-23.

3. W. B. "Pat" Spillman, *Studies in Restoration History: The Hastening Time, Volume 1* (Independence, Missouri: Herald Publishing House, 1987), 15.

4. Gregory Smith, "America at 1830," *Saints Herald* vol. 133, no. 9 (September 1986): 17-19.

5. For further reading: Richard L. Anderson, *Joseph Smith's New England Heritage* (Salt Lake City, Utah: Deseret Book Company, 1971); Whitney R. Cross, *The Burned-Over District* (New York: Harper & Row Publishers, 1950); Thomas F. O'Dea, *The Mormons* (Chicago: University of Chicago Press, 1957); Dan Vogel, *Religious Seekers and the Advent of Mormonism* (Salt Lake City, Utah: Signature Books, 1988); Kenneth H. Winn, *Exiles in a Land of Liberty: Mormons in America, 1830-1846* (Chapel Hill: University of North Carolina Press, 1989).

The Beginnings of the Restoration

On a bright day in 1820 Joseph Smith sought out a secluded grove not far from his home and knelt to pray. He found the intense religious environment in which he lived to be confusing. He was genuinely concerned about his religious condition and sought guidance, making a prayerful inquiry about the truths of religious claims. So begins the story of the Reorganized Church of Jesus Christ of Latter Day Saints.

From this and other unique and compelling experiences, which Joseph Smith, Jr., recorded as occurring between 1820 and 1829, the Restoration emerged. the experiences culminated in the publication of the Book of Mormon and in the formal organization of the Church of Jesus Christ in 1830. The first of these events, simply called the First Vision, has played a significant role in the church, for it represents both the beginning of the Restoration and defines the character of the church itself.

While the young man naturally discussed the experience with family members and with those persons close to him he felt would understand, he did not publish a report of the experience for nearly two decades. It wasn't until November 1832 that Joseph Smith was to describe the First Vision experience. Later, in 1835, he provided a short version to a "Jewish minister" identified as Joshua, as recorded by Warren Cowdery. A First Vision account was dictated by Joseph in 1838 and recorded by James Mullholland for the *History of the Church*. In 1841 Joseph made available the most considered account in a letter to John Wentworth, which was published in the *Times and Seasons*.[1]

Joseph's record tells of envisioning a sudden darkness which covered him. From it a pillar of light emerged that allowed him to see two personages bathed in a great light (his 1831-1832 account mentioned only one personage, identified as Jesus). They spoke to him concerning his confusion and his desire to do the will of God. Joseph emerged assured that the churches he had investigated were unable to provide what he was seeking and with the promise that, in time, he would be made aware of the "fullness of the gospel."[2]

In the many renditions of the First Vision one can read a growing maturity and evolution of thought as Joseph tries to place these events in perspective; a perspective which had grown and was reflected in the language Joseph used. The first account reflects Joseph as the young seeker: spiritual and inquisitive, deeply concerned with his own spirituality and his personal need for repentance. Couched in the exhaustive prose so consistent to the expression of spiritual experience in his time, it reflected his response to the experience.

By 1835 his account suggests a more reflective manner, missing some elaborate prose of the first recording, and more aware of the experience's impact on the larger concerns of religious systems and the more universal sins of humankind. Both the James Mulholland and John Wentworth accounts appear as the considerations of a unique religious leader, more restrained in language, more straightforward in presentation, reflective of larger issues and concerns of the church. They are, after all, memories of an event which, in some cases, were nearly two decades old. Joseph certainly was aware of the public nature of both these accounts, realizing they were to be exposed to a much greater audience, thus needing to reflect the full impact of the experience on that larger community.[3]

About halfway through 1838 Joseph began to dictate an account of his memories and experiences to scribes indicating how he interpreted the events of the early years of the church. By 1842 these started to appear as installments in *Times and Seasons* published in Nauvoo, Illinois. In addition to the First Vision, Joseph described events leading up to the creation of the church.

In describing these events, Joseph recorded that on the night of 21-22 September 1823, a light illuminated the room in which he was sleeping. Into this light came a personage whose name was reported as Moroni. Then, and in three additional visits, Moroni revealed that God had selected Joseph for a responsibility. A covenant made in ancient times between God and Israel would be fulfilled, but preparations would need to be made for the Second Coming of Christ. Joseph was to translate, by means of special stones called the Urim and Thummim, an ancient record engraved on plates of gold and buried in a hill not far from the Smith farm. Joseph recounted that he was unable to retrieve the plates at that time.

The criticism of this account was harsher because Joseph, like others of his period, had attempted at times to add to the family income by assisting in the location of lost articles and buried treasure. His use of a seer stone in these efforts is a significant indication of Joseph's interest and peripheral involvement in extrarational phenomena. Joseph and his father were engaged in finding lost articles by means of a smooth, oval-shaped seer stone young Joseph found some years earlier while digging a well. On one occasion, after promising to find a lost mine and failing, a lawsuit was brought and Joseph was charged with being an impostor and disorderly person.

During this exciting period of his life, Joseph met and fell in love with Emma Hale of Harmony, Pennsylvania. Despite the understandable concern expressed by her father, Isaac Hale, they were married in January 1827 and she returned with Joseph to live with him on the family farm in Manchester. She was, from the beginning, supportive of Joseph's work and, during the ensuing years, was fully involved in the work of the church.

Joseph had located the hill described to him by Moroni as close to the village of Manchester, Ontario County, New York. But again he was instructed not to take the plates. According to his account Joseph returned each year for four years until in September 1827 he was permitted to take the plates. They were an account of Jesus among an ancient people which in its retelling would, as Joseph recounts, reveal much of the fullness of the everlasting gospel.

The process of preparing an English version of the record took considerable time. The final handwritten manuscript, which in printed form took nearly 800 pages, was ready for publication in spring 1830.

There are numerous accounts of the translation process and of the nature of revelation* suggested by the preparation of the English manuscript. The discussions reflect two points of view about revelation. On the one side is the belief that the book was an exact duplicate in English of the plates as one might think of the Ten Commandments presented to Moses on tablets of stone. On the other hand is the belief that the work was a conceptual translation of ideas contained in the plates, such as a person might do when feeling he or she had been inspired to speak. Such a disagreement lies within the context of church membership and individual beliefs, and it has affected the Saints since the beginning.

We have records that suggest early translations appear to have occurred by means of the stones provided with the plates. The use of seer stones to concentrate was consistent with the methods of divination known

---

* The term *revelation* has a special meaning when used by persons commenting on the RLDS scene. Used as the name of an event or a statement, it generally means "documents" brought before the church and approved by the body as "the mind and will of God." Thus it becomes official direction and guidance to the church. It is also used in the Restoration to mean the point at which the human and the divine meet. Often both definitions apply to the same experience. In this work I use the term primarily to identify guidance or instruction brought by the prophet-president of the church. For theological discussions of the idea of revelation in the Restoration, and in the Reorganization, see Alan D. Tyree, ed., *Exploring the Faith* (Independence, Missouri: Herald Publishing House, 1987); Richard P. Howard, *Restoration Scriptures: A Study of Their Textual Development* (Independence, Missouri: Herald Publishing House, 1969); Vernone M. Sparks, *The Theological Enterprise* (Independence, Missouri: Herald Publishing House, 1969).

through the years. The method of sensory fixation helped some concentrate their intuitive powers, avoiding distraction from the physical disruptions which might interfere.

At one point it became unsafe for Joseph to continue the translation in Manchester, and he and Emma retreated to his father-in-law's home in Harmony, Pennsylvania, in December 1827. Martin Harris joined them and from mid-April to mid-June 1828 acted as Joseph's scribe in the process. It was here that 116 manuscript pages were taken to Palmyra and lost.

The record indicates that 116 pages, copied onto foolscap by means of the interpretative stones, were loaned to the scribe Martin Harris, presumably to be used to gain support from his family. While in his charge they were mysteriously lost. Joseph reported that because of this indiscretion he lost the use of the plates and the transcribing stones, as well as the pages that were translated.

Joseph was contrite about his failure to do as he felt instructed and the resulting loss of the early pages. He was assured, however, that if he maintained his faith he would be allowed to continue the work to which he was called. The loss was a significant event for the group, for it was in response to the loss that Joseph reported he prayed for, and received, revealed instructions. Thus was developed a pattern for seeking divine direction that became the prophetic means for the new movement.

During the transcribing process the plates themselves appear not to have been immediately involved and quite often were not within Joseph's sight. On occasion another person was in the room while Joseph dictated, and once in a while he appears to have separated himself from the others in the room by means of a sheet or blanket. The reports of the process presented by Emma, who often served as scribe for her husband, give us an account not unlike that of David Whitmer and others involved. In the main it reveals that because of the loss of the translation instruments, which had been present with the Book of Mormon, much of the later work was the result of seer stones that often were placed in a hat so as to darken the environment.[4]

The evidence is that the translation was not purely mechanical, at least not the part we have today. Joseph provided his scribes with what was going on in his mind, and he did so in a flowing and consistent manner, expressing what he saw in his own words. He acknowledges this fact in his alterations for the 1830 Palmyra edition, as well as the 1837 Kirtland edition, where he purposely changed words and phrases to more adequately express what he felt he had received.

Joseph reported that the plates were returned to him in 1828, but he waited until the following April before returning to the work. During the several months between the loss of the first pages and Joseph's return to translation, he became increasingly clear about his responsibilities. The work moved rapidly after that due in part to the scribal abilities of Oliver Cowdery, a young schoolteacher who came to board with the Smiths in Manchester and who undertook the task of being Joseph's principal scribe in early April.

As an eyewitness to the process, Emma reported that Cowdery and Joseph "would at once begin where he [Joseph] had left off, without either seeing the manuscript or having any portion of it read to him."[5] She added that he often sat at a table dictating hour after hour.[6]

There can be no doubt that the supernatural appearance of these plates, even in an era in which the supernatural was considered fairly common, and then their mysterious disappearance caused wide disbelief. Efforts to offset skepticism by having an expert on ancient languages look at the characters Joseph had drawn up, and pronouncing them legitimate, did not have the desired impact. For the most part the anti-Bible or false-Bible labels continued as soon as word of the book got out.

The discussion about the translation and what that tells about the nature of revelation and of scripture became part of the growing opposition to the movement. Most of the revelations that comprise Sections 2 through 15 of the Doctrine and Covenants were reported also to have been received in connection with the translation stones.[7] But in the process of working with the translation, Joseph became comfortable with a concept of revelation that came to him as impressions on his mind rather than through any mechanical means. The seer stones were put aside, and the work Joseph felt called to do now consisted of spreading the understandings he had tried to record.

During the summer of 1829, while boarded at the home of Mary and Peter Whitmer, Sr., Joseph completed the book. Two different sets of witnesses were identified. The first three—Oliver Cowdery, Martin Harris, and David Whitmer—testified that they were shown the plates by the power of God. A second group of eight members—four members of the Whitmer family, Hiram Page, Joseph Senior, Hyrum and Samuel Smith—testified they also had seen the plates. The translation was accomplished by the end of summer. A second printer's copy was completed and was marked and corrected. It appears to be the copy, held by Oliver Cowdery, that is now in the RLDS Church archives. The dictated copy, deposited in the cornerstone of the Nauvoo House, was in bad condition when recovered and only a few pages, now held by the LDS church, were saved.

Joseph sought the services of Egbert B. Grandin who operated a small printing firm in Palmyra. Payment was assured by a mortgage on Martin Harris's home, dated August 25, 1829. Type was set in biblical fashion as a collection of books, divided into chapters but not verses, and it was released as *The Book of Mormon: An Account Written by the Hand of Mormon upon Plates Taken from the Plates of Nephi.* It listed Joseph Smith, Jr., as the author, but it was clearly identified as a "translation." The completed work was finally released on March 26, 1830.

Carried about the area by members of the Smith family, or one of the small originating group, the book was accepted both as a harmless historical novel and as what it claimed to be: a translation of an ancient record of Jesus Christ in the New World. Its truth claim was inherent within it, its acceptance assumed by those for whom it spoke as promised. Many persons would echo the sentiments of George Q. Cannon, who remarked after reading it, "no wicked man could write such a book as this; and no good man could write it unless it were true and he was commanded by God to do so."[8] For those who opposed it, nothing could be said to save it from being seen as a novel with "evil overtones."

The book became a major missionary tool. As hard as it was for some to believe it, it nevertheless appeared as an answer for many who were seeking knowledge about their own spiritual lives. The Book of Mormon is a historical narrative that tells the story of an ancient community called Jaredites after their leader, Jared. They had come to the New World following the Tower of Babel scattering. This civilization endured until about 600 B.C. when there was another migration from Jerusalem. After his resurrection, Christ visited these people, presenting them with the gospel, primarily the teachings of Jesus as reported in Matthew and Mark. But despite this, the groups broke into warring factions and finally, about the fifth century of the Christian era were destroyed. The American Indians were understood to be the descendants of some of these tribes.

To believers, the Book of Mormon was more than just a historical discourse. A significant section of the book, II Nephi, provides a description of the society into which the Book of Mormon will appear. It affirms the themes not only of the larger book but of the church which emerged. In effect, it restates the experiences of Joseph's vision: the existing religious structure was unacceptable; a book of revelations would be given to a seer to share with the world; and a man named Joseph (with a name like his father) would lead the world to salvation.

The affirmations that it makes are the very reasons why many established Protestant leaders and lay persons were upset. Here was a man establishing a church in the name of Jesus Christ, who believed that his "golden Bible" was an additional scripture, and who proclaimed the will of God. His faithful followers, on the other hand, saw Joseph's translation as additional evidence of his value in the sight of God and affirmed him as leader and as oracle for God's revelations to the latter days. As the beliefs and authority of the church became clearer, they validated the Book of Mormon and vice versa. It seems reasonable then that the Book of Mormon, and the subsequent events of Smith's life, would function together to establish the authenticity of the book. Thus Joseph linked the Hebrew-Christian understanding of the world and the lives of himself and his followers.[9]

The book not only brought together the people of nineteenth-century America and the ancient ancestors of lost Israelite tribes, it united them in their understanding of Christ's soon-to-be-expected return and the beginning of his millennial kingship. These Mormonites (Mormons), as they were known, did not just separate themselves from the larger and more established Protestant churches of the time. Rather, they emerged as an exclusive inheritor of the antiquity of the gospel, which was affirmed in modern times and which already assumed the promise of Christ's return and now attributed the return to a particular place.

In relation to the Book of Mormon, the First Vision really played a minor role in the early years of church development. There are many reasons for this, not the least of which was that the scattered members did not need to be reminded of the basics of their faith—these had held strong—but rather to reaffirm the organization that would unite and guide them. Nevertheless, the meaning of the First Vision was essential to their tradition and would be a source of understanding for them in the creation of their somewhat distinct doctrinal interpretations.[10]

* * *

Legally the Restoration began on April 6, 1830, the point at which the church was organized. This was the date that legal action was taken to bring the movement—already in existence—into the position that it could function in the community in the manner many of them wanted. First called the Church of Christ, it was renamed in 1834 as the Church of the Latter Day Saints and in 1838 as the Church of Jesus Christ of Latter Day Saints.

If the small group wanted to be involved in performing the ordinance of marriage or if they desired to own land, establish trusts, or hold copyrights as a body, then they needed to form a legal entity. It was this rather than some need of formal organization that led to the meeting at the home of Peter Whitmer, Sr., in Fayette, New York. While the meeting was well attended, only six organizing officers were identified, the minimum number required by law. The group included Oliver Cowdery; Joseph Smith, Jr.; Hyrum Smith; Samuel H. Smith; Peter Whitmer, Jr.; and David Whitmer.

The church's development as a body most probably can be traced to mid-May 1829 when Oliver Cowdery and Joseph Smith reported that they had baptized one another according to their understanding of God's will in the matter and as the result of their prayers concerning religious authenticity, repentance, and the remission of sin. Joseph later described the scene[11] by saying that after a heavenly messenger descended and laid his hands upon them, he ordained them saying, "Upon you my fellow servants, in the name of Messiah, I confer the priesthood of Aaron, which holds the keys of the ministering of angels, and the gospel of repentance, and of baptism by immersion, for the remission of sins. ..." After this they were commanded to go and baptize one another, which they did. Later Joseph and Oliver were told of their need to be ordained as elders in the Church of Jesus Christ, but that it should wait until such time as their brethren could gather and express a willingness to accept them as leaders.

In the next few months others were baptized and ordained. During this time Book of Mormon materials (some copies by Christian Whitmer) were being used to convert persons to the movement. Whitmer suggested that by the time the church was officially organized, it consisted of nearly seventy members located in three branches in Fayette, Manchester, and Colesville, New York.

Thus it was that the April meeting was called and those gathered were asked to accept Joseph and Oliver as their leaders and teachers. When consent had been given, Joseph ordained Oliver Cowdery to the office of elder in the church. Then Oliver ordained Joseph, the sacrament of Communion was shared, and the other brethren were confirmed as members.

On June 1, 1830, the members returned to the Peter Whitmer home where they held the first church conference. Here in what they referred to as the *Articles and Covenants*, the methods of administering the sacraments of Communion and baptism, as well as the essence of priesthood offices, were established. Many priesthood offices are first mentioned in the Book of Mormon, though the descriptions and authority are unclear. The new church required original baptism rather than accepting letters from other denominations. Church organization was fairly simple at this point. Further organization would wait until instructions were received and would be worked out in time. The Restoration, as Joseph described it, was a process. How much the institution and the priesthood were involved in that process was yet to be identified. As steady and complex as it appears to be today, the emergence of the offices and their functions took some time.

As early as 1830 Smith and Cowdery were both identified as apostles. This office had been alluded to in an 1829 document which became Section 16:5-6 of the Doctrine and Covenants. Twelve men were to be called to preach to "gentiles" and Jews and to baptize and ordain priests and teachers. It was not until February 14, 1835, that twelve men were chosen to fill the quorum—called the Quorum of Twelve Apostles. They were identified as a traveling high council and as "special witnesses"[12] who were to preside over the church where they were. A further distinction was made, however, on May 2, 1835, when Joseph established the Standing High Council in Kirtland and instructed that the authority of the Twelve does not extend into those areas where high councils serve.

The role of the Twelve expanded again in January 1841 following the success of the Twelve in the East and in England. On their return from England, seven members of the Twelve were appointed to the city council of Nauvoo and by April 1844 four more joined them. On January 28, 1843, the Twelve had taken over publication of the *Times and Seasons* as well as all church printing.[13]

Some direction emerged from the divine guidance Joseph consistently sought and presented to the people and some developed pragmatically as it was needed to accomplish the job that Joseph had in mind. The distinction between the Aaronic and Melchisedec priesthoods first appeared in 1831,[14] but the function of the differences, as well as the offices, was not entirely clear. These were largely clarified[15] in 1835 when the Melchisedec was defined as the order "to administer in spiritual things."[16] The high priesthood was not evoked until June 1831 when Joseph ordained Hyrum and several others to this office and then, later, was ordained himself by Lyman Wight.

Branches grew wherever the church, or its missionaries, went. As the church expanded, or moved on, these branches continued to function and more and more groups needed to be united. Regular church conferences were held to bring these people, or their representatives, together so the body of the church might move forward.[17]

Notes

1. Neal E. Lambert and Richard M. Cracroft, "Literary Form and Historical Understanding: Joseph Smith's First Vision," *Journal of Mormon History* 7 (1980): 32; *Times and Seasons* vol. 3 (March 1, 1842).

2. See Jan Shipps, "The Prophet Puzzle: Suggestions Toward a More Comprehensive Interpretation of Joseph Smith," *Journal of Mormon History* 1 (1974): 3.

3. Lambert and Cracroft, 133.

4. Howard J. Booth, "An Image of Joseph Smith, Jr.: A Personality Study," *Courage* vol. 1, no. 1 (September 1970): 5-14.

5. *The History of the Reorganized Church of Jesus Christ of Latter Day Saints, Volume 3: 1844-1872* (Independence, Missouri: Herald Publishing House, 1952): 357. (This eight-volume work will be referred to simply as *Church History*.)

6. February 1879 interviews, *Saints' Herald* vol. 26 (October 1, 1879).

7. Sections 2, 6, 7, 10, 12, 13, 14, and 15 specifically.

8. As quoted by Shipps in "The Prophet Puzzle" from Andrew Jensen, *Latter-day Saint Biographical Encyclopedia* (Salt Lake City, Utah: A. Jensen History Company, 1901), 50.

9. Jan Shipps, *Mormonism: The Story of a New Religious Tradition* (Chicago: University of Illinois Press, 1985), 37.

10. See Richard P. Howard, "Joseph Smith's First Vision: The RLDS Tradition," *Journal of Mormon History* 7 (1980): 213.

11. *Time and Seasons* vol. 3, no. 19 (August 1842): 865-866.

12. Doctrine and Covenants 104:11c.

13. D. Michael Quinn, "The Evolution of the Presiding Quorums of the LDS Church," *Journal of Mormon History* 1 (1974): 25.

14. Doctrine and Covenants 68.

15. Doctrine and Covenants 104.

16. A. Bruce Lindgren, "The Development of the Latter Day Saint Doctrine of the Priesthood, 1829-1835," *Courage* vol. 2, no. 1 (Spring 1972): 439-443.

17. For further reading: Richard L. Bushman, *Joseph Smith and the Beginnings of Mormonism* (Urbana, Illinois: University of Illinois Press, 1984); Whitney R. Cross, *The Burned-Over District: The Social and Intellectual History of Enthusiastic Religion in Western New York: 1800-1850* (Ithaca, New York: Cornell University Press, 1950); Richard P. Howard, *Restoration Scriptures: A Study of their Textual Development* (Independence, Missouri: Herald Publishing House, 1969); Jan Shipps, *Mormonism: The Story of a New Religious Tradition* (Chicago: University of Illinois Press, 1985).

Early Settlements and Institutional Expansion

The message of the Book of Mormon concerned the American Indians, and Joseph anticipated taking the message to them. He was also concerned with establishing the city of Zion, as yet unidentified beyond the call to establish a city from which the message of the new gospel could be taken to the people of America, particularly to the Indians. Thus it was essential that the outreach of the church seek those places where the mission could be accomplished.

In September 1830 Joseph informed Oliver Cowdery and Peter Whitmer, Jr., that they had been commissioned to take the scriptures to the Indians. Late in September, following the second conference of the new organization, Parley P. Pratt and Richard Ziba Peterson were added to the Lamanite missionary group. According to the directions received[1] they left Manchester, New

49

York, during the middle of October, traveling first to visit the Cattaraugus Indians who were gathered near Buffalo. After a short time there the group moved on, detouring finally to Mentor, Ohio.

It was in Ohio that the missionaries met with Sidney Rigdon, a powerful ex-Campbellite pastor. Rigdon showed considerable interest in the concept of "restoration" found in the early gospel and gave careful attention to the words of the missionaries. This meeting was an early test of the movement's ability to appeal to frontier Americans. Mormonism represented a new and different response to the confusion that marked the intellectual understandings of Americans in the early part of the nineteenth century. Though not immediately sympathetic to the new gospel, Rigdon came to accept the Book of Mormon as divinely inspired and Joseph Smith as a prophet of God.

At the time he met the missionaries, Rigdon was the spiritual leader of several groups. Not only was he the pastor of a large congregation at Mentor, Ohio, he was also the leader of two communal living groups: one located at Kirtland and one at Mayfield. These groups were Utopian in intent and practiced a limited form of stewardship.

It would be hard to overestimate Rigdon's importance to the Restoration. He was not only a man of considerable influence in Ohio, but he was also an intelligent and thoughtful man who took his calling seriously. Passionately concerned with the promises of God, he applied his energies to understanding and living according to his beliefs. And, as he adapted to the new beliefs he encountered, he influenced a significant number of persons who, in fairly rapid order, followed him into baptism. Among those converted at this time were four men who were soon ordained as elders and who would play leading roles in the growth of the church. In addition to Sidney Rigdon, there was John Murdock, Lyman Wight, and Frederick G. Williams. Edward Partridge also made contact at this point, but while not immediately baptized and ordained, he was greatly impressed and soon joined.

Recognizing the necessity of their larger task, the missionary group left the converts in and around Mentor and, accompanied by Frederick G. Williams, continued on to Sandusky, Ohio, to meet with the Wyandotte Indians. After spending several days there working among native Americans, the group continued on to Independence, Missouri. The trip was a long and dangerous one as the approach of winter brought a series of violent storms. The exhausted group arrived at the frontier post in January 1831. When they arrived in Independence, Oliver Cowdery, Parley Pratt, and Frederick Williams crossed over the Kaw River into Indian territory to work with the Shawnee and Delaware. Other members of the group remained in Independence getting situated and finding some employment. They were desperately in need of resources.

Independence, Missouri, was a village built by necessity. Growing up at the end of the Lexington Trail, it had become the jumping-off point for persons planning to make the long journey into the West. While not yet known as the "Queen City of the Trails," the overland trade to Santa Fe was just beginning to blossom. For all intents and purposes, Independence marked the border between the Indians and the advancing white population. It was here that the Restoration message was preached to the Indians and where there was some limited success. But their influence on the Indians was short-lived, and after a time they were driven out of Indian territory by government-appointed agents. By now the group had given their attention to establishing the church in what was to be the Center Place of Zion.

* * *

While the missionary elders were working their way west and initiating the church's efforts in Missouri, the area around Mentor, Ohio, was becoming increasingly active. Soon church membership would exceed a thousand with members located in New York and Ohio. The Ohio region was quickly becoming the most active among the expansion efforts. It was not long before the largest concentration of members was located there.

Both Sidney Rigdon and Edward Partridge, who was not a member at the time, felt they needed to meet personally with this man Joseph who presented himself as a prophet. The two had traveled to New York in late winter 1830 for just that purpose. Both seemed impressed, finding in Joseph what they had expected. Edward Partridge was soon baptized. These men gave their loyalty to Joseph and were soon involved in leadership roles. They not only took on major responsibility in Ohio but were to make major contributions to the expanding church.

Many doctrinal concepts developing in these early days paralleled the thinking of communitarian Sidney Rigdon. Certainly the idea of holding "all things in common" was central to the community development that Rigdon had been experimenting with when he discovered the Restoration. The concept had been a significant part of the teachings of "the family," one of Rigdon's groups. Rigdon had also done a lot of thinking about church organization and discussed much of this with Joseph and Oliver Cowdery.

Soon Rigdon was putting pressure on Joseph Smith to consider moving the church's headquarters to Ohio. That was a natural suggestion, enforced by Edward Partridge, for Rigdon saw the church's greatest growth potential in the Ohio frontier. The proposal fell on accepting ears. Things were not going well in New York for Joseph or for the fledgling organization. Certainly the missionary-minded members had taken the message into several communities and met with success. Preaching and teaching were going on in several places and small branches were formed in Colesville, Palmyra, Canandaigua, Fayette, and Waterloo. But the Saints were encountering trouble as well.

Many serious and concerned citizens, flamed with the power of their own expanding religious traditions, felt that Joseph's claims about visions and sacred books were blasphemous. Many of the missionaries were prevented from preaching or, when they tried, were attacked and driven out of town. More than once growing mobs of angry men had harassed the young leader. So while Joseph did not appear too upset at the possibility of leaving the discontent in New York, he was probably more influenced by the fact that a majority of church members lived in Ohio. In addition, Ohio stood at the gateway to the northern territory where the Indian nations—the "people of the Book"—were located. Joseph was still determined that a major missionary responsibility of the church was to take the message of the Book of Mormon to the descendants of those about whom it was written.

The members gathered on January 2, 1831, for the third general conference of the Church of Jesus Christ. At these sessions Joseph addressed his small band of followers and called on them to move to Ohio. He explained that he had received divine direction which called for such a gathering. He planned to establish the official headquarters of the church in Kirtland. Acting on their commitment and trust in the leadership of Joseph the Prophet, about 190 persons, a significant percentage of the New York group, sold their possessions and prepared for the trip. For many, it would be the first of many trips required by their beliefs.

During the winter of 1830-1831, the members, divided into three traveling groups, made the long trip along frontier paths to Ohio. Joseph and Emma Smith, accompanied by Edward Partridge and Sidney Rigdon, managed to reach Kirtland on or about the first of February 1831. When the Missouri missionary, Parley P. Pratt, returned in 1831 to meet with church leaders at general conference, he traveled to Kirtland. There he told the Saints of his adventures and successes in Independence and encouraged the church to make a greater effort in Missouri. Joseph was inspired by the opportunity offered by this frontier land. Moving quickly to ensure that the church would be involved, he arranged for the organization of several missionary groups, made up of two elders each, one which included Joseph Smith. Their assignment was to make the long trip to western Missouri, each of them traveling a different route. While making their own way, the missionaries were encouraged to stop and preach whenever they had the opportunity and to spread the gospel as they traveled.

Joseph's group arrived in Independence in July 1831. Shortly after his arrival, the prophet addressed the collected Saints. In his remarks he described the full significance of their location. "This," he said meaning Jackson County, "is the land of promise, and the place for the city of Zion...the place which is now called Independence, is the Center Place, and the spot for the temple...."[2]

Members of the Colesville, New York, branch had followed Joseph and the church to Thompson, near Kirtland, Ohio. But they were soon directed by Joseph to continue their trip to Missouri. The group consisted of about sixty persons traveling under the leadership of Newel Knight. They served as the advance party for the larger group of nearly 1,200 who had gathered by 1833. The Colesville group settled near Kaw Township, about twelve miles west of present-day Independence, on land that was dedicated to the building of a community of the church.

Perhaps most important during the group's early visit was the dedication of land on which the Saints were to build a temple. On August 3, 1831, Joseph Smith, Sidney Rigdon, and other prominent members gathered where Joseph had envisioned the building of the temple. Rigdon dedicated the ground for the community and President Joseph Smith marked the site of the anticipated temple with a stone they had found nearby. It is not clear just when Joseph determined that the temple should be built in Independence. There obviously was anticipation about a temple at least among the Colesville Saints. And there is little doubt that the Book of Mormon acknowledges a temple in the life of the church. The Book of Ether describes a "literal city, 'like unto the Jerusalem of old,' should be built up upon the land of Joseph... (and the city) should contain a holy sanctuary of the Lord; or in other words, a temple."[3]

The Saints believed they were building more than a city. They were building the *city of God*, that earthly aspect of the kingdom of God—Zion. In time negotiations were conducted for the purchase of the land that had been designated, and Independence was recognized by the church as the Center Place, the New Jerusalem. The location for the temple, according to W. W. Phelps, a witness, was on a parcel of land measuring 63¼ acres. Bishop Partridge purchased the land from Jones H. Flournoy and his wife on December 10, 1831. The general location is usually known as the "Temple Lot," but it is unsure whether this was a section, a block within a section, or simply a parcel of land those involved had marked. After the dedication and brief meetings with the Saints, Joseph returned to Kirtland.

The Saints responded to the identification of Independence as the Center Place and a rapid influx of New Englanders began. By mid-1833, 1,200 members were living in Jackson County. As a group they had purchased nearly 2,000 acres of land. While the members were strengthened in their efforts by the expansion of the church community, the growing number of Saints began to cause a good deal of unrest among the original Missouri community.

There were a variety of reasons for the unrest. One significant reason was that a large percentage of the gentiles (term used by the early Saints for nonmembers) in the Independence area were settlers from Kentucky, Tennessee, Virginia, and the Carolinas. These were men and women of the Daniel Boone variety, known as the apostles of individualism, who represented the heartland of personal autonomy. They perceived themselves as solitary, self-reliant creatures of nature. To them, individual "freedom"—often interpreted in socially unacceptable ways (lawlessness and reckless behavior)—was to be kept alive even in the face of violence. The Mormons, on the other hand, were New Englanders both in birth and attitude. They reflected the increasingly cultured aspects of American society. They were a people of the village and of a society where the good of the whole had a vastly different definition than it had in the tidewater frontier or the hill country of Kentucky. The difference in their backgrounds and in their anticipations for the future—exaggerated by pressures over land, politics, and frontier economics—were soon to get out of hand.

The conversion of William Wines Phelps in June 1831 had cleared the way for the establishment of a printing office in Independence. The Saints were anxious to develop a newspaper to maintain communication among the members. Phelps, an experienced journalist, purchased a press and type in Cincinnati, Ohio, and issued the first edition of *The Evening and the Morning Star* in June 1832. It was an eight-page monthly, the first paper in Jackson County, and the most westerly in America. Fourteen issues were published, which included among other things, the *Articles and Covenants of the Church of Christ*, as well as several other revelations. The *Star* was widely distributed.

During the formative years of the church, Oliver Cowdery, John Whitmer, Joseph Smith, and others had preserved the revelations that Joseph had brought to the church. They were compiled and copied by Joseph and John Whitmer. Joseph felt it was important to print the collection, and the compilation was authorized by a church conference held at Hiram, Ohio, in November. The book was to be published as the *Book of Commandments* by W. W. Phelps in Independence. Phelps began to set the type anticipating a printing of 3,000 copies.

Throughout 1832 church leaders in Kirtland encouraged the Saints to gather in Independence. A great many responded, selling what they had and making the long journey by water and by foot to the border town. During this time the concept of the temple was growing in Joseph's mind. He had taken a trip back to New York to secure some loans for the United Order and saw buildings which affected his consideration. It also was becoming clearer that the temple would be used for education as well as a house of worship.

Basic to the Saints' plans for both the community and the eventual temple was the need for educational opportunities. In response to this, in June 1831, W. W. Phelps and Oliver Cowdery began to prepare educational materials for children. The Saints constructed a log building that was to serve as a combination church center and schoolhouse. But their concern was not only for children. Education was needed for the priesthood. A School of the Elders was organized in July 1833 to provide educational opportunities for those anxious to increase their talents. It was organized and directed by Parley P. Pratt.

In June a rather detailed plan regarding the development of the City of Zion was sent to W. W. Phelps from Kirtland. Joseph indicated he had received instructions that had initiated his thoughts and provided divine approval for their implementation. The leaders of the church in Zion met and, in accordance with the general projections, drafted plans for the creation of the House of the Lord. The plats Joseph Smith had sent them identified the size, form, and dimensions of the city and the temple. The descriptions of the first temple were suggestive of the House of the Lord that was later built in Kirtland.

But as the Saints moved ahead with their plans, trouble was brewing in Independence. As indicated earlier, the Mormons, though somewhat rough, were Eastern persons who had inherited and expanded established social moralities. They represented established standards of behavior reflecting a sophistication as yet undefined on the frontier. The Missourians were rough, violent, and unhampered. When the church began to arrive in force, members publicly dedicated land for a community and a temple. This represented the communal nature of their faith. It would be the center of the community and the mark of intended permanence. As anticipated, the idea of community was moving from vision to reality as many gathered to Zion. Some like the Colesville Branch literally moved en masse to the Independence region.

The key to the Missourian's distress lay in the scarcity of land. The gathering Saints were village dwellers, landholders, farmers, and builders of permanence. The Missourians were pioneers. They were land users and, to a large extent, land speculators. Lillburn W. Boggs, for example, was building a huge fortune on land speculation as he worked to develop the state.

The Mormons grew and collected; they converted and expanded; and the fear was that, in time, they would soon outnumber the "gentiles." There was the belief that the Mormons would drive away prospective settlers and would, therefore, soon be in a position to dictate land prices. The Saints operated under the United Order, a stewardship endeavor that gave the community economic control over, and made it the ultimate beneficiary of, all economic activity. The fear was that—given constant migration—the Mormons would soon outvote and control the Missourians, depriving them of an area which had been previously protective of their individualism and their uncomplicated society. This was not acceptable, and the Missourians were a people who were accustomed to fighting for what they wanted.

Despite the religious fervor that seemed to be sweeping many communities in the East, and even in Ohio, it is important to the understanding of what was happening in Independence to remember that border persons were notably unaffected by religion. There were no religious buildings in Independence when the Saints arrived. To the frontiersmen, church usually represented authority and discipline, not standards they necessarily liked. Among the religious persons living in the area, there were many doctrinal differences to separate them. Among the evangelical Protestants, who dominated religious morality, there was a difference of belief concerning the primary missions to the native Americans. As agent-providers they were not at all happy with Mormon ideas about, nor their interference with, the Indians.

A further concern was the Saints' fanaticism—their assurances that they were *always* right—and their use of the term "gentile" in a derogatory manner. This was represented by the Saints' association with the two minorities the Missourians had always held in contempt: the blacks and the Indians. The question of blacks was economic as well as moralistic. While the Saints were not as supportive of the black community as we might now desire, they were at least lukewarm on issues the Missourians felt passionately. The Missourians, very much aware of Nat Turner's rebellion among Southern slaves just two years before, feared the seeming support the Mormons provided.

As far as association with the Indians was concerned, the smoldering discontent in Iowa, which was to lead to the Black Hawk War in 1832, was being felt in

Missouri as well. The Indians were less aggressive than they had been a decade before, but most settlers were well aware that a new wave of violence was brewing. The Missourians believed the church's support of these people added to the discontent.

Finally, hot-tempered violence erupted. On July 20, 1833, the presses of *The Evening and the Morning Star* were destroyed, type was damaged, and previously printed materials were scattered. The unbound sheets of the *Book of Commandments*, the church's collection of divine instructions, were also scattered. The book was never completed, and thus it was never considered a standard work of the church.

Following the mob action which destroyed the printing establishment and the Gilbert and Whitney store, the Missourians forced from the Saints a pledge to leave the county. The understanding was that half the Mormons would leave by January 1834 and the remainder would be gone before the first of April. Attempts at redress through the courts failed when judges refused to issue restraining warrants against the mob. Concerned, Joseph wrote to the Saints in Missouri and encouraged them to leave and thus to avoid violence. He assured them that "Zion will be the joy of all saints & they will possess her forever & ever...."[4]

Despite the fact they had agreed they would leave Independence, the leaders there continued to hope for some other solution to their problems. In anticipation of better times, they asked for more information from Kirtland on the plans for the physical arrangements of Zion. But the Missourians remained adamant.

By late October, without waiting to see if the members would do as they agreed, a mob of armed men expelled the Saints from their homes and businesses and sent

61

them fleeing across the Missouri River. By the end of the winter of 1833 most Saints had been removed from Jackson County by force and waited just across the river in Clay County for guidance. Receiving word in Kirtland, Joseph was angry. Pushed to reaction, Joseph told the members of receiving divine instructions and issued the call for an army of armed volunteers to free Zion. They left from Kirtland for Missouri in May 1834. The Saints were reacting to the forced exile, but fewer responded than expected. When they arrived, they discovered a large force of Missourians waiting to do battle. Cooler heads prevailed, and in June Joseph reported further directions that moved them toward a more peaceful settlement. Bloodshed was avoided and Zion's Camp, as it was called, was disbanded on June 25. Some members joined the Saints in Clay County and others, along with Joseph, returned to the church at Kirtland.

As the church faced military pressure in Missouri, the events in Kirtland, Ohio, were magnifying and drawing to a head. The national depression initiated by the Panic of 1837, the collapse of the church's banking venture, the insolvency of its press, and the heavy indebtedness incurred in building of the House of the Lord, all complicated the Saints' economic situation. The joblessness of many converts coming to the Ohio area made it even more difficult. In spring and summer 1838 the crisis had reached such intensity that more than 600 members migrated westward, most to Caldwell County in northern Missouri. The county, created by the Missouri legislature in December 1836, had been set aside as a sanctuary for the Saints expelled from Jackson County.[5]

Notes

1. Doctrine and Covenants 31.
2. Doctrine and Covenants 57:1.
3. B. C. Fling, *An Outline History of the Church of Christ (Temple Lot)* (Independence, Missouri: Board of Publications of the Church of Christ, 1953), 43-44; Ronald E. Romig and John H. Siebert, "The Genius of Zion and Kirtland and the Concept of Temples," in Marjorie B. Troeh and Eileen M. Terril, eds., *Restoration Studies IV* (Independence, Missouri: Herald Publishing House, 1988): 99-123.
4. Romig and Siebert, 107.
5. For further reading: Milton V. Backman, Jr., *The Heavens Resound: A History of the Latter-day Saints in Ohio, 1830-1838* (Salt Lake City, Utah: Deseret Book Company, 1983); Roger D. Launius, *Zion's Camp: Expedition to Missouri, 1834* (Independence, Missouri: Herald Publishing House, 1984); Stephen C. LeSeuer, *The 1838 Mormon War of Missouri* (Columbia: University of Missouri Press, 1987); F. Mark McKiernan, *The Voice of One Crying in the Wilderness: Sidney Rigdon, Religious Reformer 1793-1876* (Lawrence, Kansas: Coronado Press, 1971); Warren Jennings, "The City in the Garden: Social Conflict in Jackson County, Missouri," in F. Mark McKiernan, Alma R. Blair, and Paul M. Edwards, eds., *The Restoration Movement: Essays in Mormon History* (Lawrence, Kansas: Coronado Press, 1973): 99-119; Max H. Parkin, "Kirtland, A Stronghold For The Kingdom," in F. Mark McKiernan, Alma R. Blair, and Paul M. Edwards, eds., *The Restoration Movement: Essays in Mormon History* (Lawrence, Kansas: Coronado Press, 1973): 63-98.

Seeking a Home

Originally Joseph had not planned to remain in Kirtland long, envisioning it as a stopover on his way west. But as the success of the church grew in Kirtland, and as difficulties intensified in Missouri, the Saints took more to root than expected. Homes were purchased or built, some businesses established, and investments made. The period of relative calm allowed Joseph to spend good portions of his time developing the church and working out organizations and procedures. During this seven or so years the small group from New York expanded, and in Kirtland much of what is the modern church developed.

Primary among these achievements was the expansion of educational opportunities. In a document brought to the church at Christmas 1832, Joseph admonished the members to seek "out of the best books words of wisdom" and to seek learning by study and by faith.[1] In 1833 the School of the Prophets was begun in the upstairs rooms of Newel K. Whitney's general store. Primarily created for priesthood and leaders, the school opened near dawn, and classes met until late afternoon studying both sacred and secular topics.

Within a year, however, this group was replaced by the more open School of the Elders (occasionally called the School of the Prophets and the School of the Apostles). It concentrated on religious issues and produced, among other things, the "Lectures on Faith" by Joseph Smith, later published in the Doctrine and Covenants in 1835. In their educational concern they established a Hebrew class and employed Joshua Seixas, a well-known professor of language, to teach an intensive three-month session. For the unordained the Kirtland school enrolled more than a hundred Saints in basic education resembling the high schools (academies) of that time.

Shortly before leaving New York, Joseph Smith had begun work on a revision, which he called a "New Translation" of the Bible. He was convinced that many passages of the Bible had gone through so many changes that they had lost the impact of "plain and precious truths." As he studied and sought divine guidance concerning what he was reading, he recorded a series of changes and alterations of the Authorized (King James) Version.

The eventual changes were concentrated in Genesis, Isaiah, and Matthew, although alterations were made throughout. A large number of these were Joseph's clarifications of passages that are open to wide interpretation; some changes were to clear up what Joseph considered to be archaic language. Sidney Rigdon served as a scribe for a while, and the work on the Bible moved ahead sporadically. Partial results were published originally in Independence in *The Evening and the Morning Star* in 1833. It seemed obvious that it would eventually be published as an independent document. But it was never completely finished, and considerably later the First Presidency named a committee that edited the work. The Inspired Version, as the Reorganization has called the revision since 1936, is widely used among members of the church.

After the publishing house was destroyed in Independence, *The Evening and the Morning Star* was transferred to Kirtland where the remaining ten issues were published. The first two volumes were reprinted between January 1835 and October 1836. The church was concerned that a paper be continued, and soon they were printing a sixteen-page monthly in Kirtland. Oliver Cowdery was the editor from October 1834 to February 1837, except for a short period in late 1835 when John Whitmer served in that position. *The Latter Day Saints' Messenger and Advocate* followed the general policies of the *Star*, reporting the news of the church leadership, but also providing considerably more news of the missions. When the *Advocate* ceased publication in September 1837 because of internal problems, a group of elders began the *Elders' Journal*, published in Kirtland late in 1837 and in Far West in July and August 1838. Joseph Smith was listed as the editor.

Earlier attempts to publish the revelations of the church had failed. And several new revelations had been collected since that time. In September 1834 the Kirtland High Council appointed a committee under Joseph Smith to collect and arrange the revelations addressed to the church. Their work consisted of updating and preparing materials collected for the aborted *Book of Commandments* and in adding what new materials they had received. It was approved at the general assembly of priesthood held in Kirtland on August 17, 1835, as the "Book of Doctrine and Covenants of the Church of the Latter-Day Saints." In addition to the collected revelations, the book also contained the seven "Lectures on Faith" attributed to Joseph Smith and given at the School of the Prophets, a preface, an appendix, an article on marriage, one on government, and the minutes of the assembly which approved the book. The book was printed in Cleveland. It originally sold for a dollar.

During the process of collecting and assembling the Doctrine and Covenants, sometime in July 1835, Joseph met Michael H. Chandler. Chandler was traveling with an exhibition of Egyptian mummies and ancient scrolls. He had inherited the mummies and papyrus scrolls from a relative, Antonio Lebolo, who found them near the Nile River. Chandler had come to Ohio while on tour to display his items but had been encouraged to seek out Joseph Smith and show them to him. After Joseph had given the materials a brief examination he identified them as ancient scriptures and deciphered a small portion of a scroll. They were described as belonging to the ancient patriarchs Abraham and Joseph. Smith's friends managed to raise what, under the economic conditions of the time, was an incredible amount of money and purchased the materials for about $2,400.

Shortly thereafter Joseph began the process of translating the materials. Oliver Cowdery and W. W. Phelps acted as scribes. The work as reported dealt with creation, the fall of man, and the nature of the Godhead. The result of their work was the *Book of Abraham* and a short Egyptian alphabet and grammar. The *Book of Abraham* was published in Nauvoo in 1842. The work was to have considerable meaning to the early church.

During the relative peace of this period, some major organizational changes took place, a sophistication of patterns already set. Some changes were to be expected because the church was not only growing numerically, it was also expanding geographically. Some members remained in New York, an increasing contingent was at work in Independence and Kirtland, but there were also missions scattered around these centers. To handle the increasingly complex financial matters, Joseph selected Edward Partridge as bishop in February 1831. Partridge was to be responsible for the details of the church's "Law of Consecration." When, in the summer of 1831, Bishop Partridge moved on to Independence as part of the planned migration there, Newel K. Whitney was ordained as a bishop in November 1831 and given charge of the finances in Kirtland.

Church members were, even for the times, generally very poor. Every effort was made to pool their resources so they might accomplish the goals they had set for themselves. Under the concept of stewardship they tried several varieties of the "all things in common" concept so prevalent among nineteenth-century utopians. Members of the church family shared in common much of what they had. But with the community rapidly expanding because of immigration—many of these persons arriving without funds of any kind—something more was needed.

In 1833 Joseph considered a response that he said he had received as an answer to his continual inquiries. In effect, the "Law of Consecration" called for common ownership of all property. It provided that members would continue to live on their previously held property as stewards over it. Whatever each one needed for themselves or their families should be used. But whatever existed in surplus of this need was to be kept in a storehouse from which the poor and those with limited resources could draw support.

The purpose and intention was good and under better circumstances might have worked quite well. Certainly it would help to distribute what resources they had among all the members, thus they could provide an adequate existence for even the poorest members of the community. But the greater hope that this would create a storehouse of capital for the needs of the church—as well as developing a real sense of stewardship among the members—did not work out as well as anticipated. Part of the problem was that there were more poor who needed to withdraw wealth from the system than there were wealthy persons with surplus to distribute. More difficult, in an immediate sense, was the cash value of property once consecrated to the storehouse by members who then wished to withdraw from the community. The way it was set up in Missouri under Bishop Edward Partridge, the consecration was made and, if persons wanted to leave, they were required to pay the church for whatever property—real or personal—they took with them.

Joseph Smith, Jr., was more inclined to return property to those who had left the movement. Despite efforts to clear up this inconsistency, Partridge continued his stronger interpretation. When the "Law of Consecration" was published in the Doctrine and Covenants, however, the wording was cleared up.[2] The clarification recognized that what was expected from the members was to consecrate some of their property, rather than all, for the availability of the poor and needy. It was the duty of the steward, rather than the church, to decide what was surplus.

Part of the difficulty lay in the as-yet-unclear role of the bishop. When Edward Partridge was named bishop on February 4, 1831, he was the only bishop in the church. In December of that year, Newel K. Whitney was named bishop as well. The identification of their duties, other than to receive donations for the poor, was to watch over the church and deal with misconduct.

Further guidance came in 1835 when it was learned that bishops were to serve subject to the First Presidency, and to preside over the Aaronic offices. They were identified as those persons exclusively concerned with the temporal/financial affairs of the church.[3] Whitney as bishop in Ohio and Partridge in Missouri were serving as regional officers rather than general officers. It was in Nauvoo that two additional bishops were added and the four asked to preside over divisions of Nauvoo. Soon others were added. When Partridge died in 1840, George Miller was called to replace him, and the hierarchy of the role of bishops was introduced by suggesting that Vinson Knight serve as a presiding bishop. As it turned out, he died without ever acting in that capacity.

Still no presiding bishop was named: Whitney and Miller continued to serve as general bishops, Miller as presiding officer of the high priests, and Whitney as the chief Aaronic priesthood officer. It was not until after Joseph's death that these two were referred to as the "presiding bishops." While the clarification of surplus was cleared up, the practice of "common surplus" or the redistribution of property still caused considerable ill will among the citizens of the communities where the Saints lived.

Economic disputes were not the only kind of disagreement that existed among the Saints. There were many organizational difficulties, especially because most rules and codes of conduct were local, arbitrary, and rarely written down. Frontier justice at that time was crude, and civil justice was usually dispersed through a local committee of interested persons. This same style was used by the church, and many local disputes were settled through either bishops' or elders' courts—members of these quorums asked to sit in judgment—which were both loose in their legal niceties and swift in their execution of sentence.

It was only a matter of time until high councils were identified as courts of appeal as church members wanted more defined and reasoned consideration of their disagreements. The Presidency often found itself acting as the final court of appeals in significant cases. The issues heard by all these groups centered on charges of "un-Christian conduct"—things like lying, drunkenness, or even moral transgressions—and the far more serious charges of apostasy and disloyalty.

* * *

Though the temple site in Jackson County was dedicated first, it was in Kirtland that a temple was first built. The Saints, anticipating an endowment of spiritual power, were called to action in June 1833 when Joseph acknowledged receiving instruction about a building for the School of the Prophets, to receive endowments and to prepare for ministry.

The job of building the House of the Lord was enormous, a task of funding and creation that would be hard to duplicate. The Saints were about as destitute as frontier Americans could be. They were already in debt for migration costs, for their housing, and for their efforts to rebuild lives and estates. They hardly had the tools necessary for such an enterprise. But the building committee, chaired by Hyrum Smith, gathered subscriptions and work began. The cornerstone was laid July 23, 1833. Nearly all adult members of the church worked on the building in one capacity or another: quarrying stone, finishing woodwork, making pews and furniture, weaving drapes. The general idea was to spend one day in ten on the temple, but many managed to do considerably more. The community of non-Saints was not happy with this building project, wondering at both the religious expectations of the Saints and the economic impact on the community. It was often necessary to guard the work to avoid vandalism.

The building rose on a hill, its walls standing two feet thick, fifty-nine-by-seventy-nine feet and three stories tall. The first and second stories were auditoriums, running fifty-five-by-sixty-five feet, exclusive of the stairway and the vestibule. The lower room was for sacramental offerings, and the upper was the School of the Prophets. The third floor was divided into small rooms. It cost the dedicated Saints about $40,000.

The year 1836 seemed to be better with some signs appearing that the economic situation was improving. Certainly the expanding church membership was encouraging. At an administrative conference in January, the leaders had completed the meetings in a good spirit and a sense of accomplishment. The year's promise was magnified by the dedication of the newly completed temple. It was a significant and festive occasion held on Sunday, March 27, 1836. The Saints began to assemble early, and by nine o'clock President Smith was required to order the doors closed. Every seat was filled, the aisle was crowded, and nearly a thousand people hushed to participate in the dedication ceremony. President Sidney Rigdon gave the dedicatory sermon, which lasted more than two hours. During the service Joseph Smith was once again accepted by the quorums as the leader of the church; new hymns were introduced; the general officers were sustained; and Joseph Smith, Jr., gave the dedicatory prayer.

One person described the scene: "I saw there Joseph the prophet standing with his hands raised toward heaven, his face ashy pale, the tears running down his cheeks as he spoke...."[4] Following this the gathered Saints sang "The Spirit of God Like a Fire Is Burning," shared together in the service of Communion, heard from several church leaders, and finally, after singing "Hosanna! Hosanna! Hosanna to God and the Lamb!" and a benediction, the service finished at about four o'clock in the afternoon. A second service was held the next week for those who could not get in.

* * *

To aid in the administration of the rapidly expanding church, Joseph introduced the office of high priest at Kirtland in June 1831. Parley P. Pratt, Lyman Wight, Joseph, and about twenty other men were ordained as members of this Melchisedec office. The office has always been the source from which those responsible for the administrative duties of the church have been drawn. Joseph was ordained as president of the high priesthood, a responsibility that included the office of the president of the church.

What was to become the Quorum of the First Presidency began in 1832 at the time of Joseph Smith's ordination as president of the high priesthood. He, in turn, in March 1832, ordained Jesse Gauze and Sidney Rigdon to be his counselors in the "ministry of the presidency."[5] However, by January 1833 Frederick G. Williams was functioning in the role of counselor as a result of Gauze's disaffection. The reorganization of leadership on March 18, 1833, ranked the president's counselors as first and second with Rigdon as first and Williams as second. By 1833 the First Presidency was recognized as the apex of the church structure. A revelation in 1835 specified that the First Presidency was to consist of three high priests.[6]

On December 18, 1833, Joseph, only twenty-seven at the time, gave a special blessing to his family. He blessed his father as patriarch to the church, to be a "prince over his posterity, holder of the keys of the patriarchal Priesthood over the kingdom of God on earth, even the Church of the Latter-day Saints."[7] Later that day Joseph Smith, Sr., was ordained patriarch. The role as an ecclesiastical authority was unclear at that point. Certainly his position as patriarch over the church made him a general officer. But over whom would he preside? The office was sustained at the next General Conference. At Joseph, Sr.'s death in 1840, Hyrum, as his oldest living son, succeeded him.

Of major significance to church expansion was the creation of high councils. The first of these groups of twelve high priests was constituted on February 17, 1834, and created primarily as the Standing High Council of the Stake of Kirtland. It was for the purpose of "settling important difficulties, which might arise in the church, which could not be settled by the church, or the bishop's council, to the satisfaction of the parties."[8] Joseph created a second high council in Clay County, Missouri, where the Saints had taken refuge. The council in Kirtland consisted of the three members of the First Presidency and shared in administrative and judicial matters in what was called Kirtland Stake.

Within two weeks after the organization of the Quorum of Twelve Apostles, Joseph began to select men for the Quorum of Seventy. Joseph chose men to constitute "traveling quorums, to go into all the earth, whithersoever the Twelve Apostles shall call them"[9] reminiscent of Moses and Christ appointing seventy men for ecclesiastical purposes. And while Joseph had earlier identified these men as equal to apostles, later instructions affirmed the quorum as a subordinate position. For leadership seven presidents were to be chosen from among them for the seven quorums, and from the seven, one was to serve as "President of the Seven Presidents."

The members of the Quorum of Seventy originally were drawn from the ranks of these members of "Zion's Camp." This expedition to Missouri in 1834 was unsuccessful, but in some very important ways it served to identify, for Joseph, the strongest and most loyal among his followers. Forty-five men were set apart to this office on February 28, 1835, to form the first Quorum of Seventy. Shortly afterward, seven of these men were set apart as the presidents of Seventy. They, with the First Presidency, selected new members of the quorums. They were elders of the church set apart to a special calling as missionaries.

The concept of apostolic missionary—as special witness—was a part of Joseph's testimony when he recalled his and Oliver Cowdery's ordination in 1829. In 1835 Joseph identified and organized the quorum selected by Oliver Cowdery, Martin Harris, and David Whitmer, all witnesses to the Book of Mormon plates. Nine men were ordained immediately, the rest later. Thomas B. Marsh was set apart as president of the quorum. He was succeeded by Brigham Young. The quorum had the assignment as special missionaries into places where the gospel should be taken. This included an early return to New York to organize those who had remained there. As special missionaries they were responsible, with the Quorum of Seventy, to promote expansion of the gospel.

The missionaries often reported meeting considerable indifference and even anger, and their journals report their discouragement. But there were also successes when they found willing audiences. They visited friends and relatives who aided them, preached in public meeting halls, engaged in powerful debates with other ministers or public officials, and, in going from door to door, found willing listeners. In their presentations they developed the basic and fundamental doctrines of faith, repentance, baptism for the remission of sins, and the laying on of hands for the gifts of the Holy Spirit. They explained the coming forth of the Book of Mormon and the restoration of the gospel of prophecy and the second advent of Jesus Christ. There is little evidence that the First Vision was a significant part of the message. Of course, central to their beliefs were the more traditional prophetic teachings of the Old Testament and the book of Revelation.

In June 1837 Joseph determined to send the Quorum of Twelve to missionize England. Heber C. Kimball, Orson Hyde, and five elders arrived to spread the gospel among the English people. The mission preached not only gospel fundamentals but concentrated on the role of Zion and the concept of gathering for the Saints. For Zion—in this case Kirtland but, as it turned out, Nauvoo—was offered first as a sanctuary from the ravages of the last days, as well as the promise of land, employment, and opportunities to work with God's people.[10] The appeal rested well on the hearts of the working-class British family, at this time generally illiterate and extremely poor. The message was one of optimism and hope. Within a few months Kimball and his associates had converted nearly 1,500. Many of the converts—whole families of them—began to migrate to America. A few went to Kirtland, but the majority traveled to Nauvoo, numbering nearly 5,000 by 1846.

The many changes occurring in Ohio even affected the name of the church. Originally it emerged as the Church of Christ, but on May 3, 1834, at the conference in Missouri the name was changed to the Church of the Latter Day Saints. Again, in April 1838 Joseph presented a document that called for the further change to the "Church of Jesus Christ of Latter Day Saints."

Despite the success of the House of the Lord and the unifying effect it presented, there were troubles developing in Kirtland. Criticism had followed the Saints from New York and had never disappeared. The criticism was directed toward their religious practices which the gentiles saw as peculiar, toward their economic behavior, and toward the uncompromising zeal that was attributed to members. In 1832 a mob, determined to keep Mormonism out of its community, attacked the house where Joseph was staying and dragged him into the street. While some of the mob called for his death or emasculation, they finally left him badly beaten. Rigdon also suffered in the attack and was disabled for some time with a concussion. The two men were tarred and feathered.

After the difficulties came to a climax in Jackson County, things began to get worse in Kirtland. On January 8, 1833, a mob of men fired cannon shells over the town and the Saints feared an attack. None came. But even while these differences were manifest, more and more members migrated into the valley below the town itself and, as they did, problems increased. Certainly many of the problems were economic, created by the huge debt incurred by the cost of materials for the Temple, from overly energetic land purchases designed to prevent speculation, and because of the needs of persons who had come to Kirtland without adequate resources. As well, resentment toward the stewardship program continued. Moreover, growing differences over administrative procedures and interpersonal strife between members of the leadership caused difficulty for the Kirtland Saints.

The economic situation was complex. The completion of the Temple resulted in an economic slump because of the loss of what few jobs were available. The gentiles, fearing the economic impact of the Mormons, did little to relieve these pressures. One effort that was made to ease the economic burden was the Kirtland Safety Society, conceived by Smith, Rigdon, and other leaders.

The society grew out of a perceived need for a center for temporal interests and was capitalized at $4 million. This was a typical economic response for the period and was usually held in check by the need for a state charter. The group applied for a charter, but it was denied by the state legislature. However, they had already contracted for bank notes and in order to use them had these notes inscribed with the prefix "anti" just before the word "Bank." It issued its first specie in January 1837 and was faced, from the beginning, by some serious problems: the speculation in land prices, excessive credit buying, and some unprincipled individuals. Excessive printing of currency, especially after Smith and Rigdon had resigned from the board of directors, added to the problem.

The failure to receive a bank charter led to the formation of the Kirtland Safety Society Anti-Banking Company organized by Joseph Smith and Sidney Rigdon. The directors were inexperienced and unable to meet the demands, or to save the bank as economic failure swept the country. When the bank closed in November, considerable resentment was directed toward Joseph. Over a score of wildcat banks of this type in Ohio, some even with state charters, failed during this time.

There were political problems as well. In general the Mormons supported the democratic politics represented by Andrew Jackson. The Saints associated the Whig party with special privilege and protested against what they saw as increasing government involvement. They felt they could gain support for themselves by supporting the Democrats. And in February 1835 the Saints published the *Northern Times* as a political paper. The *Times* supported the candidacy of Martin Van Buren only to discover that the state vote was against him. As well, the Mormons sought political office for themselves. By the end of 1836 they controlled Kirtland Township—further adding to charges that the Mormons controlled the elections; if not by a one-sided unified vote then by illegal counts. A statement was released by the Saints affirming their support of the separation of church and state. But it was not successful and one disgruntled Whig politician, Grandison Newell, charged Joseph Smith in 1837 with conspiring to assassinate him. Despite Joseph's acquittal, political charges continued to rise against him.

The events in Kirtland, Ohio, were approaching a crisis. The national Panic of 1837 added to the general economic problems among the Kirtland Saints. By summer 1837 the crisis had reached such intensity that nearly 600 church members migrated westward, most to Caldwell County in northern Missouri. Elder Oliver Granger remained in Kirtland as agent trying to settle claims in Kirtland, but it accomplished little. Many church members lost everything they had. And, as can be easily understood, many blamed Joseph for their difficulties. Under the pressure of an indictment for illegal banking, some vexing lawsuits, and fear of a growing mob of apostates, several leaders took refuge in Missouri.[11]

After the fall of the Kirtland Safety Society Anti-Banking Company, Joseph wrote in his journal in 1838: "A new year dawned upon the church in Kirtland in all the bitterness of the spirit of apostate mobocracy."[12] Joseph Smith and Sidney Rigdon were forced to flee on horseback on January 12, 1838, just ahead of a mob and headed for Missouri. Many Saints were to follow, leaving in Kirtland the remains of their "shattered dreams, unfilled prophesies, and an empty Temple which was used by the Gentiles as a sheep shed."[13] The hope of the church now resided in the county created by the Missouri legislature in December 1836 as a sanctuary and a home for the Saints expelled from Jackson County in 1834 and required to leave Clay County in 1836.[14]

Notes

1. Doctrine and Covenants 85:36a.
2. Doctrine and Covenants 42:8.
3. D. Michael Quinn, "The Evolution of the Presiding Quorums of the LDS Church," *Journal of Mormon History* 1 (1974): 34.
4. W. B. "Pat" Spillman, *Studies in Restoration History: The Hastening Time, Volume 2* (Independence, Missouri: Herald Publishing House, 1987): 14.
5. Kirtland Revelation Book, 10-11, as quoted in Quinn, 23.
6. Quinn, 25.
7. Quinn, 26.
8. Doctrine and Covenants 99:1b.
9. Quinn, 31.
10. See Norma Hiles, "Charles Derry: A Palimpsestic View," *JWHA Journal* 4 (1984): 23.
11. Max H. Parkin, "Kirtland, A Stronghold For The Kingdom," in F. Mark McKiernan, Alma R. Blair, and Paul M. Edwards, eds., *The Restoration Movement: Essays in Mormon History* (Lawrence, Kansas: Coronado Press, 1973), 63-98.
12. F. Mark McKiernan, "Mormonism on the Defensive: Far West, 1838-1839," in McKiernan, Blair, and Edwards, eds., *The Restoration Movement: Essays in Mormon History* (Lawrence, Kansas: Coronado Press, 1973): 122.
13. Ibid.
14. For further reading: Milton V. Backman, Jr., *The Heavens Resound: A History of the Latter-day Saints in Ohio, 1830-1838* (Salt Lake City: Deseret Book Company, 1983); Roger D. Launius, *The Kirtland Temple: A Historical Narrative* (Independence, Missouri: Herald Publishing House, 1986); Dean A. Dudley, "A Bank Born of Revelation: The Kirtland Safety Society Anti-Banking Company," *Journal of Economic History* 30 (December 1970): 848-853; Scott H. Partridge, "The Failure of the Kirtland Safety Society," *Brigham Young University Studies* 12 (Summer 1972): 437-454.

Temporary Settlement

As a result of their beliefs, the early Saints suffered from significant persecution. It began almost immediately with Joseph identified as a young man making arrogant claims. The dislike was nurtured in suspicion and distrust. After the Saints began to act collectively, amassing more goods and assuming influential positions, there was a certain degree of jealousy. The persecution was social and economic but became political as well, for the Saints represented a significant voting block at a time when politics was a more passionate endeavor.

The Saints in general suffered, but their leaders in particular seemed to bear the brunt of this dislike. Joseph Smith, Sidney Rigdon, and Edward Partridge were among those who were ridiculed, forced to suffer indignities, and run out of town. The hostilities even led to Joseph and others being tarred and feathered, a particularly painful and dangerous activity that flourished on the American frontier.

Generally, Joseph and the church responded to such injustices with passive resistance or occasionally by moving away from the source of the agitation. But after the Saints' expulsion from Jackson County, Missouri, and the violence that took place there, Joseph Smith, Jr., and many members were angered to the point of reaction. Joseph called his people to respond, affirming that "the redemption of Zion must needs come by power; therefore I will raise up unto my people a man, who shall lead them like as Moses led the children of Israel...."[1]

While declaring his peaceful intent, an army—identified as Zion's Camp—began moving toward Independence in early May 1834 gathering men along the way. It soon consisted of 200 armed men with several wagons and followed by a few women and children. Buying needed supplies as they traveled through Ohio, Indiana, and Illinois, they covered nearly a thousand miles in the next six weeks. The trip was difficult and much of their original belligerence had noticeably softened by the time of their arrival. As well, there was considerable fever, probably cholera, in camp. The Independence people, warned of the pending invasion, had hurriedly amassed an army and waited for the Saints near the banks of the Missouri River not far from Independence. As the two armies drew close, a violent thunderstorm hit which prevented battle and allowed time for reflection. A meeting, held in Liberty, Missouri, was agreed upon with hope for a compromise. No agreeable solution was found. The church members were angry and demanded payment for their lost property and goods. The Missourians, a superior force, wanted the Saints to pull back their army.

Joseph received what he considered to be further

light on the problem and assured the church members of their eventual possession of the land in question. But he did not call on them to fight. Rather, on June 30 the members of Zion's Camp were discharged and a majority of the force began to make its way back to Kirtland, Ohio. A good number stayed behind and continued to purchase land in the area, seeking to hold onto the church's position. The majority of the Saints were now located in Clay County. Talk continued about redeeming Zion, but for the moment it became a dream rather than an immediate goal.

By 1836 the tenuous peace between the church and the citizens of Missouri began to erode again. Understandably the Saints could not forget the injustices done to them, and they continued to seek redress. Just as understandably, the people of Clay County, Missouri, were frightened by the beliefs and the size of the growing number of church members, and they sought the security they felt could only come about by the Mormons' exile. Fearing more trouble, the citizens of the county gathered at a mass meeting in Liberty on June 29, 1836, and drew up a list of complaints against the Mormons. They called for an end to migration and demanded that all Mormons leave the county as quickly as possible.

Once again church members preferred to avoid violence and finally agreed to the conditions, assuring the angry Missourians they would move as quickly as they could. A committee was sent north in search of land, and finally, after negotiations with the state government, they were allowed to create a county of their own. Alexander Doniphan, a lawyer who had once represented the Saints, sponsored a bill in the legislature to set aside an organized county as a place of refuge for the Mormons. It was organized in December 1836 and called Caldwell. The county representatives were granted seats in the Missouri legislature. Far West was named as the county seat, courts were established, and a school fund developed.

When Joseph arrived in Far West in March 1838, he acknowledged it as a city for his Saints and called on the members to build a temple and once again to gather. Far West was to be the center of the movement, complete with a temple, and would serve as headquarters for the church. While the basic problems had not been resolved, many of the Saints settled in Caldwell County in hope of a more permanent location. The arrival of people from Ohio, plus the relative calm that prevailed for a short time, lured them to believe that here they could establish a community from which to await the anticipated return to Independence.

The county was already too small for the numbers arriving, and soon Mormon settlers began to overflow, seeking land, jobs, and resources in surrounding Daviess, Ray, and Carroll counties. Within a year or so Far West was a thriving frontier community boasting more than a hundred homes, several retail stores, a blacksmith forge, and a large log building that was at once school, church, town offices, and county courthouse. By fall 1838, several thousand church members were gathered about the town of Far West in Caldwell County. The Caldwell County State Militia was organized in May 1837 with Lyman Wight as colonel. The officer corps was made up entirely of church members. The following year another fifty or so homes were built and two hotels and some mills added.

A site of particular interest to those considering the move was the place Joseph had identified as Adam-ondi-Ahman, some twenty-five miles north of Far West

86

on the Grand River in Daviess County. The name came from the valley where, according to Joseph, Adam called his family together for a blessing.[2] Here, by the remains of what Smith called a Nephite altar, located on Spring Hill near Lyman Wight's home, Joseph and many of the Saints gathered in conference. Lyman Wight had settled there in February 1838.

On June 28 of that year, a stake was organized at Far West with John Smith, Joseph's uncle, as president. Joseph saw it as a location especially suited for those who were migrating from Kirtland. The settlement eventually held some 1,500 members. It had the potential of being an important city location for it rested at a point with easy river travel down the Grand River fifty miles to the Missouri. A small red brick storehouse was erected partway up Spring Hill. At the top, nearly a mile away, was the site marked for the temple block. The site was dedicated while the Saints gathered there after conflict in Daviess and Caldwell counties.[3]

The period of peace the Saints were enjoying came to an end shortly after the July 4 celebration in 1838. Several disruptions were occurring in the community. First, and perhaps most important, were the internal leadership problems that developed. Dissension continued in Missouri, because of a wide variety of reasons, but led by the powerful disillusionment following the failure to hold Zion. Smith and Rigdon responded to the weakening of the members by turning to strong affirmations of orthodoxy and by moving against those who wavered. Spiritual unity became the crusade of the church at Far West, spurred on in part by the increasing danger from angry gentiles. Rigdon in particular took a militant stand, dislodging the dissenters and determined to stamp out apostasy.

Discontent among some sections of the Missouri church reflected concerns carried over from Kirtland, some emerging from the charges of improper sales of land, overly aggressive leadership, and the growing distance between Joseph and some of the early leaders. In a series of church court procedures, several significant church leaders including W. W. Phelps, Oliver Cowdery, and John Whitmer, as well as Apostles Lyman Johnson and William McLellin, were expelled from the church in spring 1838. They were ordered to depart northern Missouri within three days. Their charges reflected the seriousness with which the members took their beliefs: violating the Word of Wisdom and the selling of their land in Jackson County. The first referred to the church's public opposition to tobacco and hot or strong drink since the 1833 revelation called the "Word of Wisdom."[4] But the sale of land considered to be sacred was equally unacceptable.

The situation became so tense that a secret organization was formed to maintain orthodoxy. The group, called the Danites after Dan "as a serpent" in Genesis 49, was led by Sampson Avard. Organized along military lines, it never contained more than 300 members and was devoted to preserving the faith. While gaining something of a ruthless reputation, the body was blatantly unsuccessful and soon became an embarrassment to the church. Avard, who left the church, became as extreme an anti-Mormon as he had been a defender of the faith.

There was, as well, a serious economic disagreement that arose from the structure of the early understandings of stewardship: the church's law of economic responsibility. The law, as then understood, was designed to encourage individual enterprise but also made available community use of surplus to meet the group's needs. In an effort to work this out, the Saints ran into trouble with the laws of the states, as well as among members and nonmembers.

The Law of Consecration, spelled out in 1831, proved unsuccessful in Ohio and Missouri in 1831 and 1832. It was abandoned in favor of consecration of surplus by 1833, and by the tithing law proclaimed through revelation by Joseph in Far West in 1838. Meeting in Far West in early August 1837 the bishop and high council voted, affirming Joseph's earlier direction, that every person would hold his or her resources as private property and assume the responsibilities as individual stewards.

There was, as well, increased friction among the gentile inhabitants of the surrounding counties. The first outbreak of violence was on August 6, 1838, when, in an effort to prevent the Saints from voting, a brawl broke out between the Saints and the townsfolk of Gallatin, Missouri, during an election campaign. The Mormons, determined to remove the anti-Mormon group from Daviess County, marched with their forces to Gallatin and set fire to the town. David Atchison, a general of the Missouri State Militia, ordered 500 men into the area to restrict the violence, but he did so without realizing the depth of anti-Mormon feeling among his troops. The result was open warfare in several Mormon areas as farms were raided, houses burned, and mills destroyed.

On October 24 members of the Caldwell County Militia, under Captain Samuel Bogart, a Methodist minister, harassed some Saints and took three prisoners. Captain David W. Patten, also of the Caldwell Militia, marched on Bogart's camp at Crooked River.

The two companies of the Caldwell County Militia faced each other across the narrow body of water, and in a hand-to-hand battle several were killed, including Patten.

The encounter, known as the Battle of Crooked River, was vastly overrated but, in the climate, was all that was needed to inflame the situation. It turned from critical to desperate when Governor Lillburn W. Boggs called 2,000 men into action with orders that "the Mormons must be treated as enemies, and must be exterminated or driven from the State, if necessary, for the public good." Armed with such an order, it is little wonder that the violence continued. On October 30 the Livingston County Militia attacked Jacob Haun's mill on Shoal Creek just a few miles from Far West with some 200 men. The decision to attack was made by Colonel Thomas Jennings who had formed a battalion of militia. For a year or so Haun's Mill had served as home for nearly twenty families. It was located just inside Caldwell County and threatened to become a stronghold for the Saints. Those who had settled there felt it could be defended if necessary.

About four o'clock in the afternoon the militia moved through the woods just north of the mill. Captain David Evans had withdrawn his pickets the day before and so no alarm was sounded. The militia moved in quickly and destroyed many of the buildings and killed about seventeen men and boys. Three Missourians were wounded. After the short and devastating attack— hardly a battle because of the weakness of the defense— Jennings and his force withdrew to Livingston County. The Saints regrouped slowly, the bodies of the slain placed in an uncompleted well, and preparations were made to surrender the land. Shortly after, the state militia under General Samuel Lucas surrounded Far West and ordered its surrender. Meeting with Lucas, five church leaders hoped to negotiate a settlement of what was rapidly becoming a war. But the five—Joseph Smith, Sidney Rigdon, Parley P. Pratt, Lyman Wight, and George W. Robinson—were arrested by General Lucas. The next day Hyrum Smith and Amasa Lyman were imprisoned with them.

After a secret military-type trial, the church leaders were quickly found guilty and ordered executed. General Alexander W. Doniphan, the military officer who was charged with the execution, was an attorney and friend of the Mormons. He refused to obey the order to have them shot. Instead he imprisoned them, holding them in Independence shortly and then moving the leaders to Richmond, Missouri. After a court inquiry held late in November, Joseph, Hyrum, Lyman Wight, Alexander McRae, and Caleb Baldwin were sent to Liberty for trial and held in Liberty Jail. An additional 136 other members and leaders were arrested during the following week, and Far West was plundered on November 2, 1838, by members of the militia. By late November most of the leaders were imprisoned in the unfinished Richmond, Missouri, courthouse.

Joseph Smith and his followers were imprisoned in Liberty Jail, a twenty-two foot square building for four and a half months. Two escape attempts were made but failed when unforeseen events foiled the effort. While in prison the men were allowed occasional visits by family and friends. Imprisonment allowed considerable time for thinking and writing and for making plans for the future. In February Sidney Rigdon was released on bail and used his freedom to make an appeal to impeach the state of Missouri. Early in April fear of their escape led to an order to have the prisoners removed to Daviess County. There on April 10 they were charged with "murder, treason, burglary, arson, larceny, theft, and stealing."[5] While traveling to the new location they were allowed to escape. After a desperate journey they reached Quincy, Illinois, on April 22, 1839.

Having lost their homes, much of their property and savings, as well as many friends, the faithful Mormons sought yet another site of refuge. The settlement, store-house, and temple site at Far West and Adam-ondi-Ahman were abandoned. So they began moving toward Illinois, stopping briefly on the banks of the Mississippi thinking they would be safe there for a while. An estimated 5,000 left northern Missouri for Illinois.

Edward Partridge, William Marks, and Sidney Rigdon had reached Quincy, Illinois, before Joseph and had suggested the Saints scatter about the area, some going to Illinois and others into Iowa. Joseph, however, favored a central location, seeking a place where they could settle and establish their headquarters and a temple. Stakes were organized in Montrose, Iowa, and other locations, but the emphasis was soon shifted to a place they had obtained called Commerce and renamed Nauvoo in April 1840. The Saints moved toward Illinois by family groups as directed by a relocation committee. The people of Quincy were kind and welcoming as people moved through. Joseph arrived in Nauvoo in April 1839.

Parley P. Pratt and Thomas Marsh had made an effort to seek redress for losses in Missouri. But they were unsuccessful, largely, it appears, because many of the strongest anti-Mormons had moved to high political office in Missouri essentially as a result of their success against the Mormons. There was a brief resurgence of hope among the Saints about reclaiming their land in Missouri when, in November 1839, an official party from the church went to Washington, D.C., to ask President Van Buren and Congress for help. The federal bodies petitioned refused to intervene in what they considered a purely state matter, and the group returned without redress.[6]

Notes

1. Doctrine and Covenants 100:3d-f.
2. The meaning of the name varies considerably. On a public sign at the Gallatin, Missouri, Courthouse it is identified as "Adam's Consecrated Land." Heman C. Smith's *Journal of History* 9:140 gives it as "Adam's Grave."
3. The significance of the location can be seen by the fact that the Pattonsburg Dam, its reservoir, and platting for Interstate Highway 35 were altered to avoid disturbing the land.
4. Doctrine and Covenants 86.
5. Leonard Arrington, "Church Leaders in Jail," *Brigham Young University Studies* vol. 13, no. 1 (Autumn 1972): 22.
6. For further reading: Alma R. Blair, "The Haun's Mill Massacre," *Brigham Young University Studies* vol. 13, no. 1 (Autumn 1972): 62; Mario DePillis, "The Development of Mormon Communitarianism, 1826-1846" (n.p.: PhD. dissertation, Yale University, 1961); Warren A. Jennings, "Zion Is Fled: The Expulsion of the Mormons from Jackson County, Missouri," (n.p.: Ph.D. dissertion, University of Florida, 1962); F. Mark McKiernan, "Mormonism on the Defensive: Far West, 1838-1839," in F. Mark McKiernan, Alma R. Blair, and Paul M. Edwards, eds., *The Restoration Movement: Essays in Mormon History* (Lawrence, Kansas: Coronado Press, 1973), 121-140; Melodie Moench, "Nineteenth Century Mormons: The New Israel," *Dialogue* vol. 12, no. 1 (Spring 1979): 42-45.

Nauvoo

The small Illinois village of Commerce was not a spectacular place either in terms of its beauty or its hospitality. It was located where the Mississippi River jogs around Iowa and forms a small arc of flat land once owned by the Sauk and Fox Indians. Here on land primarily traded for Missouri lands, or purchased from economically depressed New England land speculators on twenty-year contracts, the Saints began to settle on May 10, 1839.

The exiled believers, weakened by the difficulties in Missouri and the rigors of frontier travel, found that their new home was a marshy swampland. During the early days the fever (malaria) and other illnesses took a heavy toll on the people gathered. But as was their tradition they went to work immediately improving the situation. After securing the land they organized to create a series of drainage ditches to drain out the water. At the same time deep wells were dug for fresh water, homes were built, and the town began to receive converts—from Canada and Great Britain as well as from all over the United States—who moved into the area expecting an immediate improvement in their lives.

And the city on the Mississippi grew. The 1842 census recorded "greater Nauvoo" had 7,000 souls and by 1845, when the census was taken again, the population was listed at 11,052—making it larger than Chicago. Joseph called his new community Nauvoo, which he explained was Hebrew for beautiful place. Despite the economic burden imposed by the arrival of converts and the high demand for welfare among them, the community grew so rapidly that every kind of speculation became common. On the other hand, money was so scarce that an elaborate barter system was used and civil improvements were budgeted in terms of individual labor given as tithes.

The need for communication among the members, both at Nauvoo and among those still scattered in Missouri, Kirtland, and New York, was one of the first concerns, and the paper, *Times and Seasons*, was proposed as a monthly in July 1839. It was published privately under the editorial responsibility of Ebenezer Robinson and Don Carlos Smith. By May 1841 the paper was distributed twice a month. After Don Smith died and Ebenezer Robinson retired, the Council of Twelve purchased *Times and Seasons* in February 1842 and Joseph was named editor. The paper published its last issue in February of 1846. Control of *Times and Seasons* by the Twelve, following the death of Joseph, was important in the discussion concerning his proper successor.

Certainly the growth of Nauvoo would not have been possible if Joseph had not negotiated a remarkable city charter from the state of Illinois on December 16, 1840.

96

Several large cities in the state had charters that allowed rather extensive freedom of development. But the Mormon community was able to accomplish so much primarily because of the lack of distinction between civil and sacred government. Joseph and other leaders utilized the liberal charter so Nauvoo rivaled state sovereignty.

Before the charter the Presidency and councils served as officials in both secular and sacred affairs. Here Joseph called on the Twelve to act in the burden of administrative affairs. But under the charter, and in keeping with the church's traditional understanding, church leaders were elected and appointed as political leaders of the city. The separation of church and state, which was firmly established in the thinking of eighteenth-century Americans, appeared now to be suspect to outsiders, especially because of the strong political and sacred unity acknowledged by the Mormons. Joseph Smith, Jr., served as mayor after John C. Bennett, the first mayor, fell from acceptance, and served as chief judge of the municipal court system. Members of the Nauvoo Stake High Council also served on the city council. The political wards (the city's political subdivision and currently the LDS term for congregation) were composed of branches. It was a matter of church policy being enacted into city law, church doctrine becoming municipal policy. The only restrictions imposed on them were that the laws of Nauvoo could not violate the state constitution.

The community could not avoid becoming involved in political action, for the Saints recognized the power their numbers and unity provided them in county and state political negotiations. Realizing that for Smith and his followers the kingdom of God was seen as more and more political in the making, it is little wonder the Saints found it hard to stay out of politics. The priesthood, Brigham Young was to say later, was the "perfect governmental system."[1]

The near-even balance between Whigs and Democrats in Illinois was disrupted by the Mormon influx. The search for political favors needed to accomplish their goals meant that the Mormon community could not avoid becoming politically active. In 1842 Joseph Smith announced the Mormons would vote for the Democrats even though, because of the death of the earlier candidate, it meant the election of Thomas Ford, an opponent of the Mormon charter. The significance of their vote soon established the Mormon community as a political power in Illinois. Large and passionate criticism of Joseph Smith and his "controlled" vote followed. Smith used the vote to gain favor from the Whigs in 1843 and then changed his mind and supported the Democrats, adding more aggravation to the political unrest. The fact that the Saints were unwilling to identify with either party was even more unsettling than their vote. The Mormons gave no loyalty, paid no dues, gave no party service. The results were that both parties distrusted them. Because they could not be trusted by any group, they tended to be feared politically by them all.

One of the more colorful aspects of this balance between church and city was the existence of the Nauvoo Legion. As a frontier post, Nauvoo was granted the authority to organize and maintain a military organization. The legion was a part of the state militia, its officers commissioned by the state. It could be called to aid the state but, in effect, it was available to enforce the laws of Nauvoo and to protect its people. Unlike most militia groups, this was neither a social gathering nor a political toy. It was an army, unusual in its size and complexity and for its mission to protect the city. With Joseph Smith as a general, and its officer corps primarily made up of church leaders, the church's control of the militia was threatening to the gentile neighbors of Nauvoo, especially because the legion seemed always to be marching and training. As well, it had the habit of using live ammunition.

The Saints were generally poor, many having come from significant losses in Missouri and Kirtland, or deeply indebted to the Perpetual Immigration Company for their passage. Lack of investment capital made it extremely difficult for the community to provide jobs. This was particularly true for those skilled persons who needed mills and manufacturing. There were many small businesses (blacksmiths, tanneries, grain mills, retail, and the like) but no needed heavy industry. The Nauvoo economy was based on private enterprise and the profit motive, and as was the case in Kirtland and Independence, land prices soared as the Mormon community grew. This influx provided huge profits to a few and near bankruptcy to many, widening the economic gap.

The Nauvoo Stake was organized in October 1839 with William Marks as stake president presiding over a high council. The temporal affairs were divided into wards and administered by Bishops Partridge, Knight, and Whitney. A second stake, called Zarahemla, was quickly organized, as were nine others. But these were soon discontinued in favor of Nauvoo.

Joseph Smith owned and operated a boarding house attached to his residence, the Mansion House, and a general store generally known as the Red Brick Store.

His office on the second floor of the store soon became the headquarters of the church. Smith's income came as mayor, a per diem allowance when municipal judge, and profits from land speculation, all of which provided an adequate living.

While some church leaders, like Hyrum Smith, had been involved in Masonry before, it was in Nauvoo that a large number of church members became interested. The Nauvoo Lodge was organized in December 1841 and membership grew. A Masonic temple was completed by April 5, 1844, and dedicated. In addition, two other great building efforts were conducted in Nauvoo: the Temple and the Nauvoo House. In August 1840 Joseph contacted the "scattered Saints," calling for the building of a temple where the ordinances of the church could be practiced. Temple excavation began in October 1840 following Joseph's Conference directive. The revelation authorizing it led the way to the April 6, 1841, celebrations when the four cornerstones were laid. Anticipated rising to a steeple height, the building—larger than the one in Kirtland—included a large baptismal font. Told that if they did not complete the Temple they would be "rejected as a church with your dead,"[2] the Saints once again worked and sacrificed on a project that drew heavily on their reserves and energy.

The demands for building materials kept slowing the progress, for buildings of importance were rising up all over Nauvoo. The practice of baptism for the dead began in September 1840 and continued, using the river, until October 1841. Joseph told the Conference no more could occur until a Temple font was completed. By November the font for baptism for the dead was completed and baptisms resumed. Considerable work was done on the Temple, and it was dedicated on April 30 and May 1, 1846. The final work was never completed though it accommodated all temple practices. On October 8, 1848, it was destroyed by fire.

The Nauvoo House also was begun as a result of the document instructing the building of the Temple. The hotel was for the convenience of visitors who would come to Nauvoo—and, as it turned out, for Smith family descendants for generations to come. It was hoped they would report how well the church was doing and would be impressed with the economic growth. For a while, because of a shortage of men and material, the hotel was a rival effort to the Temple. The church broke ground for the hotel in 1841, but despite great effort, it was not completed at the time of Joseph's death in 1844.

By spring 1844 it was hard to determine what was civic and what was the purview of the church. In mid-March 1844 Joseph formally organized a secret leadership group known as the Council of Fifty. It was established as the result of two rather significant problems Joseph was trying to address. One had to do with a permanent settlement—perhaps even a country—that would allow the faithful, expanded by vast migrations of converts, to establish the kingdom on earth. And second, Joseph felt that the church needed a private, informal body of leaders who would serve as the core of power and authority for the kingdom. This body did not number fifty until about the time of Smith's death.

More than a committee or advisory group, the Council of Fifty was a policymaking body. Its meetings were held in secret and few knew of its existence while Smith was alive. Its records were limited, and what little we know of it comes from other sources that have commented upon actions of the council. It was sort of a shadow government, as Robert Bruce Flanders calls it, designed to serve as a special body of leaders in case of trouble or in emergencies. They were bound to the prophet by strong personal ties and were instrumental in advancing Joseph Smith's campaign for the presidency of the United States.

The group planned political strategies, were involved in economic development in general, and in some specific businesses, developed means for dealing with dissenters and apostates. But perhaps their most significant role was in planning for the growth of the kingdom. In this process they investigated locations for possible settlement. They negotiated with the government of Texas on the possibility of a grant for the making of a Mormon state. The Mormons were willing to trade groups of armed men to serve as protection for uncivilized sections of the country. The plan involving the Mormon Battalion, later used by Brigham Young, was influential in church growth in California.

Having received some support from Texas, Lyman Wight was commissioned to lead his Wisconsin colony to the new area during the summer of 1844. Smith's death disrupted these plans although Wight, somewhat later, carried out the colonization on his own, taking the Wisconsin group to the falls of the Colorado River in 1846 to a spot where the Mormon state was to be located.

Smith revealed some of his plan for "the imperial concept" of the kingdom to the Saints at a General Conference on April 6, 1844, envisioning with them the expanse of the church all over the United States, with Nauvoo as a center for temple ordinances. But this, like so much of their vision, was offset by the assassination of their leader. After Joseph Smith's death, the Council of Fifty played a significant role in support of Brigham Young and served as organizers of the great migration westward.[3]

Another aspect of Joseph's concern and involvement was in response to the church's mission to preach to all the world. It was only natural that the Saints, a large number with roots in Great Britain, would identify England as the location for their most extensive missionary activity. In early June 1837 Joseph told Heber C. Kimball, a member of the Council of Twelve, that he was to go to England and open up the work there. Orson Hyde and Joseph Fielding, a priest with relatives in England, were to accompany Kimball. They made preparations to go, realizing that they would need to go "without purse or scrip" and that the small group would need to find aid as they went. They made it to New York and after considerable effort, including some successful use of tracts, obtained passage on the packet ship *Garrick*. Once they arrived Joseph Fielding located his brother, a Baptist minister, who invited his American friends to use his pulpit. On Sunday, July 23, 1837, the work of the church began in England. Kimball took the opportunity and spoke to the large crowd. By the following week, now meeting in a private home, baptisms began. George D. Watt was the first, and by the end of the third week nearly thirty had been baptized. Shortly thereafter a branch was organized in Walkerfold.

The success of the missionaries is not hard to understand. Queen Victoria had recently come to the throne of England and there was a general unrest caused both by the forming of a new government and the uncertainties of this new monarch. The Church of England had been under considerable fire by the more conservative religious groups, and the scene was ripe for anyone

103

speaking with passion against the new evils that seemed to emerge out of the industrial revolution. Temperance halls, for example, were open to such men and women, and the new ministers spoke with a passion and conviction not generally heard.

By Christmas Day 1837 nearly twenty-four branches had been organized and three hundred Saints came to a conference at Preston. A hundred children were blessed. The results of the missionary activity of less than a year had been about 2,000 converts from all over England. The missionaries were well supplied for their return voyage and set sail, once again on the *Garrick*.

On their return to New York they sought out Elijah Fordham who had been of help to them earlier. They found that Orson and Parley Pratt had been active in the New York area, and that a mission of more than eighty members had been formed while the others labored in England. This was primarily the work of Parley Pratt who, while trying to find a way to reach the people of New York, wrote his pamphlet, *Voice of Warning*. Pratt complained that there was no one there to oppose him. He worked best in such opposition, but no one seemed to care enough to argue with him. After several months, and on the verge of quitting, Pratt had a breakthrough with the conversion of David Rogers, a chairmaker. Soon Pratt had several preaching invitations, and persons began to follow him. He even delivered a series of lectures in the famed Tammany Hall. When he needed to leave in April 1838, he left several branches and many members.

England continued to be an important field for the early church. Two years later Apostles John Taylor and Wilford Woodruff, accompanied by Theodore Turley, sailed for England. A few months later Brigham Young,

Heber C. Kimball, Parley and Orson Pratt, George Smith, and Reuben Hedlock followed. The General Conference of May 4, 1839, directed the Twelve to go to Europe. When it was undertaken, the Twelve did so as a council. Seven members were in England by April 9, 1840, and Willard Richards was ordained there on April 14. The mission was very successful, and by 1840 they were publishing the *Millennial Star*, which became a major publication of the movement. The impressive gains produced by the Twelve and missionaries were expressed in a significant emigration procedure that brought many British and European converts to the United States heading for Nauvoo.

Despite the growth and success at establishing a place of their own, political rivalries in Illinois drew the church into a no-win situation. The Mormons were more typically American, even Jacksonian, than most utopian-oriented communities. They were committed to the community, but they were also lower middle-class persons equally committed to a socioeconomic mobility for themselves and their children. The prevailing Mormon view of community was at the heart of the problem and was not, within the beliefs of the church, negotiable. Community was at the core of all missionary activity. Church beliefs called for expansion and for control of the community. The kingdom of God became increasingly political because it had to. But the church acted with some restraint. The Mormons had the political power to take over Hancock County but illustrated no real desire to do so. What they sought rather was freedom from government control, secular laws, and external law enforcement.

Robert Bruce Flanders has suggested that the fundamental objection was not to the unorthodox religious beliefs of the Mormons but rather how those beliefs were responsible "for the alarming success of the Saints in worldly affairs."[4] The church members' confidence in the rightness of their causes, thus their zeal as well as their limited understanding of the political reality of pre-Civil War Illinois, were to cause conflicts with the gentiles. The fact that Joseph Smith and the Council of Fifty gave consideration to plans for a Mormon state in Texas or California, and the apparent discussion about declaring Nauvoo as an independent garrison state free of Illinois, suggests that the Mormon leaders were endeavoring to prevent the failure and expulsion they had suffered so much in the past.

The effort to translate Smith's vision into political reality created a paradox—between belief and independence—that angered Illinois and frightened the Mormons. The literalism of the kingdom of God was a threat to the political pluralists who represented American thought. What followed in Hancock County was nothing less than civil war between political factions within the state. The already difficult situation was surely made worse by Joseph Smith's nomination for president of the United States on March 1, 1844, and Sidney Rigdon as vice-president, announced in May of that year. Smith campaigned for "theodemocracy," a belief that to most Americans was unacceptable. Added to these problems was the voice of dissent that emerged from persons who had been members of the Council of Fifty.

Rapidly changing doctrinal development not only caused unrest within the body but further isolated the Saints from the mainstream of Christian belief. The church had evolved in a variety of ways, some being alterations in the gospel as the members understood it. The early concerns had been directed toward church organization and with gathering and immigration. What had perhaps begun in Kirtland and Far West as a ritualistic gesture—the washing of feet, the anointing, statements of obedience and loyalty—were becoming mandated beliefs in Nauvoo. The practice of Free Masonry, introduced into Nauvoo at an early point, was seen by some as too influential, with unacceptable degrees of secrecy and ritualization.

Certainly the most significant change in terms of reaction was the introduction of the concept of celestial marriage (marriage for eternity) and its co-practice, polygamy (marriage for time). The concept appears to have originated in the Nauvoo church, probably from the nature of temple activities from about 1840 to 1844. The origins are so complex, and the documentation so vast and varied, a definitive explanation is not possible here; but a brief overview is necessary to understand the history of the church.

Joseph Smith and members of his family were concerned about those for whom the gospel message had come too late. This concern had been exaggerated by the fact that Joseph, Jr.'s oldest brother, Alvin, had died in 1823 without having "confessed Christ" and by the fact the funeral minister had affirmed Alvin was thus consigned to hell. In addition, Joseph was very aware of the effects of persecution on the Saints and the need for religious foundations that promised salvation for those loved ones who had not had the opportunity to respond to the gospel. And there was a need to promise for the future some of the security and predictability that seemed desperately lacking in their earthly life.

The pain was alleviated to some extent by Joseph, Jr.'s announcement to his dying father that the church would practice baptism for the dead. In October 1840, shortly after Joseph, Sr., died, Lyman Wight and Joseph Smith, Jr., taught the Saints at Conference about the principle of baptism for the dead. At the same time, they instructed the Saints on the need for a temple to practice this ritual. The practice appears to have gained considerable support among the members and was apparently practiced both in Nauvoo and Kirtland, Ohio. The scriptural basis for this was published in June 1841.[5] By October of that year Joseph told the church that additional baptisms for the dead would need to wait until the temple font was in place. This was accomplished in late November 1841. But baptism for the dead still did not acknowledge the long-term effects on the family in respect to priesthood expectations and responsibilities, and Joseph directed his concerns in this regard. In July 1843 the doctrine of celestial marriage (marriage for eternity) was introduced by revelation to the High Council.

Celestial marriage eventually meant that a faithful elder could be sealed to his wife and children for eternity. Thus the entire Mormon family—both the present and past members—could continue as a unit throughout eternity. This appears to have been the basis for the next logical, though perhaps unplanned step—polygamy. For in the chaotic conditions of life in the nineteenth century, men were likely to have more than one wife in a lifetime. Thus if sealed, they would be sealed to more than one wife in eternity. Understanding that a man may have two or more wives in eternity, it was an easy shift to the acceptability of two or more wives during his earthly existence. Add to this the degree to which Mormon belief diffused the usual lines between the secular and sacred world, and the connection seems obvious. By 1843 some church officials at Nauvoo were involved in what Richard P. Howard calls "an accident of history" the practice of polygamy.[6]

By 1844 a number of persons in Nauvoo were involved in plural marriage both celestially and polygamously. They were involved primarily because of deep beliefs in the implications of the law of celestial marriage as it directed their efforts toward the perpetuation of the kingdom. It was a promise that despite the turmoil, despite the separations imposed by persecution, despite the fact that they had been moved about the country in search of a safe place to be themselves, they would share together as an extended family in the promised kingdom.

The doctrine was kept as secret as possible, and what was known of Joseph's involvement caused considerable unrest. A small group distanced themselves from the church, citing the need to be more closely aligned with the basic beliefs of the gospel. By April 1844 some of those most disturbed by events in Nauvoo met together and formed a group to oppose them. This group included the following: William Law, until January 1844 a counselor to Joseph, and his wife; Wilson Law, William's brother; Austin Cowles, a member of the Nauvoo High Council; Robert and Charles Foster; and Chauncey and Francis Higbee. They decided the only way to get their message out was to publish their own paper, and on June 7, 1844, they published what was to be the first and only issue of the *Nauvoo Expositor*.

The *Expositor* was very critical of Joseph Smith, Jr., and the practice of plural marriage. The city council, which met under the leadership of Mayor Joseph Smith, saw the paper as responsible for growing criticism and on June 10 passed a resolution declaring it a public nuisance.[7] Understandably Joseph was angry, but he overreacted. The resolution calling for destruction of the paper was authorized by city policy and accomplished by the Nauvoo Legion. In identifying the *Expositor* as disloyal, Joseph Smith seems to have accepted responsibility for the practices being criticized—marriage as it related to time and eternity. He did indicate the *Expositor* authors were wrong in determining the church leaders were acting unlawfully when they were acting according to the keys of the priesthood. There can be little doubt that Joseph Smith, Jr., was aware of the existence and practice of polygamy in Nauvoo.

The difficulties came to a head with the destruction of the *Expositor*. And while both sides armed and marched about in anticipation of trouble, the trouble came first to their leader. Many non-Mormons could not understand how Joseph Smith could continue to ignore the fact that he was a wanted criminal in Missouri. As it was, many knew he prevented his extradition to Missouri by acting, in his civil capacity, to discount the warrants. At one point Joseph was even accused of attempting the assassination of the former governor of Missouri, Lilburn Boggs.[8] Joseph allowed himself, along with Hyrum and John Taylor, to be taken into protective custody by the Hancock County sheriff on charges that grew out of the destruction of the *Nauvoo Expositor*. At Carthage Jail on June 27, 1844, he was killed by a mob that overpowered jailers and shot the church leaders to death.[9]

Notes

1. Robert B. Flanders, "The Kingdom of God in Illinois: Politics in Utopia," *Dialogue* vol. 5, no. 1 (Spring 1970): 29.
2. Doctrine and Covenants 107:11a.
3. I am indebted to Robert Bruce Flanders, *Nauvoo: Kingdom on the Mississippi* (Urbana: University of Illinois Press, 1965), 292-299, for this discussion of the Council of Fifty.
4. Flanders, "The Kingdom of God," 29.
5. Doctrine and Covenants 107:10-11.
6. Richard P. Howard, "The Changing RLDS Response to Mormon Polygamy: A Preliminary Analysis," in Maurice L. Draper and Debra Combs, eds., *Restoration Studies III* (Independence, Missouri: Herald Publishing House, 1986): 145.
7. Nauvoo City Council Minutes for June 10, 1844, in *Nauvoo Neighbor* (June 19, 1845), available in the RLDS Church archives, Independence, Missouri.
8. Flanders, *Nauvoo*, 104.
9. For further reading: Robert Bruce Flanders, *Nauvoo: Kingdom on the Mississippi* (Urbana: University of Illinois Press, 1965); Donna Hill, *Joseph Smith: The First Mormon* (New York: Doubleday, 1977); Robert Bruce Flanders, "Dream and Nightmare: Nauvoo Revisited," in F. Mark McKiernan, Alma R. Blair, and Paul M. Edwards, eds., *The Restoration Movement: Essays in Mormon History* (Lawrence, Kansas: Coronado Press, 1973), 141-166; T. Edgar Lyon, "Nauvoo and the Council of the Twelve," in McKiernan, Blair, and Edwards, eds., *The Restoration Movement:* 167-206; Gordon D. Pollock, "In Search of Security: The Mormons and the Kingdom of God on Earth, 1830-1844" (n.p.: Ph.D. dissertation, Queens University, Kingston, Ontario, 1977); also, *Dialogue* (Spring 1970) concentrated on Mormons in early Illinois, collecting the works of participants at the Conference on Mormons in Illinois at Southern Illinois University. Essays on early Illinois history included materials by Stanley Kimball, T. Edgar Lyon, Robert Bruce Flanders, Richard Bushman, Leonard Arrington, Richard Howard, and John Abbot. This excellent resource should be checked for further information.

Assassination and the Crisis of Leadership

Reaction to the destruction of the *Expositor* was harsher than expected. Vicious attacks from the Illinois press added to the rampant rumors about mob action to destroy Nauvoo and move the Mormons out. Just how much potential violence was present is hard to establish, but both the Saints and the civil authorities were anxious to avoid any major confrontation.

Governor Thomas Ford of Illinois decided to visit Hancock County to avoid civil war and see if the laws could be maintained without violence. He found a large armed posse of Saints in Carthage. Believing the Nauvoo Legion had been mobilized, he called into service a third and hopefully neutral force, composed of militia from nearby Schuyler and McDonough counties. Joseph Smith, Hyrum Smith, and seventeen others were named in a writ because of the illegal use of the

113

Nauvoo Legion in the destruction of the *Expositor*.

Joseph Smith and others agreed to go to Carthage, Illinois, to be placed in "protective custody" under the authority of the Hancock County sheriff. The Illinois governor was trying to use his office to avoid bloodshed and wanted Smith detained until meetings could be arranged. It was while in the hands of the authorities of Hancock County and detained in the Carthage, Illinois, jail that Joseph and Hyrum Smith were killed and Apostle John Taylor seriously wounded at the hands of a mob on June 27, 1844. That the assigned guards left by Governor Ford did not move to protect the group was obvious. Ford said he had no reason to doubt the loyalty of the Carthage troops. He was wrong.

Following the assassinations the whole countryside was in a state of shock. Many left the area in panic because they feared the Mormons, armed and able, would seek vengeance. Others called on the state for protection. The state legislature voted 25 to 14 in the Senate and 75 to 31 in the House to repeal the Nauvoo City Charter. Almost immediately Brigham Young began to govern the city by means of the church's machinery of government. The Nauvoo Legion, declared illegal after 1845, was not disbanded, however, and with Young in command it continued to serve as a means of internal security and defense against any potential enemy.

As conflicts grew between the Mormons and their neighbors, Governor Ford appointed a commission to deal with the crisis in Hancock County. This mission was to induce the Mormons to leave the state. The commissioners took a contingent of some 300 men into Carthage late in September and discovered a Mormon force controlled it, but the force dispersed. The Mormon leaders responded unexpectedly well to the demand they leave voluntarily or be expelled, asking only that they be given time to prepare for the exodus.

Young and the Council of Fifty decided to send an advance group to the Great Salt Lake Valley. The exodus westward, in essence, had begun. For the gentiles of Hancock County the "Mormon problem" had been solved. Those faithful few who remained in the city were quiet and no threat at all. The city, once housing thousands, appeared as a ghost town. The Saints were once more on the move. But this time they left significant numbers behind, uncommitted to the leadership moving west but with no established leaders of their own.

When, in 1847, the majority of the followers moved with Brigham Young into the great westward stream, the Nauvoo experiment had come to a close. Many Saints, including Emma and her family, continued to live there but the church was broken. Alma Blair has written,

> ...a parting, nevertheless, with some choosing to create the kingdom in geographical isolation while others, individually or in small clusters, remained in the world and pondered how to find a new expression of the kingdom that would be true to the inner meaning of the concept, yet cognizant of limiting human frailties.[1]

With the death of Joseph Smith, Jr., and his brother Hyrum on June 27, 1844, the church faced a leadership crisis. Joseph failed to prepare the church for the time when he would no longer be available to lead. This meant that the vacuum would be filled by well-meaning but often unprepared claimants. The majority of church members, with a long history of following the leadership, chose to accept Brigham Young as their leader and in time moved west with him. But this was not unanimous.

Sidney Rigdon, the only surviving member of the First Presidency, was in Pennsylvania at the time of the assassination, and all but two of the members of the Twelve were on missions. All headed back to Nauvoo as quickly as they could. Rigdon, feeling confident that he was the logical successor, called a General Conference for August 6, 1844. But conditions did not support Rigdon, who had grown increasingly disaffected. Rather, the members supported Brigham Young, president of the Twelve. Many in Nauvoo were converts brought to the church by the Twelve as traveling missionaries. The Twelve were further aided by having been absent during much of the unrest that had preceded Joseph's death.

At the Conference the Twelve were supported in their calling. Young used this support to build on Joseph's earlier direction that the Twelve Apostles "form a quorum equal in authority and power to the three presidents ...."[2] Surely it was enough to guide the membership into the authorization of Young, as president of the Twelve, to lead them. And despite the protest of Rigdon and several others, Brigham Young was so recognized. But many felt power had been usurped and refused to follow Brigham. They eventually left Nauvoo with their followers to settle elsewhere and to reestablish the church as they felt it should be constituted. The extent to which the church at Nauvoo divided is best seen by tracing a few of the more significant leaders and their groups. Many of these groups were later pulled together into the Reorganization.

Lyman Wight

At Joseph's death Lyman Wight and Brigham Young disagreed over Wight's mission to Texas. Wight had been part of a special group asked by Joseph to go into Texas to secure timber for the Nauvoo Temple and to begin mission activities. When Brigham refused permission for Lyman Wight to continue with his assignment, Wight challenged his leadership. Brigham Young finally excommunicated Wight. Wight went ahead, taking about 150 persons to a spot near Austin, Texas. Finally, in 1847, they located a place of their own on the Perdinales River and named the community Zodiac. On January 1, 1849, they formally organized as the Church of Jesus Christ of Latter Day Saints with Wight as president. He was not, in his own mind, a successor to Joseph.

Soon Wight's group built a large storehouse and dedicated the upper story as a temple of the Lord. There they administered feet washing, anointing, and probably some of the Nauvoo Temple ordinances. The group practiced the same basic doctrines that had been followed in Nauvoo, including plural marriage. Wight introduced no additional scriptures nor did he attempt to expand the doctrines they had. They appear to have been more successful working with the law of consecration than many previous groups. Wight considered it his responsibility to hold the church together rather than to forge a new movement.

In fall 1849 his group joined with William Smith. Wight was chosen as a member of the First Presidency and was told to continue his work in Texas. The group, meeting in conference at Zodiac, voted to accept William Smith as their leader on a temporary basis until "young

117

Joseph" (Joseph Smith III) claimed his rightful position as his father's successor. When William Smith's group fell into disorganization, the Wight group simply continued as before. Severe flooding forced them to move in 1851, and they relocated near present-day Bandera, Texas. Wight died suddenly on March 30, 1858, and was buried at the old colony of Zodiac. After his death most of his followers joined the Reorganization.[3]

William B. Smith

As the last surviving male member of the Smith family, William had a particularly hard time with the adjustment to his brother's death. He was an apostle and had been ordained as patriarch to the church shortly after Joseph's death. But he and Brigham Young simply did not get along. Smith finally published a declaration in October 1845 in which he accused Brigham of a variety of sins, including the usurpation of authority. William Smith held that his apostolic ordination was as valid as Brigham's and urged the Saints to be careful about letting themselves be led astray. Brigham's response was to excommunicate Smith on October 19, 1845.

For a while William teamed with James Jesse Strang, but that did not work out either. William saw himself as the rightful leader and in 1847 announced himself as patriarch, prophet, and president of the church. In his new responsibilities he excommunicated the members of the Twelve who had followed Brigham. He called the Saints to gather with him in Palestine Grove, Lee County, Illinois. Isaac Sheen of Covington, Kentucky, associated with the group and began publishing the *Aaronic Herald* in February 1849. It became the official church newspaper. The name of the paper was changed to *Melchisedec and Aaronic Herald* in May and contained a revelation that named William Smith prophet and Aaron Hook and Selah Lane as counselors. It also provided for the appointment of a quorum of apostles.

In April 1850 Isaac Sheen, who had replaced Selah Lane as one of the counselors, was cut off from the church, and the Covington group broke apart over William Smith's practice of polygamy. William Smith and his followers went to Texas where they teamed up with Lyman Wight for a short time. But this union did not last either and shortly after that the Church of Jesus Christ of Latter Day Saints (William Smith) disintegrated. Later William Smith joined the Reorganization on the basis of his original baptism and was enrolled as a high priest in April 1878.

James Jesse Strang

James Jesse Strang was one of the more successful dispersion leaders to emerge after the death of Joseph Smith in 1844. He had not been a member for long; he was baptized and ordained early in 1844. Strang claimed leadership for the church based on a letter he produced, which named him Joseph's successor and ordered the Twelve to lead the members to Voree, Wisconsin. This letter, Strang claimed, was written by Joseph on June 18, 1844. On the strength of the letter, Strang convinced many members, including such leaders as William Smith, John E. Page, and William Marks, to follow him. Strang saw himself as Joseph's successor—one of the few who did—saying that at the time of the prophet's death a heavenly messenger appeared and ordained him. He led his people to Voree (Burlington), Wisconsin, but soon they began to locate on Beaver Island in the northern end of Lake Michigan, and by 1850 Beaver Island was the primary community.

In 1850 Strang was crowned king in a dramatic ceremony that designated him the head of a governmental and church organization outlined by the *Book of the Law of the Lord*. Primarily the group followed the writings in this book which, along with the Bible, Book of Mormon, and Doctrine and Covenants, supported their doctrinal beliefs. The book was first published in 1851 at Beaver Island. In terms of belief, they maintained a complex system, favored a strong sense of sacrifice, and in general accepted the beliefs of the Mormon movement.

The *Voree Herald*, a monthly, was published by Strang beginning in January 1846. At the end of that year he changed the name to *Zion's Reveille*, and it became a weekly. By 1847 it became the *Gospel Herald* and the next summer its publication passed to Frances Cooper who continued it until 1850.

Some of their accepted beliefs, such as baptism for the dead, were never practiced for the lack of a prophet in their later history. They accepted polygamy as an aspect of marriage for time and eternity, but this was not generally practiced after Strang's death.

In June 1856 Strang was attacked and mortally wounded by two men who expressed the strong anti-Mormon sentiment of the area. Following his death nearly 2,000 of his followers were forced to leave Beaver Island. Strang had not identified a successor, and the church drifted while an attempt was made to approach others, including Joseph Smith III and Charles Strang, but the church was unsuccessful. Lorenzo Dow Hickey, who eventually became the leader, and Wingfield Watson, his successor, were faithful and powerful men. The Strangites, now scattered, held together. Watson died in 1923. The church presently has several hundred members located in New Mexico, Wisconsin, and Michigan.

Cutlerites

Alpheus Cutler was born in Plainfield, Chesshire County, New Hampshire, in 1784. He was visited by Mormon missionaries there, and after what he considered a faith healing of his invalid daughter, Lois, he and several others joined the church. He appeared in Kirtland, Ohio, in 1837 where he was ordained by Joseph Smith to be "First Elder in the kingdom," a theological distinction that was later to play such an important part in his life.

Cutler, an accomplished stone mason, worked on the Kirtland Temple. He and his family followed the church from Kirtland to Missouri and then on to Illinois. After the members had been driven from Caldwell County, Cutler reported he returned on a secret mission to lay the foundation stones of the Temple at Far West. In Nauvoo Cutler again worked on the Temple, very likely serving as a supervisor. Completion, however, was interrupted by the death of the Smith brothers in 1844. In February 1846 Cutler and his family followed Brigham Young across the Mississippi in freezing weather and traversed the state of Iowa to Winter Quarters.

But the Cutler family was divided on the question of polygamy; two of his daughters, Clarissa and Emily, were plural wives of Heber C. Kimball, an apostle. Cutler refused to allow them to travel to Utah with Kimball, and they remained in Iowa, eventually marrying again. Cutler's break with Brigham started at Winter Quarters and was based on a theological disagreement. Cutler had been ordained as "First Elder in the kingdom," apart from his ordination as a high priest in the church. He believed that when Joseph died the church had been rejected, leaving only the kingdom. He thus believed he outranked Brigham. More so, however, he felt that Young was not following "the Plan," the communal economic order that was so significant to Cutler.

Few, but only a few, of the Saints at Winter Quarters accepted his claim and followed Cutler on a mission into Kansas in 1847 where he hoped to convert the Indians and establish the church. But they found the land hard and the Indians unresponsive, so Cutler moved his family back to Winter Quarters, broke completely with Brigham Young, and moved on to Manti, Iowa, in 1852. Within a year he had accepted responsibility for organizing the church, naming his son, Thaddeus, as first counselor and Chauncy Whiting as second counselor. The group accepted the church scriptures, the constitution of the United States, the Plan, and an eventual return to Zion in Independence, Missouri. But they did not accept polygamy or proselytizing. They believed the future growth of the church would come about when the Indians—who Cutler believed were members of the House of Israel—were moved by God to be involved. The group lived in Manti for seven years.

Their early difficulties arose from visits by the Josephites, as Reorganization members were called for years, who urged them to join with the Reorganization under Joseph III. Among those who responded to these overtures was Thaddeus Cutler, the first counselor.

Cutler responded to this threat by a call for his people to move on to a land he envisioned "far to the north between two beautiful lakes." Cutler himself did not live to see his promised land, having died on August 10, 1865, but the rest moved on, finally settling near the banks of Lake Clitherall. The Cutlerites, under Chauncy Whiting, were always strong abolitionists. But they unsuspectingly named their town Clitherall after a name they found carved in the bark of a tree. It was a recording mark of Major George B. Clitherall, a strong slave stater and officer in the Confederate army.

On July 31, 1865, the rest of the party arrived at Clitherall, bringing the settlement's population to some 125 individuals. They built a log church in 1870 that was replaced in 1912 by a two-story frame dwelling where a kind of abbreviated temple ceremony was carried out. The members worked hard and tried to live according to the temporal law—the Plan, a concept of Zion which held all things in common. But economic difficulties plagued them from the beginning. Other than a brief resurgence in 1912, the Plan, while strongly held, was not greatly practiced.

By far the most serious event was the arrival of T. W. Smith, an apostle in the Reorganization, who established a branch in Otter Tail County and urged the Cutlerites to join with the Reorganization. Many, including Mrs. Alpheus Cutler, associated themselves with that group. When Chauncy Whiting died at the end of the century it was assumed his son, Isaac, would accept the leadership, but he was not interested. Francis Lewis, Chauncy's brother, accepted it, but he was old and weak and the Cutlerites continued to decline in number. At Lewis's death leadership passed to Emery Fletcher and from him to his nephew, Clyde.

In 1912 the Cutlerites experienced a brief renaissance. In 1929 a second congregation was established in Independence, Missouri, where they planned to live by the Plan. But their efforts did not work out as anticipated. By 1961 the Clitherall group had dropped to five members. Today the site is a fishing village and the old church is boarded up. But the remaining members believe, as Alpheus Cutler stated, that though the members drop to very few, the time will come when they will rise again.[4]

Sidney Rigdon

As the only surviving member of the First Presidency, Rigdon felt he had every legitimate claim to lead the church. When the Twelve were sustained in their calling on August 8, 1844, Rigdon's claim as a spokesman was not voted on. However, the body did not support him, and he was eventually excommunicated by Brigham Young in September 1844. Gathering in Greencastle, Pennsylvania, his followers established a press where *The Latter Day Saints' Messenger and Advocate* was eventually published. In April 1845 the group changed its name to the Church of Christ and dropped the LDS identification from its paper.

Rigdon's group felt it necessary to take a strong stand against the Utah-bound community and announced to the public that there was no fellowship whatsoever with the Church of Jesus Christ of Latter-day Saints. Going further, they demanded that group's repentance particularly in terms of polygamy. They established a complete church organization and developed a stake at Pittsburgh. Accepting the Bible, Book of Mormon, and the Book of Covenants, Rigdon added several messages, presented as the word of God. But the group did not hold together, beginning to fall apart in 1846 when some positions taken by Rigdon were found unacceptable.

In 1863, as a result of contact with Stephen Post and Joseph Newton, Rigdon organized the remaining followers into the Church of Jesus Christ of the Children of Zion. The largest congregation was in Attica, Iowa, and Rigdon ran it by mail. The same year they issued *An Appeal to the Latter Day Saints* but it failed to attract many of the scattered Saints. In 1869 both Newton, his counselor, and John Forgeus, president of the Twelve, were excommunicated. In 1875 the main body of the church moved to Canada. The following year Sidney Rigdon died in Friendship, New York. While some of the faithful remained, the group lost most of its cohesiveness.

Disorganized

Probably hundreds of those faithful at Nauvoo were unaccepting of any of the leadership claims. A good number, it must be expected, joined other churches and continued their religious lives in that fashion. Many simply waited—often without knowing just what they were waiting for. To some the obvious successor was young Joseph, then only eleven, but who many remembered had been blessed by his father. They interpreted this blessing as an authentic claim. Joseph III, however, gave little initial indication of interest or preparation. Their disagreement, though never fully codified, tended to cover everything from church government to theology, all aggravated by twenty years of disassociation.[5]

Notes

1. Alma R. Blair, "Early Nauvoo Saints' Misunderstood 'Kingdom,'" *Restoration Trails Forum* vol. 3, no. 4 (November 1977): 8.

2. Doctrine and Covenants 104:11d.

3. Based on Steven L. Shields, *Divergent Paths of the Restoration*, Fourth Edition (Los Angeles, California: Restoration Research, 1990), 46-49. This is the best book on these many reorganization efforts, and I am particularly indebted to Shields and his work for much of the material in this chapter.

4. Biloine W. Young, "Minnesota Mormons: The Cutlerites," *Courage* vol. 3, no. 2-3 (1973): 117-137.

5. For further reading: Roger Van Noord, *King of Beaver Island: The Life and Assassination of James Jesse Strang* (Champaign, Illinois: University of Illinois Press, 1988); Annette P. Hampshire, "The Triumph of Mobocracy in Hancock County, 1844-1846," *Western Illinois Regional Studies* 5 (Fall 1982): 17-35; Marvin S. Hill, "Mormon Religion in Nauvoo: Some Reflections," *Utah Historical Quarterly* 44 (Spring 1976): 170-180; Richard P. Howard, "The Reorganized Church in Illinois, 1852-1882: Search for Identity," *Dialogue* vol. 5, no. 1 (Spring 1970): 63-75.

The Reorganization

Jason W. Briggs related that in October 1851, while concerned by the claims of various leaders, he sought and received divine guidance. Primarily it affirmed that Joseph's "seed" would be sent to preside over the high priesthood of the church. Briggs united with the church in 1841 and was ordained an elder in 1842. After Joseph's death he followed the leadership of Brigham Young, then James Strang and William Smith, but he was concerned about their claims to leadership. Once Briggs's revelatory experience had received confirming support from several leading church members, it was decided that a conference should be called.

On June 12-13, 1852, a small group of "scattered Saints" gathered in Beloit, Wisconsin, to consider Jason W. Briggs's "revelation" and to discuss the state of the church. They most surely must have been cautious about what they were to do. The group represented the remnant of Saints, many of whom felt deceived by other leaders. But in the main they were men and women who had determined to hold out until a rightful successor to Joseph Smith, Jr., could be identified. Finally the conference acted and agreed to a committee to report their action to other scattered Saints. This report, "A Word of Consolation to the Scattered Saints," identified the group's feelings and concerns. The resolution, which was unanimously accepted, contained several important declarations but most important perhaps were resolution 1:

> ...that this conference regard the pretensions of Brigham Young, James J. Strang, James Colin Brewster, and William Smith and Joseph Wood's joint claims to the leadership of the Church of Jesus Christ of Latter Day Saints, as an assumption of power, in violation of the law of God, and consequently we disclaim all connection and fellowship with them.

and resolution 2:

> ...that the successor of Joseph Smith, Junior, as the Presiding High Priest in the Melchisedec Priesthood, must of necessity be the seed of Joseph Smith, Junior, in fulfillment of the law and promises of God.[1]

Copies of the pamphlet, approved for distribution at the October 1852 conference, were distributed to members far and wide, and another conference was called for 1853 at Zarahemla, Wisconsin, on the anniversary of the founding of the church. What they were seeking was an organization that would allow them to function without a violation of their convictions concerning leadership.

At the 1853 meeting the group remained deadlocked for some time on the organization plan of Henry H. Deam. Deam had felt inspired to present a plan for organization primarily based on expanding authority from an elected leader. Finally the conference accepted Deam's presentation, and Jason Briggs was selected as presiding officer. The group maintained the beliefs that brought them together: (1) a disclaimer of all factions; (2) support of a lineal successor to Joseph Smith, Jr.; (3) recognition that the president needed to be ordained; (4) recognition that previous ordinations were legal; (5) the authority of the Bible, Book of Mormon, and Doctrine and Covenants; (6) the concept of gathering; (7) support for priesthood ministries; and (9) commitment to missionize their commitments.

According to their decision, a committee composed of Ethan Griffith, William Cline, and Cyrus Newkirk was called to name seven men as a majority of the Quorum of Twelve. The seven men named were Zenos H. Gurley, Sr., Henry H. Deam, Jason W. Briggs, Daniel B. Rasey, John Cunningham, George White, and Reuben Newkirk, with Jason Briggs as president of the quorum. In this position Briggs served as president pro tem of the church, a position he held for seven years. The conference also selected eighteen men as seventies. William Cline was selected as the stake president of the newly created Zarahemla Stake, made up of Argyle Township.

For the first two years their primary effort was directed toward consolidation. Thus in the Reorganization the first duties of the Twelve were to begin contacts with the scattered remnants. In this role they needed to accept considerable administrative authority—and to bring a ministry of pastoral reclamation. Missionaries were sent seeking the scattered members. A committee was selected to collect hymns for a hymnal, and Briggs was persuaded to write a plea to the many persons still scattered about the country waiting for a prophet. This work, "The Voice of the Captives Assembled at Zarahemla to Their Brethren Scattered Abroad," and the earlier, "A Word of Consolation to the Scattered Saints," were sent to Joseph's eldest son, Joseph III, who was still living with Emma in Nauvoo.

Perhaps of more significance than anything was the young church's response to the manifestations of the Spirit, which seemed to appear with increasing regularity among some members. The question about the difference between direction received by an individual and direction received for the church again came into question. Meeting in 1854, the body required that any such manifestations which purported to give guidance to the entire church needed to be presented to the body assembled, and such direction needed to be approved before its being accepted or circulated. In October of that same year H. H. Deam, whose dream had first given guidance about organization, apparently grew impatient with the delay and declared himself president of his own church. The Reorganization disfellowshiped him at its conference that same month.

In 1856 Joseph Smith III was approached by two men sent from the new Reorganization. Samuel Gurley and Edmund Briggs arrived in Nauvoo where they were greeted with the same respectful disdain with which Joseph greeted the continuous representatives of the Utah church. Samuel and Edmund apparently pressed their position to the point that Joseph threatened to expel them from his home. But calm prevailed, and before they left Joseph agreed to consider the letter sent from the Saints. However, he warned them he would not even consider fellowshiping with them, let alone the presidency, unless he himself felt a personal call. He promised to let them know if and when he did.

When the Saints met in their semiannual General Conference in 1859, they authorized the publication of a newspaper whose primary purpose was to inform the scattered members. This paper, edited by Isaac Sheen, was designed to rebuke the claims of false leaders and serve as a medium through which unity of the group could be established. The paper, *The True Latter Day Saints' Herald,* began publication in January 1860. The *Herald* has played a significant role in the movement ever since.

In the three years between the visit of Gurley and Briggs and when Joseph III accepted the presidency of the new reorganization, it was necessary for the young man to work out some significant problems and relationships. Just what it was that made the decision possible, and how he arrived at it, is hard to say. However, there were several problems to be faced. His mother, Emma Smith Bidamon, was married to Major Lewis C. Bidamon, farmer and shopkeeper. The Major was very much against religion, and while there is no evidence he tried to stop or even influence Joseph, there is no doubt that this man, who had been husband and father to them all, was not in favor of the church. A second difficulty, though not insurmountable, was that Joseph's wife, Emmeline Griswold, was not a member.

A third difficulty had to do with his relations with the LDS community in Salt Lake City. Joseph III had been contacted about joining with them but he had some significant reservations. First of all, Brigham Young was requiring rebaptism for those who followed him to Utah. Such rebaptism would indicate some questions about the church of his father. Accepting rebaptism could be interpreted as a statement of approval for church teachings instituted since the time of original baptism. Young Joseph did not seem inclined to do either. He seemed to have considerable difficulty with blood atonement, as he understood it was being preached, and with the question of plural marriage. There was also the matter of splinter groups, many of whom claimed some insight into the original teachings of "the Martyr," as Joseph Smith, Jr. was often referred to. But the Strangites and the Cutlerites, as well as William Smith and Lyman Wight, presented unacceptable positions. In the latter case it was primarily a question of the interpretation of Zion.

With this in mind, Joseph made his future course a subject of prayer and soon felt he had clear and specific affirmation that he should associate himself with the Reorganization. Having made this decision, he contacted his friend William Marks, whom he had known in the latter's responsibilities as the president of the former Nauvoo Stake, and indicated his willingness to serve.

As a result of further discussions with leading members of the movement and with the support of his wife and mother, Joseph III attended the 1860 General Conference held in Amboy, Illinois. There he appeared for their consideration. It was a strange meeting because Joseph presented himself with little more than his name and his own personal convictions to recommend him. Moreover, the 300 or so delegates represented a church not much larger than the Conference and one that was beset not only with financial questions but with doctrinal disagreements.

Joseph Smith III was then twenty-seven years old. He had a normal "Westerner's" experience, having tried shopkeeping and farming. He had studied law for some time, and he was, for nearly a decade, a justice of the

132

peace in Nauvoo. In this position he served primarily as a civil judge and seemed to have a reputation for fairness. But despite the obvious problems they all faced, the group accepted the young man as their leader and prophet with joy and eager anticipation. On Joseph's part he accepted the responsibility in a manner destined to predict his general attitude and behavior: "I came not here of myself, but by the influence of the Spirit." He went on to make a speech that was both cautious and imaginative, but which also caught up from the beginning his affirmations of his father's teaching. He concluded with a statement that must have been greeted with great emotion.

> I will come to you if you will receive me, will give my ability, and the influence my name may bring, together with what little power I possess, and I trust by your prayers and faith to be sustained. I pledge myself to promulgate no doctrine that shall not be approved by you or the code of good morals.[2]

The church that Joseph III was to lead was really quite scattered, not only in geography but in their beliefs and interpretations. Long left to their own devices, they had not had the advantage of discussing their beliefs with one another. As a result, the scattered Saints were quite individualistic and still maintained a great deal of skepticism garnished from years of conflicting claims for leadership. While they shared a certain isolation because of their decision to remain rather than to follow Brigham Young and their colleagues west, the very fact of that independence made it hard for them to surrender to the beliefs of a majority.

Several things were to be kept in mind in this transition. First of all, the church of Joseph, Jr., was a hierarchical one with interlocking and programmed authority leading to the president. The remnant of Saints were individualistic and less than willing to surrender all their rights to either a person or an institution. Some, in fact, still carried deep resentment against Joseph and what they considered an arbitrary authority. Joseph III, if he was to lead them, had to bring some balance between institutional loyalty, unified theology, and personal respect.

The Reorganization pulled together persons who for one reason or another had drifted away. Tapping their memories of belief and experience, men and women who had followed another path—as well as some who remained—reunited. Some followers of Brigham returned, some of those who followed Strang or Rigdon or Cutler or Thompson or Wight came together in memory of common experience. All worked together to recapture that which had first drawn them to the Restoration.[3]

Joseph III would need to gather about him more persons of leadership quality. The committee of October 1860 that was asked to select four members of the Twelve, selected only three. Joseph called his first counselor to the First Presidency in a document of 1863, and in 1865 and 1866 he added to the Quorum of Twelve by committee method. This was not sufficient, and in 1873 the calling of members of the Twelve was accomplished by documents.

The Reorganization began as a congregation, and it was the governmental philosophy of congregations that first controlled the effort. But the church—a much more generalized and unified institution—needed to operate on a larger philosophy. A philosophy of common consent rather than majority rule prevailed; a president took administrative and executive control; and general officers were responsible to the president and through him to the General Conference. And the Conference, a parliamentary body, functioned by rules governing debate.

As the church grew, some sort of organization was necessary because the concept of a centralized church was never questioned. The local groups were called branches because that is exactly what they were, *branches* of the church not *independent* congregations. Branches grew wherever the church or its missionaries went. As the church expanded or moved on, these branches continued to function and more and more groups needed to be banded together. Regular church conferences were held to bring these people, and eventually their representatives, together so the body of the church might confer and move forward together.

After the acceptance of Joseph III by unanimous Conference resolution, he was ordained as president by William Marks. The Conference recognized the membership of Emma Smith Bidamon, named Israel L. Rogers to be bishop of the church, and arranged for missionaries to move out with the news of Joseph's ordination. Joseph Smith III made it clear in his inaugural comments that he did not accept his father as the author of polygamy. Certainly he was not unaware of the belief many held that Joseph Smith, Jr., was involved in polygamy in Nauvoo. But it is documented that starting in 1879 in the *Herald*, Joseph spent a considerable amount of his time and energy in an effort to clear his father of any charges connected with the practice or inception of polygamy.

The climate for this position was strengthened first by the death of many who would have had firsthand knowledge of the events in Nauvoo. And, second, it was solidified by the development of a "them and us" move among the Reorganites. Having made the claim that the Reorganization was the true successor with the rightful leader, it became essential to represent the Reorganization as those who did not follow Brigham Young and his ideas to Utah. The Reorganization was presented rather as those who were untainted by the mistakes found in Utah. Because the Utah group had, at least to that point, continued the theory as well as the practice of polygamy, it was easy for the Saints to identify themselves as the ones who did not believe in polygamy.

The search for evidence to exonerate his father led Joseph III to Utah twice to speak to those who might have information he sought and also to seek among the Reorganization evidences and testimonies of his father's innocence. Joseph III, acting in good faith and with what must have been stout conviction, made this a central issue that was, in time, to have an effect on the church's growth and on how both Joseph and the church dealt with disagreement.

Smith and his family returned to Nauvoo where he continued to serve as justice of the peace and pastor of the Nauvoo Branch. Joseph was concerned with maintaining good relations with the citizens of those communities in which the Reorganization members resided. He was aware that opposition to Mormons—and the fear that often accompanied persons' lack of knowledge about the people—still existed. Concerned citizens remembering the years of decline and trouble surrounding the assassination had petitioned Joseph not to reestablish the Mormons in Hancock County.[4]

One early policy put forth by Joseph III that was to have a significant effect was his counsel to the church to not all gather in one place but rather to build up the church where they were. This was a departure of some note and drastically changed the idea of Zion. It recognized that church members must be involved in building their faith into the community. If members were, as their beliefs suggested, to carry the message of the gospel to all lands, they had to be out in the world where persons were. The gathering impulse, however, has remained strong in the church, and the Reorganization's move to Plano, to Lamoni, and then to Independence was always accompanied by persons who wished to settle with other members.

Because of transportation difficulties, General Conference was held in numerous places to accommodate the members. People attended where they felt naturally inclined. To implement Conference actions and carry out the wishes of the more general gatherings, districts were established, eventually with district presidents and apostles supervising clusters of districts. This relieved the need for frequent conferences of the whole church, but retained recognition of the General Conference as the one presided over by the First Presidency.[5]

The Reorganization was as missionary minded as was the early church. Soon its missionaries were sent to Utah Territory (1862); to England (1863); to the Society Islands, Scandinavia and Australia (1870s); and to the European continent (1880s).

It was the hesitation of the people of Nauvoo and the reality of practical economic considerations that were behind the guidance that members not gather too quickly. Urging men and women to live righteously where they were, Joseph cautioned he was not speaking against the gathering principle but simply recognizing that there was no value in recreating the difficult community problems of before. Later, when the church matured, they would gather.

His advice also called the members to political responsibility. In the first four or five years of his presidency, Joseph cautioned persons to avoid becoming unduly involved in the politics of their area, especially as a group, and to avoid political speeches from the pulpit. It is wisdom, he recommended, that they avoid acting as elitists or as critics of what others see as their best efforts. The role of the concerned minister is rather to play a cautious, sober approach to goodness and seek the power of forgiveness and love.

He was generally unable to follow his own advice on much of this, however, for the nation was becoming involved in the Civil War. In the face of this rending of families and states, Joseph and his primarily antislave church felt itself drawn into the conflict. After all, many who had priesthood responsibilities were of the age that the military draft was seeking. Joseph cautioned those persons not to offer themselves willingly—do not enlist—but if drafted by the government (for the church assumed the federal government was the legal one) then the responsibility was to be a good soldier, recognizing that the sin was on the nation and the individual was freed from responsibility, even for the taking of lives.[6]

While the military took some missionaries, and the ability of others to move about was restricted, they managed to bring in new members and reestablish the Reorganization's link with small branches. From as far away as England and California, groups who had maintained themselves sought to join with Joseph and the Reorganization. The membership of the group grew rapidly.

Finally by 1866, shortly after the close of the Civil War, it seemed wise to move Joseph's home—and thus the headquarters of the church—to a more centrally located spot. They selected Plano, Illinois.[7]

Notes

1. *Church History* 3: 209-211.
2. Joseph Smith III, "An Address to the Saints," *The True Latter Day Saints' Herald* vol. 1, no. 11 (November 1860): 255-256.
3. Alma R. Blair, "Reorganized Church of Jesus Christ of Latter Day Saints: Moderate Mormonism," in F. Mark McKiernan, Alma R. Blair, and Paul M. Edwards, eds., *The Restoration Movement: Essays in Mormon History* (Lawrence, Kansas: Coronado Press, 1973): 209.
4. W. B. "Pat" Spillman, *Studies in Restoration History: The Hastening Time, Volume 3* (Independence, Missouri: Herald Publishing House, 1988), 18-19. It was an indication of the church's increasing respectability that there later would be a lengthy petition from the citizens of Nauvoo asking them to return.
5. Maurice L. Draper, "Apostolic Ministry in the Early Reorganization," in Maurice L. Draper and Clare D. Vlahos, eds., *Restoration Studies I* (Independence, Missouri: Herald Publishing House, 1980): 219-231.
6. Mary Audentia Smith Anderson, ed., *Joseph Smith III and the Restoration* (Independence, Missouri: Herald Publishing House, 1952), 198.
7. For further reading: Paul M. Edwards, *Preface to Faith: A Philosophical Inquiry into RLDS Beliefs* (Salt Lake City, Utah: Signature Books, 1984); Linda King Newell and Valeen Tippets Avery, *Mormon Enigma: Emma Hale Smith, Prophet's Wife, "Elect Lady," Polygamy's Foe* (Garden City, New York: Doubleday and Company, 1984); Alma R. Blair, "RLDS Views of Polygamy: Some Historiographical Notes," *JWHA Journal* 5 (1985): 16-28; Roger D. Launius, "Joseph Smith III and the Mormon Succession Crisis," *Western Illinois Regional Studies* 6 (Spring 1983): 5-22; Roger D. Launius, "Perceptions of the Amboy Conference in the Non-Mormon Press," *Restoration Trails Forum* 6 (February 1980): 1, 11-12; D. Michael Quinn, "The Mormon Succession Crisis of 1844," *BYU Studies* 16 (Winter 1976): 187-233.

Getting Established at Home and Abroad

The new church located its headquarters in Plano, Illinois. Joseph Smith III moved there to serve as president of the church and as editor of the *Herald.* Located some forty miles from Amboy, Plano was a place where the church, long harassed and violently treated by fearful and confused neighbors, could establish itself. For it found there persons willing to give church members the time and the peace to establish the Reorganization.

The decision to locate in Plano was probably based on the presence of Israel Lewis Rogers. Rogers had joined the church in 1840. He was born in New York in 1818 and grew up around the canals of Boonville. It was there he heard about the church and joined the small group situated there. When the branch at Boonville moved to Nauvoo, he and his family followed them, locating on a farm not far from Sandwich, Illinois. He was a hard-working and ambitious young man who, in the next few years, managed to build a sizable estate.

Brother Rogers was uneasy about what was happening in Nauvoo. He first heard the story of the assassination and the breakup from persons who stopped by his farm on their way to and from Nauvoo. After the prophet's death he waited to see what would happen. In 1850 he joined briefly with William Smith but did not maintain that relationship long. In 1859 he came into contact with some of the scattered Saints in northern Illinois and Wisconsin.

After E. C. Briggs and W. W. Blair met with the Rogers family they decided to join the Reorganization. Israel Rogers accompanied William Marks and Blair to urge Joseph to join with them. Illness prevented him from being at the Amboy Conference in 1860, so he was surprised to learn that he had been called to serve as bishop to the church. Feeling his own limitations, he reluctantly accepted the position—a responsibility he would have for twenty-two years.

What headquarters existed for the church at that time, primarily a few records, accompanied Joseph who had returned to Nauvoo. During the next few years conferences were held in such places as Amboy; Galland's Grove, Iowa; and Sandwich, Illinois. But desire for a printing establishment led to consideration of a more permanent home. The *Herald*, which had been published by a firm in Cincinnati, Ohio, did not have the supervision they wished, so the October 1862 General Conference directed the purchase of a printing press. Following their instructions, and often using a measure of his own funds, Rogers purchased a small printing press which he located, in 1863, in the Henning Block in Plano, Illinois, not far from his home.

During the fall 1862 Conference, the Quorum of Twelve Apostles resolved that Joseph Smith III should assume the supervision of materials going into the *Herald*. Even at this point the leadership was well aware that the official paper of the church would be essential in building the unity they desired. At the April 1865 Conference the assembled members relieved the publication committee that had been responsible for the day-by-day supervision of the *Herald* and appointed Joseph to take charge. Originally plans had been made to locate on the Darnell farm for the Fox River Branch. With Rogers' help and considerable personal investment, the decision was made to locate the Herald Publishing House in Plano, Illinois. Joseph soon followed with his family.

Using the pages of the *Herald* and the advantages of a somewhat more permanent base, Joseph knew that several issues had to be faced by the church if it was to be what it was called to be and if the prophet's voice was to be heard as he felt it should be. On the domestic side, the new Reorganization was born in the midst of a great civil war, a war in which Americans had taken to the field of battle to solve questions of authority, government, unity, and expansion. Following the war America was well on its way to nationhood. Strong industrial development in the face of expanding agricultural growth was straining the energy of the people and the power of the government. America was rapidly moving toward a federal system and away from the implied confederacy of the early settlements. The frontier was opening up to social and industrial expansion. Reform movements arose to deal with the disastrous effects of unbridled economic individualism and state corruption.

The church was faced with a good number of unsettled doctrinal questions raised in Nauvoo and identified among the reasons for the scattering of the people following the assassination. At this point the "founding events" seemed to take on new importance. The primary push of the Reorganization was the Utah apostasy. At this point the Saints were working hard to assert their respectability and saw in the LDS both their greatest challenge and the most obvious source of disagreement with their community. Internally it appears that many leaders were persons who, in the main, had not known Joseph, Jr. Therefore, the First Vision and other founding events emerged as symbols that kept the founding leader at the center of their belief. "In time, the vision proved to be a symbol that was sufficiently multivalent to serve, on the one hand, as a 'shared community experience...that every Mormon must respond to personally,' and on the other, as a disseminator of agreement about things historical and a preserver of unity about matters doctrinal."[1] A brief comment here will identify the breadth of the questions facing the young church and its young president.

The complex nature of Divinity espoused by the movement seemed to stem primarily from the *Book of Abraham,* the King Follet sermon, as well as other writings of Joseph Smith, Jr., between 1832 and 1844. From these Brigham Young had supported and expanded on the idea of a God who had developed from the human condition. While some members of the RLDS Church accepted this in one form or another, the concept of a plurality of gods faded and was eventually silenced by Conference action in 1878. The Reorganization accepted the inheritance of "early" Mormonism and thus identified itself with a more orthodox Christian position of God, Christ, and Holy Spirit as an infinite, almighty, and all-powerful Godhead.

Also, an important question developed around the understanding of the nature of heaven and with it the temple ceremonies associated with "sealings in heaven and on earth." This included beliefs associated with baptism for the dead and marriage for time and eternity. Practice of such beliefs—understood and in some cases accepted by early RLDS members—was hampered because of the lack of a temple. But there were serious questions as well among the body about the divine nature of these practices. By the late 1870s these beliefs began to fade.

Obviously the significance of lineal authority was strong at this time. But associated with this there was perhaps far too much concern about Joseph, Jr., and the degree to which his own "perfection" affected the purity of his teachings. The concern that he be as pure and authoritative as possible led many to ignore his humanity, and they created about him a myth that would be hard for any person to live up to. The presence of Joseph Smith III among them also raised some discomfort, for his leadership meant an end to the loose and autonomous nature of the church during the interim years. Many felt uncomfortable in the larger, more centralized church after years of being scattered.

In the presence of these concerns the church felt the pull of its missionary calling. Joseph understood the need for a unified front to present to the world, but he was not going to wait for such matters to be worked out before moving out with news of the reaffirmation of the Restoration message. The earliest missionary activity of the Reorganization consisted largely of an appeal to scattered and disgruntled groups who were unwilling to associate with anyone. Now the church had to develop its own missionary arm. It consisted of getting the word out to the scattered Saints that Joseph Smith III had joined with the Reorganization. The process of spreading the word in the United States was difficult enough, but the church had been called to "go forth into all nations,"[2] and the Reorganization was anxious to be about it.

Understandably the first efforts were directed toward England where so many converts had been made during the 1840s. Charles Derry, who had himself converted in England and had come to America, returned to his home in 1863 where he located a good number of persons who had remained faithful to what they considered to be the core ideas of their conversion. There, with the help of Jason W. Briggs, Jeremiah Jeremiah, Thomas Taylor, and William O. Owen, real progress was made.

Within a short time five RLDS congregations had been identified. The missions did not grow as quickly as one might expect for a variety of reasons, not the least of which was that some converts were anxious to emigrate to America for the fulfillment of the concept of Zion which appealed to them. Converts often left the country of their conversion and migrated to America for the practical reason that life in pastoral America seemed economically superior to life in the greatly industrialized areas where conversion took place. The *Restorer,* printed in English and Welsh, was the first foreign-language publication of the Reorganization. Slowly the migration problem eased. By 1910 the mission had grown to 1,548 members.

News of plural marriage and other doctrinal difficulties in Salt Lake caused many persons in Scandinavia to reconsider their association with the church. While the RLDS were not as quick to respond to this oppor-

146

tunity as many encouraged, they did manage to send missionaries Hans N. Hansen and Magnus A. Fyrando, who were native to the area, in 1870. The promised harvest of disillusioned Mormons did not prove to be accurate, and most of the missionary work was done among the disadvantaged and those disillusioned, not by the Utah church but by state-controlled religion. The local church also had the problem of emigration. And by the turn of the century only about two-dozen members were active in Scandinavia.

Missionaries were sent as well to Germany and Italy and eventually elsewhere, but this was done primarily to reclaim lost members. The efforts were made with considerable courage and self-sacrifice, but lack of finances and training for personnel caused the work to languish. The money and people necessary for serious missionary work in these areas would have to wait until a later time.

Efforts in French Polynesia (Society Islands) had been successful when Joseph Smith sent Addison Pratt, Benjamin F. Grouard, and Noah Rogers, who landed in April 1844. Later, for nearly ten years, efforts were limited because of disagreements with the French government. In 1873, however, Glaud Rodger and Charles Wesley Wandell briefly ministered there while a boat on which they were traveling was being repaired. They located a small church made up of remnants who called their branch "Tiona" (the Tahitian word for Zion). In the few days available to them, they provided ministry to the South Sea Saints, baptized fifty-four into membership and ordained several. Unfortunately they had to move on, but others were sent in their place. First William Nelson and then Apostle T. W. Smith and his wife arrived more than a decade later.

147

Australia was another area where the church made a serious missionary try. The initial effort was by William Barrett sent from England in the 1840s to introduce the gospel. We are not sure of his success for he was never heard from again. Charles Wandell had had some success there, but he became disillusioned with the Mormon church. In 1873 he joined with the Reorganization and accepted a call to return with Seventy Glaud Rodger. After their brief but eventful stopover in French Polynesia, they arrived in Australia in 1874. Their effort was not as successful as they wished, but they managed to establish some contacts. Wandell died while there; Rodger carried on the work. In 1880 further effort was made with the arrival of men like J. W. Gillen, Apostle T. W. Smith, and Joseph F. Burton. They were disappointed by the limited success but did establish roots that would blossom into a significant Australian church. Apostle C. A. Butterworth, born in the United States, made his home in Australia from 1888 until his death in 1928.

The evangelism of the Sandwich Islands, now called Hawaii, was late in coming. In the 1890s a branch was established through the efforts of Gilbert J. Waller, Albert Haws, and a man identified only as "brother Luther." Within a couple of years the branch had more than seventy members, published its own newspaper, and was determined to translate the Doctrine and Covenants.

In North American and overseas assignments, the early missionaries of the Reorganization traveled without funds to cover even the necessary expenses of living, sometimes leaving loved ones behind to find ways to care for themselves. This required the missionaries to work at low-paying jobs to make enough money to continue to the next location, to do without, or to rely on the generosity of people whose economic status was little better than their own. But they had several factors in their favor. First of all, they were in the midst of a period in which religion was of extreme importance and when preaching and religious debates were forms of entertainment to which many subscribed. The message of the Restoration was profound enough to engage those who were aware of the basic tenets of Christianity but different enough that they stood out among others, promising salvation as the result of legitimate baptism at the hands of men of authority. It was a pragmatic religion whose tenets, among other things, promised the conservative morality that was so in fashion among the working people at the time.

One of the mixed blessings facing missionaries was the confusion between the LDS and RLDS churches. It was a blessing because it promised an introduction that often sparked the interest of those who otherwise might not have had time for the missionaries. But at the same time it meant missionaries were fighting the negative image created by the unorthodox doctrines ascribed to Mormonism. And it put the RLDS Church in the position of defending itself. The church, going to extremes to show the differences, often allowed that defense to become a submessage replacing its gospel message.

Missionary activities overseas usually began with friends and relatives who would give a good hearing to the message of the Reorganization. In many areas, however, the job was seen as bringing the message of clarity to those who still maintained their association with what was being identified as the "Brighamites." Debates, both personal and those conducted in large halls or specific street corners, were passionate and amazingly articulate. Although many of those involved in missionary work were generally uneducated and without much experience in public ministry, the level of the debates was often of high quality.

Despite the fact that conversions occurred, it was nevertheless hard work and often discouraging. Many of those to whom they spoke were unable to accept the message as delivered or remained loyal to the Utah faction of the movement. Others, of course, were consistently loyal to their own denomination, refusing the message for a variety of reasons. And in some areas into which the church went seeking converts, a state religion was maintained that was often as much social and economic as it was religious in nature.

Looking back, one is amazed at the degree of success of those who undertook missionary activity. It is important not to forget the commitment reflected in their willingness to leave their families, sometimes for years at a time, to travel into distant lands where they might or might not be accepted, and to be men and women of God among people who were often rough and uninterested.

The question of gathering was associated in the minds of the Saints with the concept of Zion. Until 1830 the word Zion was used often but was not well defined, or even its context made apparent. More definitions occurred following the conversion of Sidney Rigdon and a group of communitarians, who called themselves the "family" in Kirtland, Ohio. But early attempts in Ohio to move too quickly toward a physical expression of Zion caused problems over rights. This was eased somewhat by a restatement of the doctrine, primarily to suggest property could be consecrated for the poor, but it was unnecessary for the new members to turn over to the church all they owned.[3] However, the gathering aspect of the concept remained. And the concept of Zion as a special city grew. In 1831 Independence was identified as Zion and, for a while, Nauvoo served this function, but that ended in 1844. In 1909 Joseph III gave direction toward community living as a replacement for the idea of multiple gathering centers, but this view was never fully accepted in his time.[4]

Part of establishing their own identity was to be accomplished by accepting a new name. The early Saints tended simply to use the original name—they certainly felt they were the continuation of the original church—or to call themselves the "New Organization." However, the confusion finally moved them in the 1860s to adopt the name "Reorganized." It was not as efficient as they had hoped, and the confusion between them and the LDS church continued to be a major factor.

Relative to their assumption of originality was possession of Joseph Smith, Jr.'s "New Translation" of the Bible. At the April 1866 General Conference, Emma Smith Bidamon was asked to give the church the manuscripts that she had kept in her possession since her husband's death. A committee composed of Joseph Smith, Israel Rogers, and Ebenezer Robinson prepared the manuscript for publication. Bishop Rogers provided the $4,000 necessary for the publication. What later became known as the Inspired Version was available in December 1867 and became an important commentary on the scriptures, as well as further evidence of Joseph's faith.

Certainly one of the more important developments, and one which was to support the RLDS claim of originality, was the acquisition of the Kirtland Temple.

After the flight from Kirtland, the Temple had been sold at a sheriff's sale and used as a sheep pen. It was bought in time by Elder Russell Huntley, who repaired it enough to preserve it. He finally deeded it to Joseph Smith III and Mark Forscutt, and a limited title was acquired. In 1880, at the Court of Common Pleas of Lake County, Ohio, the RLDS Church requested clear ownership on the grounds it was the true successor of the church that built it. The case was unopposed. When the verdict was rendered, Judge Sherman clearly identified the RLDS Church as the successor and granted the Reorganization a clear title to the Temple. And, it must be understood, he granted them a significant outside encouragement in their mission.[5]

Notes

1. Jan Shipps, *Mormonism: The Story of a New Religous Tradition* (Chicago: University of Illinois Press, 1985), 32; and quoted from James B. Allen, "Emergence of a Fundamental: The Expanding Role of Joseph Smith's First Vision in Religious Thought," *Journal of Mormon History* 7 (1980): 61.

2. Doctrine and Covenants 39:4d.

3. Doctrine and Covenants 42, which is a rewriting of Section 44 in the Book of Commandments (1833).

4. See W. B. "Pat" Spillman, "On Conceptualization of Zion," *Courage* vol. 3, no. 1 (Fall 1972): 37-44.

5. For further reading: Maurice L. Draper, *Isles & Continents* (Independence, Missouri: Herald Publishing House, 1982); Roger D. Launius, *Joseph Smith III: Pragmatic Prophet* (Urbana: University of Illinois Press, 1988); Jan Shipps, *Mormonism: The Story of a New Religious Tradition* (Chicago: University of Illinois Press, 1985); Conway B. Sonne, *Ships, Saints, and Mariners: A Maritime Encyclopedia of Mormon Migration, 1830-1890* (Salt Lake City, Utah: University of Utah Press, 1987); Richard P. Howard, "The Nauvoo Heritage of the Reorganized Church," *Journal of Mormon History* 16 (1990): 41-52; Roger D. Launius, "Method and Motive: Joseph Smith III's Opposition to Polygamy, 1860-1890," *Dialogue* 2 (Winter 1987): 106; Clare D. Vlahos, "Moderation as a Theological Principle in the Thought of Joseph Smith III," *JWHA Journal* 1 (1981): 3-11.

Clarifying the Issues

The identification of Joseph Smith III as president and prophet of the Reorganization was followed by a long, difficult struggle during which differences of opinion and belief were worked out among the members. The struggle was made more difficult by the composition of the membership itself. Those who composed the Reorganization were, we must remember, persons who had broken with the early church for one reason or another. They had not followed Brigham Young westward or, if they had, many of them had left Utah to unite with the RLDS Church. Nor had many selected to stay with one of the aspirants to leadership. They held in common their various original disagreements and many had invested a great deal in their particular convictions. They would not be dissuaded easily.

These were tough-minded people who had been betrayed before by what they considered too much trust. Almost to a person, they were pleased with Joseph Smith III's alignment with the Reorganization, but they were, nevertheless, aware of the price they had paid for taking too much for granted. The variety of beliefs were more apparent because of Joseph Smith III's almost inherent understanding that if he were to unify the church, he must centralize authority. He was a practical man and appeared to have the patience to see through many of the problems that faced the church, rather than trying to argue them out. Thus he avoided the obvious disunity that could follow any prolonged battle over doctrine.[1]

One of the most obvious, and eventually pressing, concerns had to do with the nature of the presidency itself. The more Joseph succeeded in unifying the people and in centralizing the office of the president, the more this concerned some of the leaders. This is symbolized in the reform effort launched by Zenas Gurley, Jr., the son of the man who had played such a significant role in bringing the Reorganization into being. Gurley was concerned about the power of the prophet's office and was convinced that the doctrinal errors introduced into the church at Nauvoo were the result of too much unrestricted authority held by the president. Gurley was not contesting Joseph Smith III's role, nor his authority to act as president of the church. But he did believe that Smith had brought too much power unto himself, establishing a virtual dictatorship of ecclesiastical authority, and that the leader of the church—like any leader—needed to be under continued judgment.

A second aspect of this reform consideration centered on Jason Briggs, an essential member of the Reorganization, who disagreed with Joseph III on several doctrinal issues. Briggs had served as president pro tem and had played an instrumental role in bringing the Reorganization into existence. But he was concerned about the Smith family presence in the hierarchy and its tendency to rob the church of much of its autonomy. Briggs felt that individual belief and commitment were essential; thus, there must be a way to express differing views. He directed his questions by means of the *Messenger*, a missionary paper published by him in Salt Lake City, in which he argued the independence of those thinking people who differed with the prophet.[2]

The difficulty became more immediate when the Reorganization accepted Joseph Smith, Jr., and his revelations en masse. This seemed to create, at least for Gurley, a situation in which belief in Joseph Smith's revelations became a test of faith. He felt such unthinking acceptance perpetuated the mistakes imposed by the past. Gurley was determined that the conference of members and delegates impose some limitations on the power of the presidential office. It was Gurley's belief that until the church endorsed specific doctrines as presented, rather than accepting the prophet's ideas as rules of law, they were subject to more error. He hoped that he could persuade church members to his way of thinking and made every effort to establish a debate in the pages of the *Herald* to bring this about.

The debate really began when Apostle Gurley's resignation was considered in 1879. He resigned, by his own admission, to bring his issues of concern before the people of the church. President Smith would not accept the resignation and, as a result, it was taken to the General Conference for action. However, after an interpretation of the Doctrine and Covenants that Gurley felt he could live with, the Conference reinstated Gurley. Joseph Smith III made an effort to keep the disagreement with Gurley and Briggs as low key as possible. There is no doubt, however, about his hostilities to the point of view expressed by both Jason Briggs and Zenas Gurley. But Smith seemed to support the men involved. His support of Briggs in 1877, concerning an interpretation of the Conference's failure to sustain him, amounted to that action being interpreted as a silence rather than a suspension. Likewise, the president's effort in 1879 to provide a compromise saved Gurley's contribution at least for a while.

In 1880 Gurley began to push his position. He wanted President Smith to open the pages of the *Herald* to him, but Smith, as editor, refused. Smith was willing to allow deviations of thought within the church and, on numerous occasions, had editorialized about this view in the *Herald*. But he was not willing to allow such points of view to create stress in the unity he had fought so hard to accomplish and certainly not in the official newspaper of the church.

The responder to Gurley's position was W. W. Blair, the only other member of the First Presidency and, therefore, the obvious person to respond. Joseph must have felt his hands were tied. But, while Joseph had little to do with the debates, there is no doubt he was aware of—and generally approved—Blair's position. After all, when Blair spoke it carried the power of the Quorum of the First Presidency, and Smith would not have allowed that power to be used in ways contrary to his position. And, as editor, Smith would have to approve whatever Blair was to print.

As was expected, Gurley requested an opportunity to reply in the pages of the *Herald*. He did so in three articles published from February to March 1885 in which he spelled out his intended reforms—reforms primarily designed to limit the power of the Presidency. Apostles Zenas Gurley, Jason Briggs, and E. C. Briggs

156

did not attend the 1885 General Conference. The reasons why are not really clear, but for Jason Briggs and Zenas Gurley it was seen as a protest against limitations on their access to the pages of the *Herald*. E. C. Briggs's reasons are not clear. The Quorum of Twelve censured the three missing apostles. When the time came for the sustaining vote, members of the Conference asked the president for his advice. President Smith recommended that E. C. Briggs be sustained and then returned the decision on Jason Briggs and Zenas Gurley to the Conference. They were not sustained, and the Conference provided no reason for its actions.

It is hard to determine the extent to which Gurley had managed to raise support. Certainly he had that of Jason Briggs on ideological grounds. There is evidence that E. L. Kelley supported him, at least in the beginning. And some congregations, principally Pleasanton and Lone Rock, Missouri, were supportive to the extent that some members actually left the church when Gurley's reforms failed. Ironically the Conference was not in a position to expel Gurley or Briggs. Certainly the key to Gurley's argument for more defined doctrines explained why the Conference had no basis for excluding him. There were no necessary creeds or doctrinal beliefs, so it was nearly impossible to expel someone for heresy. In May of that year Smith answered a question about the status of the two apostles who were not sustained. His reply was that they were still members of the quorum and held priesthood, but because of the Conference vote they were no longer able to function as ministers in the church, nor could they do so until those limitations were lifted by the body.[3]

The 1886 Conference was saved from having to take any action on either Gurley or Briggs because both withdrew from the church. The reasons are somewhat vague despite a presentation of nine contested doctrines. Briggs probably withdrew because of being denied access to the *Herald* and the intolerable narrowness that attitude represented to him. At the 1886 assembly Zenas Gurley, his family, and Jason Briggs withdrew from the Reorganization. Documents of withdrawal and reasons were presented, trial rules dispensed with, and their names removed from the records. The dramatic exodus of two apostles for the most part was uncontested. But after the reform danger had passed, the general verdict seemed to be that withdrawal was unnecessary.

Because of the straight and forthright defense of his position in the *Herald*, many accepted Briggs's explanation for both men. However accurate Briggs's reasons were, Gurley withdrew for reasons of his own. For Gurley felt that his past successes at reform were being erased. The combination of a presidential attack and the refusal to sustain him without announced reasons meant the church was moving to its pre-1879 position. But perhaps more important, he was convinced that every opening for further reform measures were closed to him. The *Herald* could no longer be used as he saw fit, the ministerial roles of preaching and teaching were primarily closed to him, and the power of the quorum responsibility was gone. It was April before Gurley decided to withdraw—perhaps finally goaded by the Conference failure to explain its actions concerning him.

In both cases the withdrawals were probably unnecessary and very sad, considering the men's long association with the church. They were not in basic disagreement about much of the doctrine, but those they contested became so important to them there was probably no other outcome possible. Delegates to the General Conference viewed Gurley as standing in opposition to the power of the prophet and the reality of revelations themselves. He was a "denier of the faith." His views "attacked not only error but assurance."[4]

When the church accepted Joseph Smith III in 1860 they did so as their prophet. The result of the 1885 General Conference was just the opposite of what Gurley had in mind, for it reinforced that earlier decision and clearly acknowledged that the source of prophetic power was the office of the prophet. This was certainly nothing new. The prophet had been in this position since the 1830s. But it was significant because "as a result of Gurley's reform defeat, the Reorganized Church clearly defined its seat of power within the prophetic office."[5] It offset the first of several challenges to the power of the office and set the stage for the next thirty years.

Among the doctrinal concerns raised during this reform effort were several theological questions that had to be worked out. Among these was the question of plurality of gods and a main source of that concept, the *Book of Abraham*. In the early stages of the Reorganization the fledgling group published "A Word of Consolation to the Scattered Saints" which affirmed the idea of a lineal priesthood. They cited the *Book of Abraham* as their source.

Among those who retained a conviction about the book was Isaac Sheen, then editor of the *Saints' Herald*. Whether his belief in the book was the result of his convictions concerning the plurality of gods or the other way around cannot be measured with a great deal of accuracy. But both the *Book of Abraham* and the concept of the plurality of gods were popular among some who formed the Reorganization.

One example of this would be the publication of the first volume of the *Synopsis of the Faith and Doctrines of the Church*. This work had been authorized by the 1865 General Conference. It included some rather long and complex statements about the doctrine of God, including a section on the plurality of gods. The *Book of Abraham* was listed, along with the Bible, and quoted.

Apart from the *Book of Abraham* itself was consideration of the doctrine of the plurality of gods. The concept suggested that the gods, in council, decided to put humans on earth with the potential of becoming gods themselves. In the *Book of Abraham* the Son of God is pictured as saying to a group of preexistent spirits, "We will go down for there is space there, and we will take these materials, and will make an earth whereupon these [the preexistent spirits of all human beings to inhabit the earth] may dwell."[6]

On a spring day, April 7, 1844, Joseph Smith, Jr., preached a funeral sermon in honor of King Follet, an elder who had been killed in a construction accident. The most prominent doctrine discussed was that of the plurality of gods. This came as a surprise to many members, but it was not new to the discussions of the councils and, generally, was accepted by the members. It was published as part of the doctrinal belief by Orson Pratt in *The Mormon Creed*.[7] It was not totally accepted. William Law left the church in April 1844 in opposition to Joseph Smith, Jr.'s doctrines, among them polygamy and the plurality of gods.

This belief, as it eventually was defined in the LDS movement, teaches the existence of many gods—many in the sense of divine beings of pure moral character

Presidents of the Church

Joseph Smith, Jr.
(1830—1844)

Joseph Smith III
(1860—1914)

Frederick M. Smith
(1915—1946)

Israel A. Smith
(1946—1958)

W. Wallace Smith
(1958—1978)

Wallace B. Smith
(1978—   )

Kirtland Temple

Nauvoo Temple

The *Evanelia* gospel boat.

Public debates and lectures were popular missionary methods in the nineteenth century, such as this one promoted by the Clay Cross Branch in England (RLDS Archives file #T-11, used with permission).

Lamoni, Iowa, was the center of church activity from the 1870s to the early twentieth century. The historic Brick Church (top photo, RLDS Archives file #2-276) was destroyed by fire January 29, 1931. The South Woods campground near Lamoni (photo ca. 1910, RLDS Archives file #2-277) provided typical reunion experiences.

After a fire destroyed the office and printing plant of Herald Publishing House in Lamoni in 1907, the church quickly saw to the task of rebuilding (top photo). Within a short time the presses were once again busy (photo ca. 1910) printing scriptures, the *Saints Herald*, and other tracts, books, and periodicals.

The Independence Sanitarium & Hospital was established early this century in the building at left, with operations transferred to the "new" building next door in the 1940s. Renamed the Independence Regional Health Center, it now occupies a modern, 340-bed facility to the south.

Construction began directly across Truman Road from "the San" in 1954 on Resthaven Nursing Home, which provides care for many of the church's elderly members.

Auditorium construction was a slow process. Although begun in 1926, the building's interior with extensive ramps and huge conference chamber was not completely finished until the late-1950s. Work was halted completely for many years due to massive General Church debt, the Great Depression, and World War II.

The unfinished conference chamber provided the site for the 1930 General Conference (top photo, RLDS Archives file #2-1469). The 1962 World Conference (bottom photo) provided a scene no longer part of Conferences: at the final business session, church appointees received their new assignments, gathered at the rostrum, and sang the hymn, "I'll Go Where You Want Me to Go, Dear Lord."

The Laurel Club has been providing meals for church and community gatherings since the early twentieth century, while contributing tens of thousands of dollars to worthy causes and programs (RLDS Archives file #6-72).

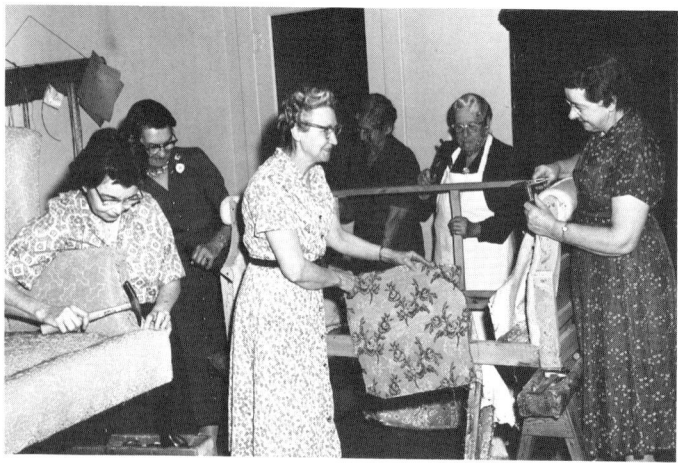

One of the many activities of the RLDS Social Service Center, supported throughout the years as a community service of the General Church and Center Stake of Zion.

Missionary work in the Society Islands (French Polynesia) began in 1844 and continued in the Reorganization. Here, Elder Clyde F. Ellis baptizes a young woman from Makatea branch in 1919 (RLDS Archives file #2-142).

Opening of the Orient mission was a watershed event in the church's missionary effort. This Korean school was one of many programs (RLDS Archives file #2-330).

Typical winter scene on the Graceland College campus.

The Park College Board of Trustees (1979).

The School of the Restoration provided the first formal training for church appointees.

Church expansion in India (top photo, RLDS Archives file #2-254) and Africa (RLDS Archives file #2-3.1) since the 1960s has challenged the church to rethink its understanding of being a worldwide communion of Saints.

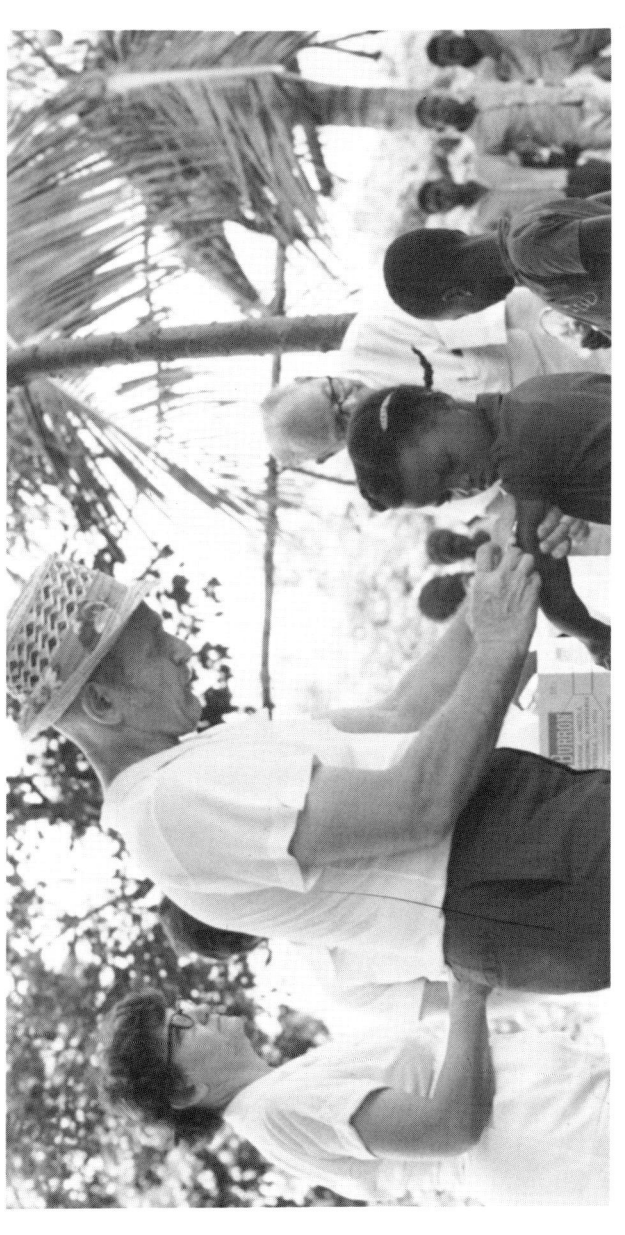

Medical and dental teams sent to the poverty-stricken island nation of Haiti in the 1960s has led to the establishment of one of the fastest-growing missions anywhere in the entire World Church.

The Temple in Independence, Missouri.

who work in harmony for a common end. It is defined by the term "plurality of gods," which avoids the more common term polytheism and its unacceptable definitions. The nature of the gods—and our God—is in the process of "becoming" rather than "being." This is affirmed in the King Follet sermon in which Joseph Smith taught, "God himself was once as we are now, and is an exalted man, and sits enthroned in yonder heavens!"[8]

The idea of the plurality of gods was strong in the Reorganization, and in 1865 the Council of Twelve debated the issue and finally concluded they considered it divine. Joseph Smith III prevailed on the Twelve with the view that the belief was not a requirement for "membership in good standing" nor was it to be taught as a general doctrine of the church. In time those members of the council—and of the church—for which this doctrine carried much significance began to die out. Thus, instead of a major debate over the issue, it simply faded away as the more orthodox Christian view of God, that of the Trinity, became the primary belief of the movement. By 1890 the plurality of gods was referred to as a "doctrine of man."[9]

Somewhere in this process the *Book of Abraham* began to fade into the background. There are at least two reasons that might explain this. The first has to do with the treatment of blacks in the *Book of Abraham*. Joseph III was far more open in his acceptance of blacks in terms of membership and priesthood than was Joseph, Jr. In early 1836 Joseph, Jr., pleaded for noninterference with the Negro-slave policy of the South. He supported the basic prejudices of the time, linking the peculiar institution of slavery with the biblical stories of Canaan. In what was written in the *Book of Abraham*, it seems as if Joseph Smith, Jr., expanded the usual curse of servanthood to include the inability to hold priesthood. Joseph III came much closer toward an acceptance of all persons when in May 1865 he delivered a document that announced it was wise to ordain persons of every race who had received and responded to the teachings. This did not mean the immediate baptism or ordination of large numbers of blacks, but it did begin the process of moving in that direction. Again, this was accomplished without undue effort or fanfare; thus, it was accomplished without major debate. He simply allowed it to happen.

A second reason for the decline in acceptance of the *Book of Abraham* lies in the comparison between the Reorganization and the LDS church. As the LDS faction put more and more stress on the *Book of Abraham*, canonizing it as part of the *Pearl of Great Price* in 1880, the RLDS position became more significant as a means of differentiation. Probably the most definitive statement came from President W. Wallace Smith in March 1970[10] when he indicated that the Reorganization did not consider the *Book of Abraham* inspired.[11]

Yet another issue that had to be dealt with was polygamy. Many early members of the Reorganization wanted the issue cleared up. Sidney Rigdon had been one of those who, later in his life, felt the need to address the issue. He explained that the leaders of Mormonism had introduced the idea of plural marriage and that it was practiced secretly by the Twelve even after the assassination. While this might have been easily explained away as harsh feelings between the leaders, he was not alone. Others, including W. W. Blair, Charles Derry, Isaac Sheen, William Law, and the Cowles brothers, offered additional testimony.

By 1867 the response to polygamy—by those associated with the Reorganization—was more a stand against polygamy than a defense of Joseph the founder. In the vast amount of antipolygamy rhetoric from 1852 until 1860 when Joseph Smith III assumed leadership, there was little effort to disassociate Joseph Smith, Jr., from polygamy as it developed in Nauvoo. The availability of materials like William Clayton's diaries associate Joseph Smith, Jr., with celestial marriage, but they also acknowledge that he was disturbed by the power of plural marriage as the theological implications manifested themselves in polygamy. Richard P. Howard, church historian, put the best light on it when he wrote, "Once Joseph Smith, Jr., came to see the harm being done to the church, he sought the help of Marks to use all their combined power to put down polygamy in the church. However, by that time things had gone too far."[12]

When Joseph Smith III came to the Reorganization, he did so as an avid foe of polygamy. In his first sermon preached before his new followers at Amboy, Illinois, on April 6, 1860, Joseph acknowledged his utter abhorrence to the concept of plural marriage. His determination to free his father from the burden of polygamy became a major focus of the Reorganization's claim for self-identity. The source of his position emerged from a simple syllogism. Major premise: My father was a good man. Minor premise: Good men do not practice polygamy. Conclusion: Therefore, Joseph Smith, Jr., was not involved in, nor did he initiate, polygamy.[13]

This was the established position, and Joseph III held it through his life, spending considerable time and effort following leads and attacking accusers. Smith believed that maintaining his family honor was essential not only to the Smith family but to the Reorganization. For to clear his father was to identify once again the separation that existed between Utah Mormonism and the mainstream of Protestantism to which he was more closely aligned. The church moved into the period of Joseph Smith III's presidency acknowledging along with him that if indeed his father had been involved in polygamy, then he was wrong. Polygamy was a violation of both civil and church law. The reorganization of the scattered Saints—many of whom scattered because of this particular doctrinal issue—was not accepting polygamy in any form, neither as a celestial necessity nor an earthly consideration.

It is most understandable why the Reorganization—seeing itself as the successor to the original message—would place polygamy outside the mainstream and want assurances that its founder was not associated with it. There is no blame attached to Joseph Smith III's response other than, perhaps, in his insistence that by freeing his father from any responsibility at all, he pushed the Reorganization into making the issue more significant than it should have been.[14] But even with the concern about Joseph the founder, the RLDS Church was opposed to the doctrine of polygamy primarily on the grounds it was not of God. It was only opposed secondarily on the grounds that Joseph Smith, Jr., was not responsible for it. Joseph III even made the modest assertion that if his father had been responsible, he would be punished.

At a Joint Council of the Presidency and Twelve in 1867, the whole question was officially discussed. Joseph failed to support a motion that affirmed Joseph, Jr., had been free from all responsibility for polygamy. He recognized the "almost universal opinion among the

Saints that Joseph was in some way connected with it" and felt that any such affirmation would be of little value.[15]

While the differences between the RLDS and the Utah-based LDS had always been important, with polygamy a central issue, the rivalry increased during the 1870s and the polygamy question became more and more important as a symbol. Joseph III addressed the issue with a two-prong attack: first, to affirm himself and his presidency as the rightful heir and to expose the false doctrine of polygamy; second, to work with non-Mormon forces to destroy plural marriages by breaking the Mormons' power to live with the doctrine unchallenged in Utah.[16] By 1880 or so Joseph's view had become so generally accepted that the great majority came to recite it without much consideration.

The Reorganization's pressure on Utah and on the federal government concerning the practice of polygamy led Smith's friends in the late 1870s to petition President Ulysses S. Grant to name Smith as governor of Utah Territory. Just how serious this was is questionable, but at least one supporter, Edward W. Tullidge, claimed that Joseph Smith III as governor and 200 missionaries would soon convert 20,000 Utah Mormons to the antipolygamy cause.[17] Even the *Weekly Argus* of Sandwich, Illinois, supported Joseph, reporting in 1881 that he was a "true, loyal citizen, a practical Christian, a temperant [sic] man, an able leader, and bitterly opposed to that 'peculiar institution.' "[18]

His concern about polygamy led Joseph to make several trips to Utah. The first visit occurred as a stopover in 1876 after an extended trip to California and Nevada. In Utah he met with his cousin, Joseph Fielding Smith, Hyrum's son who had been born in

November 1838 while Joseph and Hyrum were in Liberty Jail. Joseph III, ill and tired from a long trip, found the meeting difficult. It was made more so by his first experience coming face to face with polygamy.

The fight against polygamy continued in Washington, D. C., and in February 1882, Joseph Smith left for Washington where he supported a petition affirming that the Reorganized Church be recognized as a separate organization from the Utah LDS. The Reorganization had sent representatives to Congress to testify at the hearings of the Edmunds Bill, which passed and was signed by President Chester Arthur on March 22, 1882. Their purpose was to be sure that the bill, directed against the practices of polygamy, did not limit the privileges of the Reorganization. President Smith had appeared in Chicago to address a group supporting the Edmunds Act and, while well received, further expanded the antagonism with the Smith family in Utah.

This came up in correspondence between Joseph III and Joseph Fielding Smith. While the two Josephs corresponded most of their adult lives, they met only briefly after that. In 1885 when Joseph III went west, Joseph Fielding was in the Sandwich Islands avoiding arrest for polygamy. In 1889 Joseph Fielding was still in hiding. In 1905 Joseph Smith III was at the LDS conference and saw his cousin, but they apparently did not meet. Their letters were primarily about polygamy but, to some extent, about authority as they represented conflicting views of that as well. While frank and sometimes harsh, the letters portrayed something of the bond the two leaders must have felt. Joseph III continued to press the argument that he "headed the church that his father had restored, and the Utah church was in error."[19] The strained relationship continued into old age when, as presidents of rival churches, the two met once again in November 1913. Joseph Fielding was in the Midwest and stopped to visit Joseph III.[20]

Joseph assumed a victory when Wilford Woodruff, the LDS president, instructed his people in 1890 that members should no longer undertake any marriages in violation of federal law. This may have ended the immediate cause of the concern, but for Joseph and the Reorganization it did not end the argument.

The practice of baptism for the dead was another doctrinal issue that needed to be worked out. Practiced first in the muddy waters of the Mississippi and then in the font of the Nauvoo Temple, many members of the Reorganization—often only a short generation from Nauvoo—had no serious question about the practice. William Marks recalled that at one point Joseph Smith, Jr., had halted baptism for the dead stating it should not be practiced until there was a baptismal font built in Zion (Independence) or Jerusalem.[21]

Baptism for the dead first appeared publicly on August 15, 1840, in Nauvoo, during the funeral sermon of Seymour Brunson. Based on the assumption that God loves all people, it recognized that if baptism is required for salvation, many who had passed away would die unsaved. The solution—theologically and personally—was the acknowledgment that the dead may be baptized by proxy. The concern, a strong one for the Smith family because Joseph's eldest brother Alvin had died in 1823 without baptism, was formalized in a January 1841 document and published in the 1844 edition of the Doctrine and Covenants. It became a temple ritual in 1841.

In keeping with their pluralistic approach, the early Reorganization took no clear stand on the concept of baptism for the dead: permissive but unstated. By 1865 it was identified as representing a special local need but was not a first principle. By 1886 it was specifically identified as having no General Church emphasis unless "reiterated or referred to as binding" by revelation.[22] Throughout Joseph III's life he recognized baptism for the dead as legitimate in principle but, particularly later in his life, did not push it as a doctrine. However, as late as 1892, the members of the Twelve expressed their willingness to respond to the ceremony if directed by revelation, but no Conference action was taken.[23]

Another significant problem to be dealt with concerned the Saints' reaffirmation of their role in Independence, Missouri. Up to this time the general return of members to Independence had been slow. One of the early persons, and a significant one, was Henry Etzenhouser who arrived in Independence in 1870 with his wife, Hannah, and eight children from Sacramento, California. He believed the church should be built up in Independence, and he was tired of waiting. With his efforts a branch was opened on May 25, 1873, with Henry serving as pastor. They met in the county courthouse. Later they moved to the second floor of the Chrisman-Sawyer Bank building. Construction began on a brick building, some thirty-six-by-fifty feet, at the corner of East Lexington Avenue and Pearl Street in 1879. The Brick Church was dedicated by Joseph Smith III in July 1884. But with seating for 350, it was already too small. Attention was given quickly to the construction of a larger building. On a lot given by Daniel Bowen, the Saints began work on what was to become the Stone Church. The foundation was laid in 1887 and the cornerstone set by President Joseph Smith III on April 6, 1888.

The financial burden grew and when, in 1890, the holder of the mortgage pushed for payment, the General Conference authorized the bishop to raise money throughout the church to finish the building. A special fund was raised that met the mortgage and promised completion. By September 1890 plasterers were finishing the interior. In March 1892 the *Herald* announced to the church that the Saints, at a cost of $40,000, had finished the building which, with the upper auditorium, could seat 1,500. On April 6, 1922, General Conference was held there for the first time.

The years between 1860 and 1890 were extremely important years for the Reorganization. In these years the doctrines of the movement were worked out, as was the organizational structure and the early centralization of authority in the First Presidency. These issues were not solved as much as they were worked out and, in years to come, there would be additional adjustments to be made.[24]

Notes

1. Alma R. Blair identified Joseph Smith III as a moderate, Clare D. Vlahos showed him as legalistic, and Roger D. Launius portrayed him as pragmatic. Each has made an excellent case and their opinions should be read.

2. "Skepticism—Its Use," *The Messenger* 2 (Salt Lake City, Utah, 1876): 32.

3. *Saints' Herald* vol. 32, no. 42 (October 1885): 674-676.

4. Certainly one of the best accounts is found in Clare D. Vlahos, "The Challenge to Centralized Power: Zen[a]s H. Gurley, Jr., and the Prophetic Office," *Courage* vol. 1, no. 3 (1971): 141-158.

5. Ibid., 154.

6. O. Kendall White, Jr., *Mormon Neo-Orthodoxy: A Crisis Theology* (Salt Lake City, Utah: Signature Books, 1987), 59-60.

7. Van Hale, "The King Follet Discourse: Textual History and Criticism," *Sunstone* 8 (1983): 5-12.

8. White, 63.

9. Hale, 6.

10. *Saints' Herald* vol. 117, no. 5 (May 3, 1970): 7-10.

11. For an excellent discussion of this topic see Richard P. Howard, "The 'Book of Abraham' in the Light of History and Egyptology," *Courage* (Pilot issue, 1970): 33-46.

12. Richard P. Howard, "The Changing RLDS Response to Mormon Polygamy: A Preliminary Analysis," in Maurice L. Draper and Debra Combs, eds., *Restoration Studies III* (Independence, Missouri: Herald Publishing House, 1986): 145-162.

13. Roger D. Launius, "Method and Motives: Joseph Smith III's Opposition to Polygamy, 1860-1890," *Dialogue* vol. 20, no. 4 (Winter 1987): 106.

14. Howard, "The Changing RLDS Response to Mormon Polygamy," 157.

15. Council of Twelve Minutes (April 9, 1867): 34.

16. Launius, "Method and Motives," 113.

17. Ibid., 116.

18. Ibid., 115.

19. Linda Newell, "Cousins in Conflict: Joseph Smith III and Joseph F. Smith," *JWHA Journal* 9 (1989): 13.

20. For an account of RLDS anti-Mormon (polygamy) efforts see Roger D. Launius, "Politicking against Polygamy: Joseph Smith III, the Reorganized Church, and the Politics of the Antipolygamy Crusade, 1860-1890," *JWHA Journal* 7 (1987): 35-44.

21. Roger D. Launius, *Father Figure: Joseph Smith III and the Creation of the Reorganized Church* (Independence, Missouri: Herald Publishing House, 1990), 115.

22. General Conference Resolutions 282, 308.

23. *Church History* 5:188.

24. For further reading: Richard A. Brown, *An Illustrated History of the Stone Church* (Independence, Missouri: Herald Publishing House, 1988); Francis M. Holm, Sr., *The Mormon Churches: A Comparison from Within* (Kansas City, Missouri: Midwest Press, 1970); Roger D. Launius, *Joseph Smith III: Pragmatic Prophet* (Urbana: University of Illinois Press, 1988); Roger D. Launius, *Father Figure: Joseph Smith III and the Creation of the Reorganized Church* (Independence, Missouri: Herald Publishing House, 1990); M. Richard Troeh and Marjorie Troeh, *The Conferring Church* (Independence, Missouri: Herald Publishing House, 1987); Alma R. Blair, "Joseph Smith III: Prophetic Son of a Prophet," *Joseph Smith, Sr., Family Reunion Souvenir Program* (Salt Lake City: Smith Family Reunion, 1975): 6-12; Paul M. Edwards, "The Persistent Pretended," *Dialogue* vol. 18, no. 2 (Summer 1985): 128-139; Wayne A. Ham, "Truth Affirmed, Error Denied: The Great Debates of the Early Reorganization," *JWHA Journal* 7 (1987): 3-11.

Lamoni

On October 7, 1881, Joseph Smith III and his family left Plano with their household goods for Lamoni, Decatur County, Iowa. There they established themselves in a large wooden frame house, built just west of town. In time the home became known as Liberty Hall. With the move Joseph brought the church headquarters and Herald Publishing House to Lamoni from Plano, Illinois, after nearly twenty years there. The first issue of the *Saints' Herald* was published in Lamoni on November 1, 1881, making the transition complete as far as facilities were concerned. In that issue Joseph Smith wrote: "We sit down amid the *debris* of building, and the unorganized chaos of an office removed, to greet our readers from our new home in Iowa. We bid our contributors and correspondents a hearty welcome to our new quarters."[1]

All the Saints may not have understood the reason for the move to Lamoni. Plano had been good to the church and, for once, no angry mob waited to expel them. The Reorganization had gained some respectability. Later, Joseph would take a moment in his *Herald* editorial columns to remind his readers of "the reasons for locating the business center and 'the seat of the First Presidency of the church' at Lamoni, Iowa."[2] Not only was it important for the church to establish an area of its own but the revelation concerning gathering to Jackson County, Missouri, and "regions round about" was renewed in Section 117:11 and affirmed on March 3, 1873.

Late in 1869 Joseph had advanced the idea that the Saints gather in a communal experiment and—to avoid many of the previous difficulties—suggested creation of a body along the lines of a joint-stock company. The corporation could select and hold land, making it available on equitable terms. Such an effort could avoid the problems associated with church management, which were the cause of the destructive sides of Nauvoo, Kirtland, and Far West.

The United Order of Enoch was authorized in 1869 at the October General Conference. It was primarily a joint-stock company. The order was a tool designed to help the church accomplish its mission, not a fulfillment of that mission. By February 1870 the order was active with Elijah Banta, Israel Rogers, and David Dancer selected as a Committee on Location. The 1875 Conference adopted a resolution appointing a committee of five to select land and support a gathering. The committee was composed of Joseph Smith III; Israel Rogers, bishop of the church; David Dancer of the Presiding Bishopric; W. W. Blair of the First Presidency; and J. H. Lake of the Council of Twelve.

When committee members first reported they had located some reasonable sites, they also admitted they did not have the money necessary to purchase the land.

They issued a call for persons who were willing to loan or consecrate money to the cause. The promise was that after the land was purchased, these persons would be repaid from funds made available through individual sales. They recommended between $25,000 and $50,000 be made available before purchases began.

During summer 1877, Joseph Smith made a tour of the land suggested along the Missouri-Iowa border and secured forty acres of land for a family home near Lamoni. In September 1877 the committee reported it had decided to purchase "a tract of land now open for sale, of some two hundred acres, lying in the vicinity of a tract lately purchased by Brother Moses A. Meder, and by him deeded to the church, situated in the southwest portion of Decatur County, (Fayette Township) Iowa."[3] Joseph was later to point out that when the Saints were in Jackson County, Missouri, in 1833, the area of Fayette Township (Iowa) was located in the adjacent county to the north, and thus the land met the requirement of "round about."[4]

At the April 1882 Conference the location committee reported that, in accordance with its instructions, it had accomplished the following: decided to move the business center of the church to Lamoni, Iowa, following the completion of the railway through Decatur County, Iowa; purchased land; established a brickyard, burned brick; bought lumber; hired workmen; and constructed a building thirty-by-sixty-five feet in size, two stories high, with an engine room of sixteen-by-sixteen feet attached. The building cost was $5,541.14 with $400 for furnishings. It was to serve as the home of the Herald Publishing House and to provide offices for the First Presidency. The report also indicated that the Herald office in Plano had been sold and the equip-

175

ment and employees moved to Lamoni. Articles of incorporation were filed on February 3, 1882, and the move accomplished.[5]

The Saints had been gathering there for some time. When the headquarters moved, nearly a thousand members were in the area. While many Saints gathered with great anticipation, and the days marked an increase in spiritual growth, material prosperity, and religious activity, the early years at Lamoni were not as pleasant as perhaps anticipated. The *Herald* reported "fevers of more or less virulence have laid siege to the health, patience, and faith of the Saints, and some good and fair ones have died."[6]

Other things were not going according to plan. Among the difficulties was the change in the location of the main wagon road from Lamoni to Eagleville; the settlement of an unexpected number of non-Saints, including a large Methodist contingent in the area; a final decision by the railroad to locate the track north and east of town; and the establishment of several taverns in the village. The latter problem was partially resolved when the saloon owners found the business to be either morally or financially unprofitable and left town.[7]

At the 1881 General Conference a report on representation was accepted. It was amended in 1883 and included giving ex officio status to all general officers and a representation of one delegate for every twenty-five members. It was at the 1882 Conference, however, when the first credential committee report appeared certifying the legality of participation. Earlier, the Reorganization had had little formal agreement. But as the church grew larger and more scattered, an effort was made to identify Conference representation and procedures. In 1878 the church published *Rules of*

Order and Debate for Ecclesiastical Deliberative Assemblies. But by 1880 it was still not clear who acted with ex officio rights in the legislative assembly, and the General Conference appointed a committee to report to the next Conference. The report identified all general officers and elders (priests were specifically excluded by later amendment) and made specific instruction for the selection of delegates, voting rights, and responsibilities.

In 1882 George A. Blakeslee was ordained presiding bishop. He had united with the Reorganization in 1859 and had served in a variety of assignments since that time. He replaced Israel L. Rogers, who resigned because he believed the bishop should be near the printing press and felt unable at age sixty-four to make the move to Lamoni. Rogers had played a significant role in the formation of the Reorganization. In 1890 E. L. Kelley, who had served as Blakeslee's counselor, became acting bishop on Blakeslee's death. Later he was ordained presiding bishop. Kelley's father had been a church member before the assassination, and E. L. Kelley became acquainted with the Reorganization when he was ten. He was a lawyer and had served the church as a missionary.

The annual General Conference convened April 6, 1883, at Kirtland Temple, the first held by the Reorganization in the Temple. At the Conference the church recorder listed 15,061 members, an increase of 420 during the year. Of perhaps greatest lasting significance was the recommendation for local "reunion meetings." The first reunion was held at LeLands Grove, Iowa, on September 15-23, 1883. These were really designed as reunions for those who, in the early Reorganization, always met together but who tended to lose contact as the church grew. And for periods of spiritual renewal, care was taken to prevent "swings, shows, or intoxicating liquors" on or near the grounds.[8] The success of the first reunion led to a resolution that it be held annually. The reunion quickly replaced the semi-annual Conference.

At the April 6, 1884, Conference one of the early signs of a lasting disagreement between the Twelve and First Presidency emerged. At Stewartsville, Missouri, the Twelve entered their concern about their role as "traveling presidency." Districts had been created with district presidents named and to be sustained at the annual and semiannual Conferences. In May 1866 Joseph III had published a statement on the duties of the Twelve and Seventy, indicating that for the Twelve to serve as presiders was inconsistent with their responsibilities and that they should work under the influence of the Spirit and direction of the First Presidency.[9]

But in 1867 the Conference limited the power of such districts by denying them the authority to send missionaries beyond their own geographic limits. The following year the Conference determined that districts had the authority to elect their own presidents and district officers.[10] In a resolution supported by the General Conference, the Twelve affirmed its right to preside over branches and districts. The apostles resolved that their calling was to serve as presidents over the field in which they served, and this included making decisions on laws and usage. Also, they affirmed their right as presidents to preside at local conferences. The General Conference agreed in principle. While it made little immediate difference to the church, the issue would be raised time and time again.

While this agreement seemed to work fairly well, the conflict continued for the next twenty years. What appear as Sections 118:3 and 119:8 of the Doctrine and Covenants deal with this conflict among the First Presidency, Twelve, and standing ministry in organized areas. Then, in May 1887, the Twelve set forth the duties of the presidents of the districts and branches in a document that met with considerable opposition. The First Presidency and the elders were against it; the Twelve and Seventy endorsed it.

Failing to come to some acceptable solution, the apostles called on President Smith to seek light on the issue and to lead them in a disposition of the problem. His response, now Doctrine and Covenants 120, announced that branches may be presided over by Melchisedec or Aaronic priesthood chosen by the branches, and districts presided over by an elder or high priest.[11] The Twelve and Seventy are "traveling presiding councils."[12] Despite this guidance, the Twelve asked again, in 1894, for further clarification. The answer was received in what became Section 122, dated April 15, 1894, at Lamoni, Iowa. It admonished the Twelve to leave the care of local organizations to local officers and engage in pushing for more missions.[13]

On December 7, 1884, a group of Saints under the leadership of Lars Peterson and James Brighouse organized the "Order of Enoch" at Independence, Missouri. This group, which had determined that all procreation cease, should not be confused with the economic body of that name.

One of the accomplishments of 1884 was the introduction of the Sunday school lesson system. The first Sunday schools in the Reorganization appear to have been organized in Nauvoo in 1860, and then in 1864 in

St. Louis, Missouri, and 1866 in Pittsburgh, Pennsylvania. There was some opposition to the idea of Sunday schools, however, many feeling that the education of the young should be conducted by the priesthood in preaching services. But by 1865 the First Presidency recommended that a Sunday school be established wherever practical. The 1869 General Conference felt strongly enough to direct the creation of *Zion's Hope*, a church paper specifically for youth.

By 1871 the Conference had voted to establish Sunday schools, and in 1876 reaffirmed this view by asking all local jurisdiction leaders to push for the adoption of such a school. Once serious instruction began, it quickly became evident that materials used by the adults—primarily the scriptures—were not sufficient for children. In 1881 the Conference recommended a committee of three to consider how best to develop and use Sunday school materials. Thus it was that in 1884 a Conference resolution called on the Board of Publication to furnish suitable lessons for "Sabbath school." Those interested in a churchwide organization met in 1889, and in 1890 recognition was given for the General Sunday School Association to organize and arrange for the proper conduct of Sunday schools. At a convention in Kirtland, Ohio, on April 4, 1891, the General Sunday School Association was organized. The organization finally unified the work of the local schools and aided in preparing material, teachers, and district representatives. Four years later the *Saints' Herald* introduced a column dedicated to the work of the organization.

Young people in St. Joseph, Missouri, had organized a group known as the Young People's Mutual Improvement Society and soon they were seeking General Church membership. The Conference agreed, and in

1893 a churchwide society was formed named Zion's Religio-Literary Society (called the "Religio"), which was immediately successful. *Autumn Leaves,* owned and published by Marietta Walker, began in 1888 and was taken over by the church as its own, beginning with volume eight in 1895. It was published as a special magazine for the young people. By 1898 the Society had more than 2,000 members, and by 1900 more than 3,000 members were located in forty-four district organizations, including one in the South Sea Islands. By 1911 the Religio was working in cooperation with the Sunday School Association, issuing a *Religio Quarterly* with more than 7,000 subscribers.[14]

At the 1904 convention of the association, provisions were made for a primary and, soon, a graded curriculum to be established. A Home Department was established for those members who were too far away to be associated with a regular class. By 1914 the association's membership exceeded 33,000 with 6,000 more in the Home Department. The first quarterly was dated September-November 1892 and was written by Christiana Stedman Salyards. In 1906 the first *Sunday School Exponent* was published with T. A. Hougas as editor. He also served as superintendent of the association. In 1913 *Stepping Stones* was started, coedited by Marietta Walker and Estella Wight, for older children.

One great tragedy of the church during the 1880s was the illness of the beloved David H. Smith, Joseph's younger brother, born some five months after his father's assassination. In 1869 he and his brother Alexander had gone as missionaries to Utah to contact Saints living there. The experience was most difficult for David; he was sensitive, insightful, and deeply hurt by charges raised there. Despite the unpleasantness, he made a second missionary trip to Utah. Shortly after his return, on March 3, 1873, he was set apart as a member of the First Presidency. David was an extremely able poet, singer, and preacher whose work enlivened the early church. In 1875 a book of his poems was published, *Hesperis*. His hymns were a mainstay of the early hymnals and his "The Pebble That Dropped in the Water" ("Let us shake off the coals from our garments") was long considered as the most popular hymn in the movement. But he was troubled by a melancholia that he seemed unable to control.

David Smith's illness worsened. He spent a good deal of time resting in Nauvoo and was away from church activities for several years. But still that did not prevent the impending breakdown. Finally it became necessary for him to be under constant care, and he was committed to the Illinois Hospital for the Insane on January 10, 1877. At his release from the First Presidency in 1885, Joseph Smith III, in answer to one of the many questions about David's well-being, replied, "The voice of the Spirit is that David H. Smith be released. He is in mine hand." David spent the remainder of his life in the institution and died on the afternoon of August 29, 1904.

Because the increasingly legal workings of the church required better records, the 1886 General Conference called for the publication of the rules and resolutions enacted by the Conferences. They were available for the annual 1887 Conference, which met in Kirtland. In the reports of the church's missionary activities, it was identified that missions were moving ahead successfully in Australia, the Society Islands, Germany, and Denmark. Domestically the church was growing everywhere in America, with the exception of Alabama. The work in Utah was difficult as always but some increase was noted.[15]

The 1888 General Conference met in Independence. Among other things the Twelve passed a resolution affirming that it would not call persons to appointment who were addicted to tobacco or strong drink. They were also concerned about the fact that the quorums—especially the Twelve—remained unfilled. The membership in the Twelve was down to seven, and Joseph was asked to seek God's direction. In response to the concern Joseph presented a document to the quorums for consideration; it was then adopted by the Conference. It named James W. Gillen, Heman C. Smith, Joseph Luff, and Gomer Griffiths to the Twelve but informed the body that it was not yet time to fill the quorums.

Something must be said here about women's organizations in the Reorganization. The Nauvoo Ladies' Relief Society of Nauvoo, organized in March 1842 in the upper room at the Red Brick store, was the first women's group developed. Emma Smith was president of the group created primarily to give relief to the destitute, poor, widowed, and orphaned. In addition, they fed and clothed the workmen of the Temple, as well as raised money to buy nails and glass.

Under Joseph III's direction, women first organized on a local level, the first being the "Society of Gleaners," which met in 1867 in Sandwich, Illinois. The Sisters of Dorcas, in St. Louis, were developed as a Sunday school auxiliary that trained teachers and comforted the sick. Certainly one of the most significant moves was Marietta Walker's "Mother's Home Column" (written under the pen name Frances), which began appearing in 1886 in the *Herald*. It became a loose-knit support system for women—aimed at home duties but also serving to communicate and share feelings—which lasted for seventy-two years until 1958.

In 1888 another support and assistance group, the Prayer Union, was developed. It was designed to develop a prayer life as well as to be a support group for women church members. They reached a watershed at the 1890 Conference when it was decided to sustain the Prayer Union.[16] In 1892 the union became a cause of controversy. At the 1892 Conference it was strongly supported, but the union lost its heart when restrictions were imposed on the selection of its officers. In response, following the April 6, 1893, General Conference, a group met to organize a society among the women of the church. A committee consisting of Anna Stedman, Catherine (Cassie) B. Kelley, Emma Elizabeth Smith, Abbie Horton, and Marietta Walker worked to develop its structure. The group was called the United Daughters of Zion. The association was immediately successful and in 1894 reported 400 members in twenty-three local societies.

At the 1890 April Conference the First Presidency and Twelve met at Lamoni to address questions of disagreement and to come to the point where they could issue a statement of unity.[17] When it came, it concentrated on the growth of the church—more than 2,000 converts that year—and the increasing opportunity for missionary work, as well as an improved financial stability. It then affirmed the harmonious manner in which the leading quorums had dealt with disagreement and avoided any obstacles thrown in the way of progress by the "'cunning craftiness' of him that lieth in wait to deceive."[18]

In 1882 the members of the Church of Christ in Independence, Missouri, fenced in a portion of what had been identified as the Temple Lot. Nine years later, claiming its rights as the true successor, the Reorganization brought legal suit for clear title. In an unpleasant trial in the Western District Court of Missouri, Judge John F. Phillips favored the RLDS, but on appeal the case was reversed on the grounds the Reorganization had not acted to make its claim in a reasonable time. Many Saints have held that because the decision of originality was not reversed, the earlier decision stands. Nevertheless, the Church of Christ (Temple Lot) has maintained title since.

Isaac Sheen was the first president of the Quorum of High Priests in the Reorganization. At the time there were few members of the quorum—twenty-nine in 1860—and the quorum did not grow to any measure until 1890 when ordination was closely defined.[19] The need for a standing ministry grew, as well. The most difficult problem had to do with the organization of the Standing High Council. This was an essential part of the organizational discussions held by the Presidency, Twelve, and the Quorum of High Priests during the late 1880s. Haste in ordination was slowed by the Presidency's concern. But the 1894 Conference accepted the twelve persons recommended, ordained them, and thus reconstituted the Standing High Council.[20 21]

Notes

1. *Church History* 4:374.
2. "The Regions Round About," *Saints' Herald* vol. 40, no. 3 (January 1893): 34-38.
3. *Saints' Herald* vol. 24, no. 20 (October 1877): 307.
4. *Saints' Herald* vol. 25, no. 9 (May 1878): 135.
5. *Saints' Herald* vol. 29, no. 9 (May 1882): 139.
6. *Church History* 4:376.
7. *Church History* 4:379.
8. *Church History* 4:434.
9. *Church History* 3:438-439, 483.
10. *Church History* 3:495.
11. Doctrine and Covenants 120:2a-b.
12. Doctrine and Covenants 120:4b.
13. Doctrine and Covenants 122:5, 7.
14. Richard P. Howard, *Joseph Smith III, A Study in History* (Independence, Missouri: n.p., 1974), 93.
15. *Church History* 4:561.
16. The material is based on the work of L. Madelon Brunson, "Precedents Lost: A History of the RLDS Women's Organization, 1842-1974" (M.A. thesis); and *Bonds of Sisterhood: A History of the RLDS Women's Organization, 1842-1983* (Independence, Missouri: Herald Publishing House, 1985).
17. *Church History* 4:653.
18. Richard P. Howard, *Joseph Smith III, A Study in History*, 145.
19. *Church History* 4:644.
20. *Church History* 4:654-655.
21. For further reading: Joseph H. Anthony, *Lamoni's Passing Parade* (Lamoni, Iowa: Blair Printing Company, 1948); Roger D. Launius, *Joseph Smith III: Pragmatic Prophet* (Urbana: University of Illinois Press, 1988); Roger D. Launius, "The Mormon Quest for a Perfect Society at Lamoni, Iowa, 1870-1890," *Annals of Iowa* 47 (Spring 1984): 325-342; Sara J. Hallier, "Spreading the Word—A Survey of 19th Century RLDS Publishing," in Marjorie B. Troeh and Eileen M. Terril, eds., *Restoration Studies IV* (Independence, Missouri: Herald Publishing House, 1988): 164-170; Gregory Prymak, "Toward Nominalism: Doctrine and Covenants 156:7-9," in Marjorie B. Troeh and Eileen M. Terril, eds., *Restoration Studies IV*: 202-207.

Joseph Smith III's Final Years

By 1890 Joseph Smith stood out as the primary spokesman for the Reorganization. Having solidified leadership through his role as editor of the *Herald*, as chairman of major committees, and as the presiding officer of the General Conference, Joseph was in a better position than ever to guide the movement. While Joseph III was a milder and far less authoritarian man than his father, he nevertheless used the power of his office, as well as his own charismatic abilities, to direct the church and to meet those who would challenge either his leadership or the direction of his guidance.

The world into which the church was moving during the closing decade of the nineteenth century was a world so vastly different than that of 1830 that it was hardly recognizable. In America a nation had been born, forged on the anvil of Civil War, expanded by conquest against the American Indians and the people of Mexico, industrialized to an unbelievable level, and thrown into its first world conflict in the Spanish-American War. Men and women who had come to the church by sailing ships, oxcarts, and on foot now moved as missionaries in railroad cars, on steamships, and soon in automobiles. The telephone and telegraph made it possible to communicate in a matter of minutes. Each advancement brought the world of the Saints closer and closer together. With the unity came a new meaning to the concept of "headquarters."

Lamoni, Iowa, which served as the headquarters of the church, had itself grown from a sleepy post office to the social and religious center of the church: the home of its college, the location of its library and publishing plant, and site of its welfare homes. The population of Lamoni had grown by 1895 to nearly 1,200. By the turn of the century, Lamoni's several businesses included dry goods and general stores, two drug stores, two banks, three butcher shops, buggy dealers, restaurants, millinery shops, and a grain elevator. The community sponsored the Chautauqua Society, Odd Fellows and Masonic lodges, a chapter of the Grand Army of the Republic, the Ladies Mite Society, the Lamoni Silver Band, the Mandolin Band, as well as baseball and football teams. Lamoni, however, was not the central location Joseph III desired. The president interpreted the Lamoni experience as a stopping point on the journey to Independence where the Saints were slowly gathering. He encouraged quiet and gradual settlement in the areas in and around Independence, Missouri, anticipating that the time would come when Zion might be reestablished there.

In the 1890s the question of a church college was raised, a continuation at least in intent of the School of the Prophets and the University of the City of Nauvoo.

With a few students in its first class, and meeting originally in the French Building in Lamoni, the college opened in 1895 and graduated Frederick Madison Smith as its first graduate in 1898.

The 1891 General Conference, the thirty-ninth of the Reorganization and fifty-fourth of the Restoration, met in Kirtland at the newly redecorated Temple. The Conference was preceded by the first meeting of the General Sunday School Association. The members' desire to learn was tremendous, and most branches operated large and successful Sunday school programs. The Sunday School Association was a separate but inherently allied organization that took responsibility for the education of members. The association served as a separate body in every meaning of that word; it had its own leaders, organization, and curriculum production facilities, as well as financial control. It was so successful financially, the members not only paid their own way but were able to provide large and consistent donations to the general funds of the church.

When Joseph III came into the presidency he was obviously inexperienced and knew little of his responsibilities. Nor did he have well-defined goals or directions in mind. It is perhaps enough to suggest that he wanted the church to be strong, to accomplish the mission of bringing people to Christ. It was Joseph's understanding, however, that an individual assumes religious leadership by developing administrative machinery, establishing theological consistency, and promoting hierarchical leadership systems that funnel decision making to the top. Regardless of his early inexperience, Joseph III consolidated much of the power of leadership and, when the time came, to pass that along to his son and successor, Frederick Madison Smith.

The earliest step was to accept responsibility for the publishing house and the church magazine, the *Saints' Herald*. It was a natural move and began with his October 1861 request that the Conference grant him the authority of "examination and supervision" of all matter going into the *Herald*.[1] By 1865 theory had become fact when Joseph was affirmed as the working editor of the *Herald* and manager of the publishing division. Throughout his administrative career he would take an active part in what went into the *Herald*. He always played a determining role as editor both personally and as the Quorum of the First Presidency itself became the chief editors.

Joseph also recognized the amount of control inherent in administrative procedures. He realized that the distinction between administrative and legislative function lies in the source of power. Through his leadership and constant involvement, he moved much of the authority for daily activities from the legislative to the administrative function and thus assumed more direction of the church. Like his father he understood that some decisions must be made administratively rather than by Conference action and recognized that once administrative officers were sustained, the membership as well as the headquarters' functionaries should respect the authority of the executive.

Over the years Joseph moved to develop policies and procedures which, at the surface level, seemed of little significance. But in this fashion he eventually created administrative channels that required presidential approval of the routine business of the church. These policies included the manner in which local leaders were selected, the way local persons reported to supervisors, the hiring of paid employees who reported directly to the Presidency, the manner in which records were kept, the selection of Sunday as the Sabbath and how it was to be celebrated, the legalization of the marriage ceremony, the scope of official jurisdictions, and the clarification of priesthood authority. A central part of this emerged around the procedure for reporting and the identification of supervisory personnel. Administrative control had been lost early because it was the habit of department heads and committee chairs to report directly to the General Conference. In doing so they bypassed the administrative quorum involved. On more than one occasion they took items to the Conference for actions that had been expressly denied by the administration. The idea that all departments, commissions, and quorums were to report to the Presidency—and that they did so not as a courtesy but as a requirement—was hard to establish. But this "right of presidency" was sufficiently worked out so that by 1914 the *First Presidency's Report* to the Conference included the reports of all other departments and commissions as well as the quorums. The right to report directly to the Conference was limited to those institutions that were primarily independent of the church.

Another way in which presidential authority was centralized was in the development of administrative committees and the affirmation of primary assignment rights of the Presidency. Over the course of the years, Joseph III built on the Conference's reluctance to accept substantial assignments by accepting much of that work himself. As the church became more complex, it naturally became more bureaucratic, and just as naturally standing committees increased. Besides being the obvious choice to chair these committees, Joseph began to assert his right not only to be a member of any significant committee but also to name most, if not all, of the members. With his own people working these committees, Joseph became executor as well as administrator.

By the close of the 1902 General Conference, the Reorganization was more complete than it had been previously. The leading quorums were full, and President Joseph Smith, though now in his seventies, was associated with younger and stronger men. After the death of W. W. Blair in 1896, Alexander H. Smith, as president of the Twelve, was called to act in the Presidency as counselor. This continued until 1902 when Frederick Madison Smith and Richard C. Evans were called and ordained as first and second counselors to the president. The role of the presiding patriarch was more clearly defined. Agreements were reached and the groundwork was laid for the formation in 1908 of the Order of Bishops. Perhaps most significant was the clarification of field administration.

The ordination of non-American apostles as well as the assignment of apostles to foreign missions—Peter Andersen to Scandinavia, John W. Rushton to the British Isles, and Cornelius A. Butterworth to Australia—raised again the question of field authority. Related to this was the development of stakes where local officers were required to report to the First Presidency rather than the Twelve. The emerging Order of Bishops and the development of a strong corps of presiding high priests appeared to usurp authority that the Twelve believed rightly belonged to them.

As the church grew in size and geographical complexity, apostles found the scope of their administrative responsibilities expanded. They needed to work with local men who were capable of giving guidance to the local area. The term "district" was adopted in the 1860s to identify local jurisdictions, and the boundaries of the apostles' assignments became more stable over the years. What eventually emerged was an organizational structure for the "field" in which branches were rather flexibly gathered into districts headed by the apostle or, eventually, an elder or high priest who served as his spokesman.

The relationship between an apostle and his expanding field continued to cause disagreement. At the head of the disagreement was how they related to the First Presidency. In the early years the role of the apostle, and thus the assignment, was not particularly clear. They were primarily involved with missionary work. Sometimes they took on responsibilities as members of important committees and, even on occasions, had local assignments as pastors. But as the size of the church grew, the fluid nature of the Twelve's assignments left many unanswered questions. One of the most significant had to do with reporting responsibility. Some assumed local leaders reported directly to the First Presidency. Others felt they should go through their apostle. Still others saw the district as fairly autonomous and thus capable of acting independently on many issues.

Joseph III's response was to draw attention to the missionary aspects of the Twelve and of the Quorums of Seventy and thus to assume they should not be limited by involvement in presidential functions. The Conference agreed, and during October 1887 a resolution was received to that effect, calling upon all those who held such offices to be released from administrative responsibility. But further disagreement continued, and in 1890 President Smith addressed the issue in what became Section 120 of the Doctrine and Covenants. The document acknowledged the existence of districts that were themselves composed of branches. They were to be created either by Conference action or by the missionary and were to be presided over by a local high priest or elder. The presidential function in local jurisdictions was to remain with those in the local jurisdiction.[2S] Still not totally clear, this position was reaffirmed in Section 122 in 1894. It went further to define the role of the Twelve and Presiding Bishopric in financial matters. A new understanding was made between what has been identified as the "standing ministry" and the "traveling ministry," the first being the local officer while the second represented missionaries who worked for the General Church. This matter seemed settled, for the time being, in a manner acceptable to those involved. Later generations would raise those same questions again.[3]

Certainly the matter was not completely settled. The Twelve and the Seventy had rethought their positions—and the changing needs of the church—and affirmed their role as presidents of the church abroad in all the world. This being true, they felt the presidents of branches and districts should turn to the Twelve and Seventy rather than the First Presidency for their reporting.

In 1901 the confusion was expanded when the church further organized two stakes—in Lamoni and Independence. The members needed little other encouragement, and soon Independence surpassed Lamoni as the primary membership location of the church. The 1906 Conference took action to affirm that the district president had the primary right to preside locally, acknowledging that recognition of the general officer was a courtesy not a right.

In what proved to be the opening salvo of the second phase in the long and heated argument between the other quorums and the First Presidency over authority, Joseph Smith III published a special issue of the *Herald* in 1905.[4] In an article called "Safeguards in Church Government" (subtitled, "Are the People Safe?"), Joseph raised questions about the balance of power. Smith was aware that the growing church required an administrative leadership unhampered by the need for constant consultation with local leaders. But he was concerned that the administrative officer, as delegated authority, not impose on the rights of persons who, because of the nature of the system, could not safeguard themselves.

Because all members cannot have equal information, Joseph argued, they could not share the responsibility for making decisions. Therefore, those upon whose shoulders it falls to make decisions must take into account the protection of those for whom decisions are made. The power of the quorums rests in their internal agreement as to their action. Each quorum is therefore offset by the power of the other leading quorums. The First Presidency was offset by the Twelve, "a quorum equal in authority and power to the three presidents ... [and that of the seventy who] form a quorum equal in authority to that of the twelve ... ."[5]

Within this balance the theme of presidential authority remains. The balance of power was not a balance of assignments but rather a challenge to any quorum's usurpation of power. For the Twelve there appeared to be little authority left as a "second presidency"; thus, they rose to guard the responsibility for missionary activity. Their position, made initially in a series of preambles to resolutions prepared for General Conference, stated that the Doctrine and Covenants[6] gave the

Twelve the right to take charge over all important missions. Joseph, seeking clarification, asked that the Twelve define what they understood was meant by "under the direction of the Presidency" used in Section 104.

Failing to get an acceptable reply, the Presidency proposed a carefully worded statement called "The Right of the Presidency to Preside." In the statement the laws and principles involved in the Presidency's relationship to the Twelve — as well as to other quorums and departments — was expounded. The statement was never approved by the quorums, nor was it ever considered by the Conference. But it has, at least historically, rather well defined the relationship ever since.

In brief, it states that the First Presidency has the right to officiate in all the offices of the church. There are no restrictions on this right. This must "necessarily be active as well as passive supervision in and over all the offices of the church, else the word 'Presidency' does not carry with it its legitimate meaning."[7] It acknowledged that one person should be appointed to preside over the priesthood of the church. This appointment must necessarily invest this person with an authority that is not only advisory but also supervisory over all things domestic and in the mission field. It concludes that the First Presidency stands at the head of both the missionary and local quorums, and it is in this light that the Presidency administers the affairs of the whole church all over the world.[8]

The Twelve, meeting in pre-Conference sessions in March 1908, rejected the Presidency's statement on "The Right to Preside" on the grounds it did not deal with the question: that is, the First Presidency had acted in the mission field by naming R. C. Evans as minister in charge of Canada without consultation with the Twelve. Discussion at this meeting did not provide an acceptable answer.

At the pre-Conference session the following year, the Twelve failed to sustain R. C. Evans in the First Presidency. The question of presidential control was open again. The Twelve felt that any action or communication with their field should be through the appropriate member of the Twelve. In a letter addressed to the Twelve dated April 8, 1909, Joseph reaffirmed his position.

> It is the opinion of the Presidency that it is within their rights and privileges as the presiding quorum of the church, to have an oversight of and interest in both the missionary work of the church and the local work of organizations, districts and branches as well; that in the exercise of this right they may properly look after the administration of affairs in both districts and branches...."[9]

Joseph assured the Twelve that in stating the opinion he did not intend to give it as the expression of a dictatorial decision or to infringe on the rights of the quorums possibly affected by the opinion, but he affirmed the role of the Presidency as the primary presider. The law clearly favored the Twelve exercising strong influence over the church by involvement in administrative matters. But it is equally true that Joseph's efforts to direct this influence toward missionary activity rather than administrative control would be followed up with presidential directives over missionary activity. There was no doubt, however, that at this time the power of presiding officers on the local level was on more solid ground.

When local ministers were asked to report directly to the First Presidency, the apostles and seventies saw it as an unwarranted disregard for their position. But the idea was continuously stressed, and the outcome of convenience, the flow of information, and the availability of line and staff communication all worked against the Twelve. Finally, apostles were assigned to serve as ministers in missionary activities by the First Presidency. While this was a short-lived solution to the larger problem, it did help to solidify the Presidency's position.

Joseph Smith III took a realistic view of his own increasing age. In 1906 he began the process of delegating a larger amount of his work to his counselors. His age and reoccurring illness meant he could not meet all the demands of his office. It was at the 1909 Conference when President Joseph Smith III presented his work-worn gavel to the assembled delegates. Recounting how he had used it as presiding officer for nearly fifty years, he now recognized he was no longer physically able to lead Conference business. It was a characteristic gesture for him. The General Conference genuinely loved and trusted the old man who was their leader. They accepted the gavel, approved his stepping down as presiding officer of the Conference, and then wholeheartedly reaffirmed him as their leader—prophet and president—of the church. His son, Frederick Madison, was acknowledged as his father's stand-in and presided at the 1910 Golden Jubilee Conference.

In 1909 Joseph reaffirmed the church's need to organize into a colonized Zion.[10] From this document, and inspired by the United Order of Enoch which organized the settlement of Lamoni, another group emerged. The United Order of Enoch was organized in Independence, Missouri, on October 26, 1909. There was some opposition to this, but it was incorporated in Kansas City,

Missouri, on May 11, 1910. According to the charter the

United Order of Enoch is a helping and benevolent association, organized for the benefit of the poor and needy, dispensing its charities by furnishing equal opportunities to the needy, upright, and industrious in a financial, educational, and social way, with those who are more fortunate, and the supplying of stewardships and homes or inheritances to the worthy who may lack.[11]

The order purchased about eighty acres south of the present Auditorium, developed it, and offered the land for sale at terms church people could afford. The Summit Addition (Enoch Hill) was connected to the area by a bridge constructed by the city and the order over the Missouri Pacific Railroad tracks. Despite the fact many sales occurred, and some building was accomplished, the order was chronically short of funds. Much of the order's financial resources went into the maintenance of the United Order of Enoch House, a combination visitor's house and temporary shelter for the poor located at 102 North River Boulevard in Independence, directed by Charles and Amy Gurwell. The order also provided start-up money for new businesses needed to provide employment for the Saints in Zion. Despite the limited success of the order in Missouri, its facilities were reproduced in Lamoni, Iowa, when Fred M. Smith and forty-six residents organized in late June 1914. Elbert A. Smith served as president, John F. Garver as secretary, and Oscar Anderson as treasurer.

Joseph had suggested that the order in Missouri could properly hold and manage church properties and recommended that the Committee on Incorporation in

Stakes, of which he was chair, be dissolved. By the close of the 1913 General Conference, a committee was established to organize a body to hold church properties. Meeting in the United Order of Enoch House in Independence, they drafted the incorporation of what was to be the Independence Mutual Building and Loan Association. In June 1921 seventy acres of land known as Gudgell Park (or the Golf Links) was purchased by the order for development and sale to the Saints.

Most of the tasks of the order diminished over the years both because it grew increasingly autonomous and because the Presiding Bishopric took on more responsibility. Bishop Benjamin McGuire was less aggressive in his support of the order and pushed the local areas, as well as the bishop, to assume more responsibility. When Albert Carmichael became presiding bishop in 1925, much of the work of caring for the poor and needy reverted to the bishops, and the care of church property became the concern of the church's holding company, the Central Development Association.[12] On March 6, 1928, Bishop Carmichael challenged the order to disorganize and transfer its assets—estimated at $72,000—to the church. The board declined but did soon sell a great deal of its property and allowed the Presiding Bishopric to become trustees of many of their assets for the church.

During 1910 and 1911 Joseph was confined to his home and to local travel only. During this time President Frederick M. Smith was assuming more responsibility, including the reorganization of the quorums of elders and the Aaronic priesthood, a move which led to their reporting to their local conferences rather than to the General Conference. The transition was further eased when, during the 1912 Conference, Joseph resigned publicly from all the committees on which he served, replacing himself with his son.[13] The years were taking their toll, and his declining ability to hear, as well as failing eyesight, was making effective service difficult.

Joseph III was well aware that much of the success of his leadership, and the continuation of the unity he had fought so hard to develop, would depend on the choice of his successor. The question was not really if the church would accept his son Frederick Madison, but if he could, in fact, pass on the power of the Presidency. There appeared to be no doubt whatsoever in Joseph's mind that he would be a primary factor in the selection. He was "particularly anxious to avoid the trauma and confusion over succession to the presidency that plagued the early church after 1844" and did not want his successor to have to reinvent the administration of the church.[14]

Despite the fact President Joseph had raised the question of Fred M.'s succession on at least three different occasions, he sent a questionnaire on January 3, 1912, to the leadership asking what they thought about succession. After consideration of the issue, Joseph proposed the "Letter of Instruction" which made his wishes very clear.[15] The significant aspect of the "Letter" was the inclusion of a statement about the leadership procedure of the church, which affirmed that as long as two members of the First Presidency remained, it was still a quorum and could act as the Presidency. The Twelve had no role in this whatsoever.

But Joseph was aware that the idea of linear succession in the priesthood was larger than simply the First Presidency and could not be allowed to run rampant. Thus, President Smith made it clear that the assumption of father-to-son priesthood was an abstraction to be interpreted as meaning the essence of the father's priesthood was carried in the son. It was not a promise that the son would inherit his father's priesthood office.

The years Joseph was president produced many changes and considerable growth. At his installation the church was small and divided. At the time of his death there were more than 71,000 members located in several countries. The quorums were filled with experienced men and more than 5,000 priesthood were functioning in their appointed offices. Under Joseph's leadership a system of courts had been established to maintain standards among the membership. Organizationally the church had been developed into stakes, districts, and branches. More than this, of course, was the fact that the Reorganization had an identity, stable doctrines, a working organization, and an efficient and dedicated priesthood and membership. As well, Joseph III had defined the relationship to the church of his father by rejecting polygamy, softening the idea of gathering, and urging his members to a community relationship designed to assimilate rather than challenge the gentile community.[16][17]

Notes

1. *Church History* 3:298.
2. Doctrine and Covenants 120.
3. Doctrine and Covenants 122:7.
4. *Saints' Herald* vol. 52, no. 12 (1905):266-267.
5. *Church History* 6:151.
6. Doctrine and Covenants 122:9 and 123:23.
7. "The Right of the Presidency to Preside," *Church History* 6:248-250.
8. Minutes of the First Presidency (1907): 201-207.
9. *Church History* 6:307-308.
10. Doctrine and Covenants 128.
11. *Church History* 6:659.
12. *Church History* 6:673.
13. *Saints' Herald* vol. 59, no. 17 (April 1912): 391-392.
14. Larry Hunt, "F.M.S., The Formative Years of an RLDS President," *Journal of Mormon History* 4 (1977): 70.
15. *Church History* 6:559.
16. See "Joseph Smith III, 'Pleasant Chat,' " *Saints' Herald* vol. 9, no. 9 (May 1, 1866): 129-139; Roger D. Launius, "Joseph Smith III and the Quest for a Centralized Organization, 1860-1873," in Maurice L. Draper and A. Bruce Lindgren, eds., *Restoration Studies II* (Independence, Missouri: Herald Publishing House, 1983): 104-120.
17. For further reading: Paul M. Edwards, *Preface to Faith: A Philosophical Inquiry into RLDS Beliefs* (Midvale, Utah: Signature Books, 1984); Paul M. Edwards, *The Chief: An Administrative Biography of Fred M. Smith* (Independence, Missouri: Herald Publishing House, 1988); Norma Derry Hiles, *Gentle Monarch: The Presidency of Israel A. Smith* (Independence, Missouri: Herald Publishing House, 1991); Roger D. Launius, *Father Figure: Joseph Smith III and the Creation of the Reorganized Church* (Independence, Missouri: Herald Publishing House, 1990); Maurice L. Draper, "Apostolic Ministry in the Early Reorganization," in Maurice L. Draper and Clare D. Vlahos, eds., *Restoration Studies I* (Independence, Missouri: Herald Publishing House, 1980): 219-231; Wayne Ham, "The Musical Legacy of Mark Hill Forscutt," in Marjorie B. Troeh and Eileen M. Terril, eds., *Restoration Studies IV* (Independence, Missouri: Herald Publishing House, 1988): 156-162; Roger D. Launius, "Joseph Smith III and the Quest for a Centralized Organization, 1860-1873," in Maurice L. Draper and A. Bruce Lindgren, eds., *Restoration Studies II* (Independence, Missouri: Herald Publishing House, 1983): 104-120.

The Church Enters the Twentieth Century

Historically many people date the twentieth century from the beginning of World War I, for the outbreak of that cataclysmic event marked the end of the Victorian period and ushered in an age of industry, expansion, and violence. For the church the twentieth century began about the same time. With the death of Joseph Smith III, who died in December 1914 and who had been its beloved leader since the Reorganization, and with the ordination of his son Frederick Madison Smith as president, the church began a new era. This marked a departure point from the leadership of an "old world" man, born and raised in the traditions of the nineteenth century, to a leader who was the product of the "new world," the world identified with the modern era.

Joseph's declining years had been fairly peaceful. And though the church continued to grow and sponsor missionary activity, the last years of the aging prophet tended to be maintenance ones. The effects of his long and able leadership continued without much involvement. Fred M. Smith, a longtime counselor to his father, had considerable time to formulate his own responses to the direction of the church. He must, at times, have been frustrated by the need to accept his father's slower and even hesitant methods. Certainly Fred M. had anticipated what his role would be and how he would deal with many of the unanswered questions that remained from his father's presidency.

Frederick Madison Smith was raised to be president. Fred M., as he was generally known, was "to the manor born." The third child of Joseph III and Bertha Madison, he was born while the family was in Plano, Illinois, and baptized in 1883. He attended Graceland College and the Iowa City Academy. He married Ruth Lyman Cobb, taught at Graceland for a year, was editor of the *Lamoni Chronicle*, and served as a counselor to Bishop Anderson of Lamoni.

From a small lad following his father about the dusty roads of Lamoni to his early assignments as church historian, librarian, assistant editor, and missionary elder, he was trained by his father for this new role. Certainly the "Letter of Instruction" both outlined his responsibilities and clarified any misconception he might have had about his future with the church. But he was concerned, as his father had been, about the transition. He did not want his father's death to bring about a period, however temporary, in which there was no leadership. In such a vacuum men often step forward, seeking to take authority. Fred M.'s earliest experience with the responsibilities of being president, a period in 1903 when Joseph and R. C. Evans were in

England, had given him a taste of being president without power and he wanted no more of it.[1]

He started his formal training in 1902 when he was ordained as first counselor to his father. The call was timely for it closely paralleled Joseph III's declining health. Over the next dozen years the aging president came to count on Fred M. more and more. As the older man's blindness became debilitating and his facial neuralgia took its toll, Fred M. found himself taking on most of the daily responsibilities of the office.

Fred M. was a man known for his complexities: He was often warm and sensitive, yet sometimes gruff and disagreeable; he could be charming and personable but, on occasion, curt and short-tempered. He was always the student, teacher, scholar, and president. Determined and occasionally arrogant, he was indeed a dreamer and man of vision but was as well a reflective man with an intensely pragmatic style. He was a traditionalist who nevertheless held modern views, a social reformer and innovator as well as staunch defender of the faith.

Under his father's growing insistence, Fred M. pursued his education and, after working it out with the office, sought a graduate degree. He attended first the University of Missouri and then the University of Kansas. He journeyed to Worcester, Massachusetts, with his wife and two daughters to continue his studies. The doctor of philosophy degree in sociology and organizational psychology was granted by Clark University in 1916. He received the degree shortly after assuming the office as president of the Reorganization.

His view of the church was a strict one that demanded a great deal from the people, sometimes more than they had to give. Thus, he often met with disappointment and sadness. Caught as he was between two major world wars, he faced unique problems that quickly formed the rapidly changing world in which the church would function. Certainly the events of the two world wars, and the Great Depression between them, produced an environment that made the years of his presidency more difficult than they might have been in some other time in history.

Fred M. brought to the presidency his own administrative style and an even more clearly stated centralization of authority. Throughout his public life he spoke out openly against what he considered to be disrespect for authority. Standing firmly against "revolutionaries and shortsighted reformers," he argued that lack of respect was responsible for the social disorganization of the times. It would, if unchecked, lead to chaos. He was not unaware of the totalitarian dangers that sprang from too much power, but he believed that the more immediate danger was the flagrant violation of the law.[2]

If the church was sometimes restless under Joseph's slow "working through," which the older president exercised in his democratic and patient way, it was often rebellious under Fred M.'s control. Obedience to the law and to the power of the First Presidency was stressed by Fred M. as early as 1903 when he used the *Herald* to remind the church that obedience to the leadership was essential and demanded in every case.

It has been observed that this

> ...seemingly natural movement from father to son was natural only in expectancy. These were vastly different men each who led and inspired the church in his own manner. Drawn to this position by a lifetime of expectancy and seasoned with the maturity of those who acknowledge power, Frederick Madison Smith came

prepared. A man with a diversity of interests and abilities that would make him forever restless, he emerged as the most controversial figure in Reorganization history.[3]

While Joseph III had made massive strides in developing the church, there were still some serious internal questions demanding solutions. One problem Fred M. inherited had to do with the dispute between the Twelve and the Presidency. The Twelve's position was that they should be administrative vice-presidents, assigned to geographical areas, and that in these positions they were the church authority. Fred M. could not recognize this view. As he understood the law, the Twelve were called as special witnesses and traveling missionaries. They were only secondarily administrators. According to Fred M.'s perspective, the church was already far too decentralized and thus too inefficient. The proper directing of the church called for a strong administrative leader.

The role of the Twelve in church administration had been a problem for Joseph III as well. His father, while organizing the early church, had given the Quorum of Twelve both witnessing and administrative authority and had often used them as a "second presidency." And while this was seen as a product of necessity, it was nevertheless on this basis that Brigham Young legitimized his actions following the death of Joseph, Jr. But as the Reorganization grew, and its organizational structure was formalized, Joseph III dealt with this by limiting the Twelve's authority to preside over local conferences. But neither this nor a careful spelling out of quorum duties[4] really solved the problem. The Twelve resented the fact that once the areas in which they worked had progressed to the point of developing congregations, they then lost administrative control over them. The fundamental problem emerged from the understanding of what was meant by the "second presidency" and how this was to be exercised by the Twelve. As presidents in their fields, they felt the collective right to review and determine field policy in their own right.

Fred M. did not wait long to emphasize his point: The president of the church was the presiding officer, and it was inefficient for others to assume this position. The president was, and by rights needed to be, the primary authority and administrator; all others served at the discretion of the office. All those who work within the church structure must of necessity report to the president. President Smith's view of church government was labeled Supreme Directional Control. An unfortunate, but basically accurate title, it became the rallying cry of those who felt the theocratic side of theocratic-democracy was overemphasized.

A forerunner to this confrontation was a disagreement between Smith and R. C. Evans, a man who had served as Joseph Smith III's other counselor in the First Presidency. Evans was disturbed with Fred M.'s increasing involvement in the quorum. The break was further emphasized by the fact that in 1909, under pressure from the Twelve, Joseph III released Evans and called him to be the "Bishop of Canada." In that position Evans continued to fight what he considered the increasing and unchecked power of the Presidency. The riff became so wide that in 1917 Fred M. found it necessary to silence Evans, who shortly after withdrew from the church.

The conflict with the Twelve was rekindled by a reinterpretation of the role of the Standing High Council. President Fred M. Smith saw it as the supreme judicial body for general officers, and it was the First Presidency (or Presiding Bishopric if the Presidency was involved) who would decide just what cases they would hear. A basic change had been made in the council. Custom was that the Standing High Council met during Conference so distant high priests could serve with the council. But in 1916 their workload was too heavy, and by Conference action, the council was reorganized with only high priests resident in Independence. That same year the Conference authorized the reorganization of Independence Stake so as to form the Independence, Kansas City, and Holden stakes. In 1920 what had been Independence Stake was renamed Center Stake of Zion and placed under the direct supervision of the First Presidency. President Smith's use of the council was seen by the Twelve as a further invasion into their area of responsibility.

Some sort of final agreement on the final role of the Presidency and its relationship to the Twelve was needed. In the 1919 Joint Council—composed of the First Presidency, Presiding Bishopric, and Quorum of Twelve—personal feelings became heated and at one point the president resigned as chair of that body. The issue, however, was not personal. It had to do with the authority for administering the work of the church in the field. But the commitment was deep and often was exhibited in ways that were taken personally.

In a powerful forty-page document, the "Brief," the apostles insisted the Quorum of Twelve had administrative jurisdiction over the ministerial work of the field. As was his inclination, Smith decided to meet the problem head on. He addressed the 1919 General Conference on the issue indicating the nature of the

211

split. He expressed deep concern both for the disagreement and the effect of the disagreement on the work and told the Conference he saw no means to compromise. In all concern for the church, he could not be president if he were not the presiding officer. Because they had been unable to come to a working agreement, he felt he had no other alternative than to resign his position. He did so.

The delegates were greatly disturbed. They continued to meet for several days, hearing both sides of the argument and considering President Smith's resignation. Finally the Conference reached a compromise that, realistically, supported President Smith and rejected the apostolic position. They then refused to accept Fred M.'s resignation. After discussion with the delegates sent to meet with him, Fred M. returned to the Conference and his responsibilities.

The crisis was over but the problem was really not solved. The 1920 General Conference, while without discord, was nevertheless important. The gathered Saints celebrated the centennial of the 1820 vision reported by Joseph Smith, Jr. President Smith's message called for the release of two members of the Twelve who were ill and brought Myron McConley and Thomas W. Williams to the quorum. He also admonished the Twelve not to be "unduly concerned with the work of the standing ministry... and [to] let contention cease concerning the prerogatives of the leading quorums."[5]

Having in mind the need for adequate meeting facilities, the Conference also acted to build a General Conference auditorium in Independence, and officially identified Independence, Missouri, as the "Center Place." The area was to function under the First Presidency and Presiding Bishopric. The Standing High

Council was to take the place of the Stake High Council. Between Conferences President Smith, accompanied by Apostle Thomas Williams, traveled to Europe and Palestine, visiting the Saints and developing a missionary plan. The extended trip lasted more than a year. Because of a delay in the president's return, it was necessary to postpone the 1922 General Conference until October.

During this time there was further dissatisfaction felt concerning apostolic assignments and, as is often the case, the larger and more significant concern was expressed in picking at other unrelated discomforts. There had always been the feeling that Fred M. spent more money than necessary, and there was probably some truth in that fact, given the limitations of church finances. His expenditures on his extended trip to Europe, and then on to Palestine, provided a case in point and the Twelve raised this as an official issue. On his return he met with the Twelve and while the outward concerns were about finances, the underlying difficulty that kept surfacing had to do with apostolic roles and responsibilities. A pre-Conference meeting failed to solve either problem. Fred M. defended his expenditures and reaffirmed his position on presidential authority. The meeting accomplished little, for no satisfactory solution could be reached on any of their differences.

At the beginning of the 1922 General Conference, President Smith presented a document that called for massive changes in the leading quorums: calling Floyd McDowell into the First Presidency, releasing four other apostles, and calling John Garver and five young men in their twenties or early thirties to the Twelve. Then, acting contrary to tradition, he bypassed the oldest

213

member of the Twelve and named James A. Gillen as its president. The Twelve felt the issues between the Presidency and their quorum should be dealt with before any changes in personnel. With this in mind they asked the assembled delegates to delay action on the document until the other problem was solved. There were several days of debate over the document and some initial quorum rejection, but the delegates decided to accept the document as the mind and will of God.

The 1923 Conference convened with serious questions still being raised about administrative relationship. On this occasion disagreement arose about the rights of nomination, but difficulty was avoided by a compromise suggesting dual responsibility between the executive and the legislative body.

There was no General Conference in 1924 in accordance with the agreement to meet every two years. However, the off-Conference Joint Council sessions were particularly important. There President Smith received acceptance, though hardly unanimous, for his ministerial administrative authority. His statement had been straightforward:

> In organic expression and functioning there must be recognized grades of official prerogatives and responsibility with supreme directional control resting in the Presidency as the chief and first quorum of the church.[6]

His authority for this was the authorization of Doctrine and Covenants 104 and 122:9.

At the close of these sessions the Twelve asked Fred M. to provide them with as clear a definition as possible about how he saw the relationship between the First Presidency, the Council of Twelve, the Presiding Bishopric, and the Quorums of Seventy. Without delay he prepared for them a statement on "Supreme Directional Control," which appeared somewhat later in his presentation to General Conference. There was some discussion, even in the Presidency, about the wording, but Fred M. felt the need to be open and direct. For the next two years the church administration argued the issue in the *Herald*, in private publications, and in letters. Sides were taken by both members and quorums. The members of the Presiding Bishopric found themselves siding with the Twelve on this issue, fearing that taken literally the theory of Supreme Directional Control would in fact remove the checks and balances and jeopardize the bishops' ability to meet their responsibilities.

During this disagreement, and in some respect because of it, the church experienced a serious operating deficit from 1921 through April 1924 that called for high-level attention from the Joint Council. When in April 1924 the Joint Council met to discuss action to be taken, the disagreement between the president and the Twelve expanded to include the bishops. The First Presidency had affirmed its right to overrule administrative decisions made by the Presiding Bishopric. The bishops requested that President Smith prepare a statement on church government that restated his position. When it was considered, it finally passed, but the Presiding Bishopric was vitally concerned over a lack of any clear means of checking presidential action. An "open letter" was published in the *Herald* signed by two members of the Twelve, the three members of the Presiding Bishopric, the presiding patriarch, and twelve other well-respected lay leaders of the church. It took the position that the charge of temporal affairs must of necessity lie with the bishops and that they alone are responsible to the General Conference for the accumulation and disbursement of funds. They were the ones accountable, and they were directly accountable to the Conference, not to the First Presidency.

The opening of the 1925 General Conference had all the tension of a political convention. Individuals quickly took sides on these issues, and as the Conference drew near, a good many of the delegates were selected to represent one side or the other of this issue. Some were even instructed by their local conferences. Meeting in the Stone Church on April 6, 1925, the Conference began immediately to tackle this problem. President Smith was not one to sidestep an issue, and he felt this issue had to be decided one way or the other. The debate went on and on as every detail was heard. The passions of the moment were reflected in long debates and caustic comments. But when it came time to vote, the weight of the Conference supported presidential authority as outlined by President Smith. And in the end the delegates accepted the president's position, voting 919 to 405 on a "yea-and-nay" vote.

Under the circumstances the Presiding Bishopric felt it could not continue to function and asked the Conference for release. The Conference asked the prophet to seek light on the issue and, after President Smith had had time to seek guidance, a document was provided and accepted by the Conference. The three bishops were released and Albert Carmichael was called as presiding bishop. But Fred M. required more from the Conference. There was still the matter of editorial policy to be settled. After a considerable debate, a motion was presented and passed giving the First Presidency control over the editorial policy of church publications.

While the majority certainly favored the Presidency, there were a significant number unwilling to maintain their church membership under the circumstances. Just how many separated is not known, but the 1925 General Conference caused a serious breach and from it several separatist groups were eventually founded.

Another concern Fred M. faced had to do with the Auditorium. There was a need for the members to meet together in conference. He had long visualized a building to seat them all during General Conference, which would serve as a symbol of unity and permanence for the members. Under Fred M.'s leadership, the church moved ahead with its plans for expansion, unaware of the growing economic chaos forming around them.

The Auditorium, as it was to be known, was an enormous building designed so the Saints could assemble without any internal supports to deny access or sight. The construction was begun in 1926. It was a massive effort with a seating capacity for 5,800 persons (once permanent theater-type seats were installed thirty years later), a lower auditorium for smaller assemblies, and accompanying offices and facilities. It was an amazing project for a church of no more than 125,000 members. The 1927 General Conference met in the partially completed basement. There the body voted sufficient funds to complete the building in time for the 1930 Centennial Conference. It was enclosed enough that the large celebration prepared for the centennial was performed in the upper chamber, but completion of the Auditorium would have to wait for a better time.

By 1930 the church was in financial trouble. The Order of Bishops had been set up as the Board of Appropriations in 1913, and in 1919 a financial policy was established which asked for, and received, approval by the General Conference. But the Conferences, concerned about programs and General Church personnel, repeatedly voted for budgets larger than they could raise by tithes and contributions. By 1920 the church was unprepared for the unfavorable economic situation and addressed the "little depression" of the early 1920s by releasing nearly seventy appointees and cutting family allowances by 10 percent.

In the midtwenties a temporary solution was found in borrowing from the money collected to build the Auditorium. And, while it allowed the church to avoid debt and the payment of high interest to an external organization, it seemed to have done a disservice to the church by hiding the seriousness of the problem from the members. Perhaps if the members had understood the extent of the problem earlier, they could have at least avoided some of the debts. When the building program began in 1926, the money that was set aside was unavailable. And, as the depression grew and income decreased, the church was unable to pay back the building fund.

The Auditorium served as a symbol of the church's determination but became, as well, evidence of its difficulty. The building of such a structure was approved by General Conferences in 1917 and 1920, but in 1921 the bishops warned against starting such an effort when finances were so poor. However, two years later, the building was approved and in another two years it was ordered built without delay. The 1927 Conference met on the slab that has become the lower assembly room floor, but almost immediately it was evident that there were not enough funds to complete the building. A bond of more than $300,000 was authorized and construction continued, off and on, until late 1930 when it was agreed that the money could not be expended for this purpose. All construction halted in January 1931.

So while the depression from 1929 to 1931 hit America hard, it was harder on the church because it had not been paying its way as it went along. The expanding church created needs that had not been met earlier; depreciation of equipment and buildings and the planned retirement of employees were not properly offset with reserves. Thus, it became more and more difficult to deal with this hidden debt, as well as the loss of income, to meet operating expenses. The full impact of this position was made even more difficult by the fact that the value of church buildings, held as offsetting assets, were depressed along with the markets and were not worth what was anticipated.

Income did not meet expectations; the Auditorium costs drew heavily on what little income was available. But in January 1932 the first $15,000 payment came due and was met promptly. It was a significant payment. The collection of the money was difficult, and there were other expenses against which it could well have been used, but this signaled to the financial community that the church intended to meet its obligations. Because of this the banking community gave the church some room and refinanced it in December 1934. The bonds were retired in January 1941.

The Presiding Bishopric was reorganized in February 1931, and the budgets for 1931 and 1932 were cut by nearly a third. Before it could be halted, the debt level rose to nearly $2 million. Acting on the 1931 retrenchment program, the church brought an end to deficit spending in 1934 and attention was turned to attacking the debt. The Presiding Bishopric of L. F. P. Curry, N. Ray Carmichael, and G. Leslie DeLapp proposed a thirteen-paragraph plan for recovery, which was approved.

Basically it was designed to arrest expansion—building only as cash was available—and to stop the leaking of much needed funds by unwise and unnecessary expenses. This would require the liquidation of assets not absolutely necessary for the work of the church and maintenance of the balanced budget, which included major debt payment and the creation of resources for special accounts like retirement as well as an operating reserve. It was essential, as the bishops knew, that any plan adopted not be the cause of impoverishing the members but rather would establish financial security.[7] Recognizing it would not be easy, DeLapp had said, "We do not believe that deathbed repentance insures immediate entrance to the celestial kingdom, we surely ought not to expect the economic law to be more elastic than the spiritual law."[8]

During the next few years this hard and restrictive financial plan was administered with courage and impartiality. It was difficult and called upon every leader to limit spending, prevented building projects in which extended funds would be used, halted all work on the Auditorium, and restricted the number and incomes of appointees and employees. To meet increasing financial responsibilities the church was forced to sell a large amount of property and put many of its employees and appointees on leave. The cost in terms of personnel and programs was immense.

The Joint Council was retained at President Smith's insistence, despite its members' willingness to resign. He felt it was essential to keep a cadre of involved and active full-time church leaders. When the church began to recover, these key men, along with stake leaders, would be necessary to reestablish the programs of the church. All other appointees under age fifty-two were released or given leaves of absence. The courageous acceptance of such measures by these persons and their families was remarkable as they found themselves back in the job market at a time when the economy was so poor. As hard as it was on all concerned at the time, the long-range effect was even more disruptive to the church. The loss of these young ministers would be felt for decades to come. But the church held to the plan, and slowly but surely it began to make a difference. The policy remained in effect until 1942 when the Presiding Bishopric announced with pride that at long last the final debt was paid.

Another of the organizational understandings that needed to be worked out was the changing role of the Quorums of Seventy. For many years these "missionary elders" had been self-sustaining—meaning they, or the field in which they worked, would cover their expenses and those of their families. Many carried on other jobs to support themselves. And often these men would leave the mission field to work to support their families. But the church needed full-time ministers who could be sent into areas where the church was working to expand its influence. Frequently the needs of the field and the inability of the local jurisdictions to pay for their support led to the adoption of General Church allowances for such persons. While this was a good and usually workable policy, it was nevertheless true that when contributions were inadequate the number of General Church appointees was curtailed.

The two systems overlapped for a while with paid members of the quorum working side by side with those on a self-sustaining basis, but the appointee system and allowances prevailed. Those unable to take regular field assignments were honorably released. From 1915 to 1926 the active membership of the quorum fell as new men who were unable to take full-time assignments were not named. As the Quorum of Seventy increased and the activities of its full-time paid members expanded, there began to be some questions about their jurisdictional authority. Several attempts to work this out had failed. Fortunately an increasing number of former members entered the Quorum of High Priests and assumed administrative roles. They understood the work of the Quorums of Seventy and the needs they had in relation to their jurisdictions, and a good working relationship emerged on an informal basis.

One program Fred M. had been working on was the consolidation of the Sunday school and Religio materials. By 1921 they were being produced under the direction of a Consulting Board in Religious Education. The next year they were brought under the First Presidency. The superintendents of Sunday schools were recognized as pastoral assistants in charge of religious education. By 1930 the General Conference had approved the new program in religious education, which gathered all the producers and resources under a single program. Many of the persons brought together to maintain the programs were among those lost in the personnel releases of the early 1930s. Fortunately many programs were maintained.

Underlying President Smith's concerns with the working of the organizational church were his beliefs about Zion and the cause of the kingdom of God. One effect of this interest was a resurgence of the idea of gathering and stewardship promotion. These were articulated and presented as fulfilling the major church objectives: the building of Zion and evangelism of the world. When he became president in 1915, he brought with him his own views on the meaning and purpose of Zion. He was highly educated in both sociology and organizational psychology, as well as having grown up under the influence of his father, and had formed some powerful convictions.

Given his intense interest, there is surprisingly little reference to Zion in the several additions made to the Doctrine and Covenants during his administration.[9] His most complete statement concerning Zion, which appeared in the Doctrine and Covenants in 1940, came in his last such statement to the church near the end of his life. In this document he admonished the church "...that the task of establishing Zion presses heavily upon us. Barriers and hindrances to the achievement of this goal should be removed as speedily as possible and practicable."[10] His interpretation of Zion was that it was a place where the Saints were free and safe to pursue their love of God. Zion was, as well, a people characterized by their purity in heart and by their intelligence and spirituality. Thus it was a condition, a condition that constituted a perfect society where the relationship of men and women, group to group, should be defined by a social order akin to that foreseen by God.

Until 1830 the word Zion was often used but was not necessarily well defined, nor its context made apparent. But the idea of Zion as a special city quickly grew. In 1831 Independence was identified as Zion and, for a while, Nauvoo served this function. But that died along with Joseph and his brother in 1844. In 1909 Joseph III replaced the idea of Zion as a special place of community living. Instead, he urged the idea of multiple gathering centers. While this is what happened, the idea was never really well accepted in his time.[11]

Fred M. believed Zion would come about when humans emphasize the social aspect of religion, not forgetting God but incorporating divine and human knowledge for the benefit of all. Late in his life he distinguished between ways in which the kingdom of God theoretically could come about. One means would be by cosmic crisis, where the city drops from the clouds as a result of a people becoming so righteous that they merit such a city. Another way would be by starting where the people were and working, despite their limitations and imperfections, to fulfill the Zionic possibilities in all persons. With respect to the best intentions of the people of the church, Smith felt there was no promise for the first and that all needed to work diligently on the second.[12]

President Smith believed it was humanly possible to create the social conditions necessary for Zionic living. It was not a Pollyanna concept, and he was more than willing to deal with the sins and transgressions, as well as the laziness and faults, of humankind. But he felt if humans could overcome the selfish motives of greed and individual advancement, they had a chance to bring about physical salvation and thus, in time, the spiritual salvation of all persons. Not only did he acknowledge that selfishness and ruthless competition were everywhere, but he recognized that they led to increasing polarization between the interests of capital and labor. And, he acknowledged, capital had assumed far too large a share of those interests. He wrote in the 1930s, "[The church must be more] ... than a performer of ceremonials, or a funeral home. The pulpit must stand for social reform, denounce selfishness in all forms and in all places, ... and free itself from the charge of being subservient to the interests entrenched behind the bulwarks of individualism."[13]

Fred M.'s response suggested that the Saints, whether capitalists or laborers, were responsible for the godly use of their resources of time, money, and energy. The vision of the kingdom of God called the Saints to voluntarily donate their economic surplus for the benefit of the community. The ultimate result of this process, which Smith and the church have always labeled stewardship, were the roots of the literal kingdom in which economic and social justice would prevail.

There were those, of course, who saw Smith's views as socialism or even limited communism and raised opposition to him. But Smith replied that he was neither socialistic nor communistic, but rather Zionistic—an order where private property and private responsibility functioned for social, not individual, aims. The whole idea of all things in common did not apply to that which was needed for reasonable existence and life-style but was, rather, the rule of surplus.

Central to his views on Zion was Fred M.'s concern about gathering. From the beginning he had supported the "cause of Zion," meaning by that an economic gathering to promote spiritual growth. The new stakes of Zion were eager to cooperate but were aware that unprepared gathering would simply rekindle the difficulties the Saints had experienced before. The desire to collect with other Saints in Independence was to be fulfilled by working through the Presiding Bishopric. Persons were admonished to keep in mind both the needs of the congregation they were leaving and the opportunities for economic as well as spiritual growth in Independence.

As a part of this preparation, Fred M. saw the church's responsibility to aid the gathering process by encouraging economic opportunities in Independence. In seeking a way to accomplish this, he said,

> I have finally concluded that perhaps the solution lay in calling into counsel with the spiritual authorities of the church the men who have become experienced in business, men of affairs, men who have shown themselves to be equals and even the superiors in some instances, to men in similar industries in the affairs and activities of the world.[14]

His organization of the stakes as the "Center Place" and the official move of church headquarters to Independence in 1920 all reflected his concern. It was reflected as well in his interpretation of stewardship, defining stewardship as the means by which persons use the talent and resources God gave them to bring about economic harmony. In this way the poor, the economically enslaved, and the disenfranchised are allowed to take part on an equal footing with all others. This stewardship is tied to Zion in terms of industrial might, business enterprises, and community ownership. Therefore, the church became increasingly involved in supporting business, underwriting new professionals, and economically encouraging culture and the arts.

As the years passed and Fred M.'s energy was expended on other issues, the industrial nature of his views moderated. He became more concerned with the demands and limitations of the concepts of a physical Zion. He acknowledged growing criticism of his emphasis on the physical, and he reluctantly saw financial demands requiring the church to pull out of business and industrial ventures. He admitted that when he thought of buildings he always thought in terms of spiritualized persons to occupy them, and when he spoke of roads and streets within a community they were only to connect the like-minded who gathered.

He came to understand Zion more as a spiritual condition necessary for the physical building and gathering. The Zionic condition is a condition of love, humility, moral goodness, and unity in the cause of Christ. The elusive goal—the cause of Zion and the kingdom of God—would come about through persons who are involved in the process, for Zion is both a place and an attitude, it is both material and spiritual, immanent and transcendental. While his dictum, "from every man according to his ability, to every man according to his needs," sounds socialistic, Fred M. Smith felt that the full solution to the problem, thus the proper use of profit and surplus, lay in the Zionic motivations of individuals whose hearts were filled with the love of Christ. The church's role was to create a pervasive social conscience, a consciousness that can be developed through education, but education with a strong emotional content. [15]

Fred M. addressed the difficulties of living the pervasive social life in his sermons and writings. But it was more than that. He made considerable effort to encourage others, to provide educational opportunities, and to prepare the priesthood to the greatest degree possible. [16]

Fred M. was beset by personal problems as well. The tragic death of his wife in an automobile accident in 1926 hurt him deeply. The development of facial neuralgia—a disorder that had affected his father—caused him severe discomfort and frequently forced him to be away from the office for several days at a time.

While the years between 1927 and his death in 1946 were devoted to maintenance, President Fred M. Smith was deeply concerned with the internal unity of the Saints. A constant theme of his documents had to do with the need to stop internal strife and commit oneself—and thus the church—to the task of evangelizing the world and establishing the cause of Zion.

Fred M. died in 1946 without accomplishing the many dreams he envisioned. Rather, he emerged as the man who held the church together during crisis after crisis—some internal, some external—leading the church through two world wars, a depression, and the administrative battles of the twenties. Fred M. provided a great service, for he pulled the church into the twentieth century and called it to meet the problems of its day. His progressiveness was not simply reorganization but new direction—calling the members to be not only a spiritual people but a people with a social commitment.[17]

Notes

1. *Saints' Herald* vol. 50, no. 23 (June 10, 1903): 521.
2. Frederick Madison Smith, "Christianizing Society," *Saints' Herald* vol. 71, no. 6 (February 6, 1924): 124.
3. Paul M. Edwards, "Theocratic-Democracy: Philosopher-King in the Reorganization," in F. Mark McKiernan, Alma R. Blair, and Paul M. Edwards, eds., *The Restoration Movement: Essays in Mormon History* (Lawrence, Kansas: Coronado Press, 1973): 341.
4. Doctrine and Covenants 120 and 122.
5. Doctrine and Covenants 133:2b.
6. Paul M. Edwards, "Theocratic Democracy," 353.
7. G. Leslie DeLapp, *In the World...* (Independence, Missouri: Herald Publishing House, 1973), 159.
8. Ibid., 160.
9. There is no mention in Sections 132, 133, 134, 135, and only peripherally in 136:3c and 137:1b.
10. Doctrine and Covenants 138:3a-b.
11. W. B. "Pat" Spillman, "On Conceptualization of Zion," *Courage* vol. 3, no. 1 (Fall 1972): 37-44.
12. Norman D. Ruoff, comp., *The Writings of President Frederick M. Smith, Volume 1: Theology and Philosophy* (Independence, Missouri: Herald Publishing House, 1978), 129 and 273-280.
13. Frederick M. Smith, *Foundations of Zion* (Independence, Missouri: Herald Publishing House, 1951), 73.
14. *Church History* 7:385.
15. Norman D. Ruoff, comp., *The Writings of Frederick M. Smith,* 152-153.
16. Larry E. Hunt, *F. M. Smith: Saint as Reformer,* 2 vols. (Independence, Missouri: Herald Publishing House, 1982).
17. For further reading: Paul M. Edwards, *The Chief: An Administrative Biography of Fred M. Smith* (Independence, Missouri: Herald Publishing House, 1988); Norma Derry Hiles, *Gentle Monarch: The Presidency of Israel A. Smith* (Independence, Missouri: Herald Publishing House, 1991); Larry E. Hunt, *F. M. Smith: Saint as Reformer,* 2 vols. (Independence, Missouri: Herald Publishing House, 1982); Norman D. Ruoff, comp., *The Writings of President Frederick M. Smith,* 3 vols. (Independence, Missouri: Herald Publishing House, 1978); Ruth Lyman Smith, *Concerning the Prophet: Fredrick [sic] Madison Smith* (Kansas City, Missouri: Burton Publishing Company, 1924); Karen E. Troeh, "Zion's Praises: The Changing Concept of Zion as Reflected in the Hymns of the Restoration," in Marjorie B. Troeh and Eileen M. Terril, eds., *Restoration Studies IV* (Independence, Missouri: Herald Publishing House, 1988): 225-235.

Church Institutions

During the years of growth in membership and in the affirmation of beliefs, the church continued to meet its community expectations. A brief description of some of these efforts will be helpful at this point.

Graceland College

The church has always considered education very important, as a tool to aid persons in understanding God's world. And it increased their comprehensive participation in the work of the church. Just a few years after the Reorganization a call went out to build a college where students could work (farm) and study. There was little immediate follow-up on this suggestion made at the Stoles Hall Conference in St. Louis in 1869, but the idea remained. By 1888 E. L. Kelley drew up some articles of incorporation and proposed subscriptions to establish a college in the liberal arts tradition in Lamoni.

The 1890 General Conference was held in Lamoni. With nearly $10,000 subscribed for a college, serious consideration was given by the delegates. Lamoni, then the location of church headquarters, was selected as the site. At the 1893 Conference the land was received: a key twenty acres from Marietta Walker's farm east of town, some thirteen acres from W. A. Hopkins, and six acres from Minnie Wickes. The decision was made to open on September 16, 1895, in rented facilities.

Beginning only a day late, the eleven students, outnumbered by dignitaries, met in the French Building in Lamoni. Tuition was set at $1.00 a week for a curriculum of collegiate, didactic, preparatory commercial, music, and art in three terms. Eventually thirty-four students registered, including Fred M. Smith who was to be the first graduate. Three faculty served with T. J. Fitzpatrick as senior professor. Ruth Cobb, later to marry Fred M., was the elocution instructor for the second term.

Early in 1895 the trustees had given the go-ahead for the construction of a building on the "graceful" land. C. R. Cunham was the architect and Adam Jessiman was selected to build it. The dedication was an elaborate ceremony in November with Joseph Smith tapping the cornerstone in place. The Ad Building, as it has been affectionately known for nearly a hundred years, opened for classes in 1897 with ninety-six students beginning their studies. From the beginning the college had to fight for funds. The dedication of church people was not in question, for many had given large contributions. However, the cost of the college was a heavy burden for the small church. There were several reasons for this. First of all, the college was not seen as having a direct relationship to the work of the church, thus tithes and offerings to the church could not be used for the support of the college.

A second problem stemmed from the fact that the number of students anticipated was not available. In the minds of many people preparation for work in the church did not require college training. And while the nation was generally becoming more interested and increasingly dependent on higher education, many of the church people were having trouble seeing this connection.

A third reason was that higher education was more costly than anyone at first imagined. The board knew the college would need to operate at a loss each year, hoping to meet the difference out of grants from the church or from individual subscriptions. But the single building they occupied had cost twice what they estimated—nearly $20,000. In addition, the cost of improving grounds, the wide diversity of faculty needs, and the service on the debt were heavy drains on operating funds.

The coming years saw expansion in the curriculum. Fred M. Smith had, in spring 1898, been the lone, as well as the first, graduate. The event was celebrated, and Fred M. made a remarkable, if somewhat grand, speech as both salutatorian and valedictorian of his class.

General Church concern about the college's continued debt was so strong that the 1904 General Conference in Kirtland passed a resolution to close the college. The job of closing was left to the board of trustees, but they refused to take the steps necessary. That year 120 or so students faced a difficult year. The 1905 Conference met in Lamoni and the college dismissed classes so the students could be in attendance. After a long and occasionally emotional debate, the Conference voted 1,207 to 697 to continue the official sanction.

From then on, to the beginning of the Great Depression, the college experienced a period of slow and consistent growth, both in terms of students and curriculum. The industrial department allowed students to be involved in successful work programs while at the same time continuing their studies. A rather important milestone in the life of both the college and the church occurred in 1913 when the General Conference faced the question of academic control. It was suggested that the Conference appoint a committee to consider the textbooks being used by the college. Their hope was to keep from students those things not appropriate for members of the church, or at least not consistent with its mission. The Conference voted no, realizing that if an honest education was to be provided, young people had to deal with the world.

In 1912 Graceland joined the junior college movement, an educational program that was just being recognized in the United States. It was accredited in 1917. From 1912 to 1929 the college, under the able leadership of G. N. Briggs, was involved in an expanded building program which was slowed, then halted, by the depression. Following World War II, however, Graceland went through an amazing boom as returning veterans swept toward colleges to take advantage of the GI Bill.

In 1946 Edmund J. Gleazer, Jr., was named president, and Graceland expanded its offering, meeting the challenge of growth with the same persistence with which it had faced the challenge of debt. In 1960 the board decided that Graceland should regain its baccalaureate degree status; the college was accredited as a four-year institution, with its first major in religion. William T. Higdon became president in 1966, leading the college in its second major period of growth. During this time the Frederick M. Smith library and the Closson Center were completed, as well as numerous academic departments and programs. The nursing program, long associated with the Independence Sanitarium and Hospital, became a part of the Graceland academic program in 1971.

As Graceland looks toward its centennial in 1995, it recognizes nearly a hundred years of superior academic preparation. Among its graduates are ministers, professors, lawyers, ambassadors, a recipient of a Pulitzer Prize, physicians, a gold-medal Olympic decathlete, educators—nearly 23,000 individuals of public and private service.[1]

Independence Institute

Fred M. Smith was concerned about the education of the lay leadership as well as the priesthood of the church. Many were limited in their service because of restricted education. He understood that many leaders, especially in Independence, were not free to take regular college or even high school work. In response he started the Independence Institute of Arts and Sciences to meet this need. Some preliminary classwork was done at the Stone Church Annex beginning in October 1916. Established under the authority of the Educational Commission, it was designed to provide high school and college-level instruction for adults. A majority of the training was conducted in the evenings or on weekends.

At the time of the second commencement more than 130 persons had taken instruction under eighteen instructors and artists who worked without compensation. By 1920 there were more than a hundred students under President Walter W. Smith and his faculty. On September 23, 1922, the institute opened for classes as an accredited academic academy. It was centered at the Campus, located east of the present site of the Auditorium, on an expanse of land that was once the Swope Farm. The site was purchased for $50,000, raised by donations from church members and citizens of Independence. The Campus consisted of twenty acres plus the mansion house with sixteen large rooms and an auditorium that seated 250 persons.

The academy was successful both with the members of the church and the citizens of Independence. An excellent and well-credentialed faculty and adequate facilities allowed students—at little cost—to complete high school or even begin college work. Increasing economic difficulty forced the church to close the Independence Institute of the Arts and Sciences in 1931.

Children's Home

The revelation of 1906 made provisions for a children's home in Lamoni, "...the efforts of the Daughters of Zion should be approved and carried unto completion as soon as is consistent with the necessary demands of the work of the church in other directions."[2] Sufficient funds ($7,000) were raised to provide a building which, as a General Church effort, was to be operated under the direction of the presiding bishop. The General Conference agreed and a committee of women was appointed as a board: Emma E. Smith, Callie B. Stebbins, Ruth Lyman Cobb Smith, and Emma G. Hougas. The home was formally opened in

Lamoni on August 15, 1911, located in the old Elijah Banta home on South State Street. The Daughters of Zion assumed responsibility for the costs. During 1915 the Children's Home had served as many as nineteen children at one time, and in 1916 the debt on the home was liquidated. The majority of the children were of school age and attended school during the day. Some, too young for school, were cared for by a series of nurses who volunteered their time. Most of the children worked at the home to help with the chores and expenses.

The home was closed by General Conference action in 1926. Two reasons were given: It was believed the children could be better cared for by private families, and the administration had been encountering legal difficulties because of differing state laws. About forty children were in residence when it closed, and they were placed in foster homes. The building, used temporarily as a dorm for Graceland College students, burned in December 1927. While no further effort was made to provide a home for children, Center Stake maintains an adoption agency, Center Place Child Placement Services, begun during the 1970s.[3]

Resthaven

Over the years the church was involved in a variety of rest homes and sanctuaries for older persons. Homes for the aged were provided by the church at Kirtland, Ohio; Lamoni, Iowa; Holden, Missouri; and Independence. In 1898 the Saints Home opened in Lamoni for the care of the elderly. The home was supervised by Bishop Kelley and built primarily by volunteers. It was a two- story building of about fifty rooms located a mile or so west of Lamoni on land given by David Dancer.

Alice Dancer was appointed matron and served in that capacity until 1926 when she entered the home as a resident. Huldah Braby was matron until 1943. In 1905 Liberty Home was taken over by the Saints Home. In 1909 two houses in Independence were retained on Blue Avenue (Truman), one called Kensington and the other Bonheim.

In 1915 the Saints Home and Liberty Home were operated under a Board of Control and reported sixty-five persons as residents in the homes. Two years later the church purchased the old St. Cecelia Seminary in Holden, Missouri. Located on a little more than five acres, it was a beautiful setting for a rest home, which could house a hundred persons. The Kirtland (Ohio) and Kensington (Independence) properties were sold and those living there, along with the residence of Bonheim, were transferred to Holden. The residents who had been living in Holden were transferred to the Lamoni Saints Home in 1933, then, eight years later, to Liberty Home, which had been reopened for that purpose. The Saints Home was converted into dormitory space for Graceland College.

The church purchased two large homes set on seven acres on Winner Road in Independence. The first of these rest homes was opened in 1945 and the second in 1948. Collectively they were known as Resthaven. Purchased with Oblation funds, they were established for physically incapable women, but they expanded to become a home for the handicapped elderly. They were licensed by the Missouri Board of Health. In 1949 property on Truman Road was made available to the church, and the house there, the previous Mark S. White home, was refurnished as a rest home. But the demand for space soon made it necessary to provide more rooms. In August 1954 construction began on a new facility, completed and occupied in 1956. That same year the Saints Home in Lamoni was demolished. The property vacated on Winner soon became the headquarters and classrooms for the School of the Restoration, the church leadership training establishment. In 1973 the property became the Graceland Independence Education Center. Today Resthaven is a modern facility on Truman Road that provides care for persons in an atmosphere best described by its motto: "Only gentleness spoken here."[4]

Independence Regional Health Center ("The San")

Joseph Smith III rather reluctantly left Lamoni and moved to Independence in 1906. That same year he called on the people to provide "a sanitarium, a place of refuge and help for the sick and afflicted...."[5] The Independence Sanitarium and Hospital was to play an essential role in Independence and the church. In conjunction with this, Joseph named Dr. Joseph Luff, then a member of the Council of Twelve Apostles, as the administrator.

After consultation, Bishop Kelley purchased a suitable piece of land in Independence on Van Horn (later Truman) Road, and construction began there in August 1907. By December 16, 1909, the building was finished and sufficiently equipped, at a cost of nearly $53,000, to permit its formal opening. In the remaining two weeks of 1909, the San (as it soon became known) treated three patients. For the first few years patients only used the first floor, but in 1916 increasing need caused an expansion of facilities to all three floors.

In a move to keep the San, the 1920 General Conference reorganized its board to consist of the First Presidency, Presiding Bishopric, and the church physician. The original building had grown too small and $50,000 was raised, to be matched by the community, to begin work on a new building. In 1930 the church matched the $132,000 raised by the community. Despite the fears of the Great Depression, plans went ahead to build a new addition to the Independence Sanitarium and Hospital. The cornerstone was laid in 1930 and four walls and a roof were added before the church was forced to stop construction. The depression hit with all the impact feared, and it was not until 1946 that the debt was repaid.

In 1941, having received U.S. government help and local contributions plus earmarked church support, the hospital completed construction of the first two floors. With the upper floors of the "old" hospital, it housed 102 beds. The new San opened for formal inspection in December 1942. As construction moved ahead, facilities were moved to the new building and the brick hospital became the nurses' home. By 1946 the sixth floor was ready for occupancy.

But hospital use demanded further construction, and in 1966 work started on a new diagnostic center and twenty-five bed addition. It was completed by June 1968. In that same year the board was expanded to fifteen members. At the beginning the board consisted of the church leadership, but in 1930 it was enlarged to include the mayor of the Independence and the eastern judge of the Jackson County Court, the political administrators of the county. The 1968 revision added lay persons from the community. This was also the year that Graceland College announced its bachelor of science (B.Sc.) degree in nursing which, in 1971, replaced the San School of Nursing. The diploma school at the San had, by this time, graduated 1,046 nurses.

During the 1970s and 1980s the hospital expanded again with the addition of the South Tower and the Truman Forest Professional Building, the North Tower Extended Care Facility, and the final destruction of the original hospital in 1985. Symbolic of the church's growing outreach to the expanded community, the San was renamed the Independence Regional Health Center in June 1986.

Herald Publishing House

Joseph Smith, Jr., embarked on a major publishing effort, the Book of Mormon, even before the church existed officially. Early interest in the availability of scriptures unique to the Restoration suggested the necessity of maintaining church presses, presses that would make the movement independent of outside publishing firms.

After the assassination and dispersion, the need for communication was greatly expanded. For those still interested in reviving the church, it was essential. At the autumn 1859 Conference the assembled group authorized Zenos Gurley, William W. Blair, and William Marks to publish a newspaper for six months. Thus, *The True Latter Day Saints' Herald* came into being in January 1860 under editor Isaac Sheen. By 1865 Joseph Smith III was serving as editor and drawing his only wages from that effort. While the early *Herald*s were compiled in a shed in Illinois, the actual publishing was accomplished in Cincinnati. This was neither convenient nor reliable, and the church soon purchased its own presses and established them in Plano, Illinois, where the church headquarters were being located. At first, printing was accomplished by hand, but soon the Herald Publishing Company graduated to a steam press. During the eighteen years it was located in Plano, a rather ambitious publication program was maintained.

In 1872 the publishing division of the church was formally incorporated by the Board of Publications. When Joseph Smith III decided to move the headquarters to Lamoni, Herald Publishing House went with it. By 1881 it had a publishing plant with its own power source printing the first issue of the *Herald* in November 1881. In the new location the Reorganization continued to print journals, tracts, memoirs, sermons, polemical works, and Sunday school supplies, as well as meeting demands for scriptures and hymnals. In 1907 the binding and publication building of Herald House burned to the ground, destroying most of the church's administrative records as well as its library and limited archives. Local support enabled Herald House to rebuild almost immediately; actual construction got underway before the close of the year.

Church headquarters moved to Independence, Missouri, in 1920—many leaders had lived there since 1906—and Herald House soon followed. In 1920 they purchased the Battery Block Building less than a hundred feet from the spot where *The Evening and the Morning Star* was destroyed in 1833. The first *Herald* was published in Independence on May 24, 1921. During the week of September 12, 1965—just one hundred years after Joseph III became editor of the *Herald*—new facilities for Herald House opened with considerable fanfare. Today Herald Publishing House, under editor Roger Yarrington and manager James Hough, is located in a modern printing establishment. The *Herald,* one of the oldest continuously published church magazines in America, is the main voice of the institutional church.

Park College

In November 1974 President Kenneth Beyer of Park College and Apostle William T. Higdon (former president of Graceland College) met to discuss Park's future. A fine Presbyterian college, Park had fallen on hard economic times. Eventually a five-year transition was agreed upon in which Park, retaining its own identity, would operate under Missouri Higher Education, toward potential RLDS ownership. A special committee to discuss Park, Graceland, and higher education in the church was named and reported in 1979. It called for the creation of a Higher Education Advisory Board to advise the First Presidency on the most complementary use and relationship of the colleges.

But the idea of a merger did not bear fruit and control of Park was returned to its board of trustees, the college becoming instead affiliated with the RLDS Church.[6] Since that time Park College has continued its strong affiliation with the Reorganization. In 1983 the church's appointee education and orientation program was consolidated in the master of arts in religion program associated with the Graduate School of Religion at Park College. First under Harold L. Condit and then Donald J. Breckon, Park College has continued to make a significant contribution to the church's educational program.[7]

Notes

1. Paul M. Edwards, *The Hilltop Where...* (Lamoni, Iowa: Venture Foundation, 1972).
2. Doctrine and Covenants 127:3.
3. "Daughters of Zion," *Autumn Leaves* vol. 21, no. 8 (August 1908): 362-367; "The Children's Home," *Autumn Leaves* vol. 24, no. 3 (March 1911): 129-131.
4. "The Passing of the Saints' Home," *Saints' Herald* vol. 104, no. 23 (June 10, 1957): 536-537.
5. Doctrine and Covenants 127:1a.
6. 1982 World Conference Resolution 1171.
7. For further reading: Roy Cheville, *Through the West Door* (Independence, Missouri: Herald Publishing House, 1946); Paul M. Edwards, *The Hilltop Where...* (Lamoni, Iowa: Venture Foundation, 1972); Barbara J. Higdon, "The Present Time of Past Things," in Maurice L. Draper and Debra Combs, eds., *Restoration Studies III* (Independence, Missouri: Herald Publishing House, 1986): 335-339.

World Consciousness

The post-World War II years were marked by significant growth of the church as it moved toward an increasing worldwide involvement. Following the death of President Frederick Madison Smith and the ordination of his brother, Israel A. Smith, as president, the Reorganization entered a phase of expansion. Israel's role centered on unifying the church and moving it from the long winter of debt and disillusionment toward participation in the world left by world war.

This development has been described as,

> the church's moving through cycles of, on the one hand, housekeeping functions (symbolized by church building construction and fiscal, legislative, administrative, and judicial policy revisions), and on the other hand servanthood (illustrated by sharing ministries offered to "the world" with little or no expectation of economic return). These two categories, it should be noted, are not mutually exclusive.[1]

When Israel became president in 1946, the debt had been paid and the church was beginning a period of

financial security. But most of the destructive conse-
quences of more than a decade of financial struggle
remained. One of the most obvious and significant was
the vastly depleted quorums and ranks of full-time
appointees. This became a major concern for President
Smith, and the councils turned their attention to it.

One characteristic of the post-war period was the
strong feeling of self-affirmation held by the church. It
had moved through a devastating depression and still
held on to the membership and to the major assets
needed to continue its mission. It had held together
through a vast world war in which member was
matched against member as national concerns pulled
them into the field of battle. And with this new self-con-
fidence members began to recognize the merits of their
own identity, though they had not yet freed themselves
from the desire to prove the LDS wrong. There was
apparent in this post-war era, however, a dynamic and
positioned self-image that affirmed the church as the
body of Christ for its people.

While Israel A. Smith was aware of the continued
struggle to identify the Reorganization on its own terms,
he was equally aware that the Reorganization's beliefs
needed to be considered in light of its expanding interest
in taking the message of the church into new cultures.
The military service of many church members had
brought them into contact with the cultures and peoples of other lands. This firsthand knowledge, as well
as numerous personal friendships, were instrumental in
expanding the interest of church members in the missionary task. As a result of these contacts, several opportunities opened up for taking the church into lands and
cultures previously closed. They would wait, primarily,
until the expansion periods of the sixties and seventies.

The history of the church during this time was, to a large degree, a history of internal inquiry and adjustment that resulted from our external efforts. New theological understandings, expanding evangelical efforts, and concentrated domestic growth all centered around an increased understanding of what it meant to be the church in a world still suffering from several decades of depression and war.

When President Frederick Madison Smith died, his brother, Israel Alexander, was seventy years old. While Fred M. left behind an oral statement naming his brother as his successor, there was no written document to that effect. The Council of Twelve asked Presiding Patriarch Elbert A. Smith to seek direction before the 1946 General Conference, which would consider the question of a successor. The Conference's response affirmed Israel as "president, prophet, seer, and revelator." Apostles John F. Garver and F. Henry Edwards were set apart as his counselors, and the new First Presidency was complete.

Both the pause in leadership and his advanced years made Israel concerned about his own successor to the prophetic office. As might be expected from a lawyer who had served the church for so many years, he centered his response in the law and tradition. He was concerned with avoiding any confusion about leadership and any loss of dignity that might emerge from an extended consideration of the succession question. While covering the issue he avoided any premature disclosure of his feelings or his May 28, 1952, document that named his half-brother, W. Wallace Smith. The document identified the procedure by which succession should occur.

Israel came to the presidency by way of heritage and long service. He had been a lawyer most of his adult life and had served in a variety of legislative commissions, including the Missouri Constitutional Convention of 1943. But his primary commitment was with the church. He had served for a time as his father's secretary, and from 1920 until his resignation in 1925, was a counselor to Benjamin McGuire in the Presiding Bishopric. He had been associate editor of the *Herald* for some time and was eventually called into the First Presidency in 1938. Born in Plano, Illinois, on February 2, 1876, he was named after his father's good friend and longtime church bishop, Israel Rogers, and often called "Dutch" by his contemporaries. President Israel was raised in Lamoni, studied at Graceland College, and read for the law, having been admitted to the Missouri Bar in 1913.

He came with the insights available from long association with the office via his family and with experience in both the legal and financial affairs of the movement. For the first time in decades, the church's financial condition was reasonably stable, and the future promised the funds necessary to accomplish some of the programs that had been so long delayed.

Relieved of the pressure of having to seek financial cuts and blessed with a balanced budget, the new president turned his attention to program needs. He sought immediate improvement in the church's programs and activities, pushed for repairs for the more than 600 churches that had suffered from deferred maintenance.

Work on the Auditorium moved toward completion, and funds were expended for other facilities long put on hold. Work was done at Graceland, Resthaven was expanded, and construction at the Independence Sanitarium resumed.

The completion and financing of the Auditorium was one of the tasks to which L. F. P. Curry and G. Leslie DeLapp turned their attention. For many years the Auditorium had been symbolic of the burden of debt and appeared to many as a "great white elephant."[2] The building, sitting on a lot that proved too small for it, was displeasing to the eye and reminded members of their struggle. For many years a picture of the Auditorium, with a dark cloud hanging over it, appeared in the *Herald* as a reminder of the need to clear the debt. As the members gave more and more of their resources and the debt was paid, the cloud disappeared.

During the recovery process, work on the building continued: a steel railing on the balcony, east and west wings faced with brick (financed by the Laurel Club and brick from the Old Columbian School), the foyer completed, a copper roof covering the dome, the building faced with limestone, and improvements inside made the building more usable and turned it from its incomplete state to the worship and legislative center so many had envisioned.[3]

The year following Israel's ordination, the First Presidency, in a report to the 1947 General Conference, provided a statement of goals for the church. The plan drew attention to three major concerns and made a three-pronged proposal. The goals were designed to reestablish the church's mission. It called for the establishment of immediate and long-range programs for branches, districts, and stakes. The program called on the church to harmonize the missionary task by means of local support for overall and expanded missions. And it called for effort to advance the gathering while being constantly aware of the ministerial needs of those away from Independence.

To accomplish this President Israel A. Smith dedicated himself to elevating standards of home and family life and to calling and training local leaders in expanded tasks so they might release general officers for their distinctive work. In addition, he proposed to establish and make use of departmental work at the General Church level to expand and integrate programs throughout the church.

Missionary work was emphasized with rapid increases in the size of the appointee force and encouragement to members to share their testimonies in local evangelistic activities. The Twelve were again identified as responsible for opening the work in new places. The counsel from the president was to push for balanced growth with new areas constantly being reinforced by affirming the center of religious life: the home and family. Of special significance was the calling, once again, of self-supporting members of the Quorums of Seventy.

By 1953 the number of seventies had decreased alarmingly: and the first and second quorums merged and the third disbanded. The presidents of Seventy were calling men from among the appointee force only, but this considerably limited the number available. President Israel addressed the problem in 1954 in a document accepted by General Conference that altered the guidelines by which quorum members were called. The guidance allowed self-sustaining seventies to be ordained. The quorums were slow to issue the call however, and years later this situation led President W. Wallace Smith to urge the greater use of those with talents and calling as self-sustaining ministers. Israel pressed this in his message to the 1948 Conference[4] in which he encouraged the Quorums of Seventy to increase their efforts in opening the work in distant and undeveloped areas, thereby releasing the apostles to concentrate on their special responsibilities.

Leaders and members sought a better understanding of and deeper immersion in the act of worship. The decades of the 1930s and 1940s were often discouraging and humbling. The people sought ways to express their belonging and participation. The results of expansion and increasing self-awareness also led them to understand that they did not have all the answers and that they desperately needed to increase their ability to worship together.

As a part of the First Presidency's desire to train local and General Church leaders for their roles in an expanding world, the School of the Restoration was established. During the depression years education, like other activities, had suffered. In 1951 the Joint Council established an expectation of two years of college for all General Church appointees. In 1956 the School of the Restoration was created and eventually housed at the old rest home property on Winner Road. It was established for the training of leadership within the priesthood and to provide theological and historical understanding for the church at large. By means of correspondence materials it provided additional training for leaders and members all over the country. At its residence campus in Independence "an institution of voluntary adult education" was maintained, which graduated students after a nine-month course with a diploma in religion. The School of the Restoration was the forerunner of Temple School.

Part of the task facing the church as it moved toward expansion was the need to clean up some theological loose ends. One of the most interesting of these was the question of baptism for the dead. President Israel Smith had voiced opposition to the doctrine as early as 1940, and shortly after he became president he initiated the idea of removing references to it from the Doctrine and Covenants. By 1950 the question was all but solved simply by lack of acceptance. Finally it was challenged, though such a challenge was probably unnecessary, by Russell F. Ralston, one of the presidents of Seventy (he would later serve as senior president of Seventy before being called into the Council of Twelve in 1964) who could see no theological or biblical base for the concept or its practice. Several church leaders, as well as a significant segment of the membership, resolved that whatever its value in the early church, it had no place in the twentieth-century Reorganization.

President W. Wallace Smith was also opposed to the doctrine and, as a part of his 1968 document concerning the Temple, he indicated that no secret ordinances would be practiced in the Temple. The whole question of baptism for the dead was resolved at the 1970 Conference. The First Presidency originated the proposal to move those sections dealing with the ceremony[5] to an historical appendix of the Doctrine and Covenants. Delegates gave their assent. Certainly the ease with which this was accomplished is an indication of the fact, despite some disagreement, that this was no longer a significant issue. A final step was taken by Conference delegates in 1990 when the historical appendix was ordered removed from the Doctrine and Covenants.[6]

As a part of the development of the domestic field, and in keeping with President Israel A. Smith's view of "potential Zionic gatherings," centralized administration of population areas was increased. When he became president there were five stakes in existence, all of them close to Independence and Headquarters. His 1950 proposal, brought to the General Conference for action, created two more stakes, one in Los Angeles, California, and the other in Detroit, Michigan. Both were prime population centers for the church.

When President Israel A. Smith was in French Polynesia he informed the people that local gathering was in order. While he certainly had not given up the larger gathering principle, he did realize the value to the Saints of permanently locating in areas of their homeland:

> It would be wisdom for my people to withdraw from those places that are farthest removed and gather in large numbers in those islands nearer the centers of trade and business when such changes can be done without material loss.[7]

This had the effect on the church, and its Zionic concept, of recognizing various population centers meeting the purposes of Zion. Certainly the development of stakes and metropoles (large urban congregational groups in Papeete, Tahiti; Honolulu, Hawaii; Toronto, Ontario; Portland, Oregon; and Washington, D.C.) was in keeping with the spirit of this interpretation.

Through this effort the church expanded moderately in North America, growing from 134,000 in 1950 to more than 174,000 at the time of Israel's death in 1958. But it was still very much a domestic church with the massive percentage living in the United States or Canada. In 1960 there were only nine regions abroad that had reported church members: Great Britain, Germany, Australia, and French Polynesia accounted for ninety-five percent of the 9,842 members outside North America. A small group maintained itself in Grand Cayman Island but there was little activity. Unfortunately there were no longer members reported in Jerusalem, Switzerland, or Poland where in 1947 there had been at least core groups. And none were located in Latin America, an area which was to respond dramatically in the following decades.

There was some activity, however, as the expanded missionary program began to establish seed groups in a whole range of foreign assignments. The first Korean citizen joined with the Reorganization in 1954; the first conversion from India and Pakistan was in 1958; and the work in Mexico expanded from a mission in the Rio Grande Valley of Texas. However, the major expansion efforts would take place during the presidencies of W. Wallace and Wallace B. Smith.

President Israel A. Smith was only president of the Reorganization for twelve years, the shortest period of all the presidents. Despite his age he managed to keep quite active until his death in an automobile accident on June 14, 1958, at the age of eighty-two. No one expected him to show the same vigor anticipated by a man half his years.

During his presidency he was assisted by men of strength and influence. F. Henry Edwards and John F. Garver were his original counselors. After Garver's death in late 1949, W. Wallace Smith entered the First Presidency in 1950. To a large extent they carried on the daily business of the church.

His primary concern was to strengthen the unity of the members and to reestablish a healthy agenda of domestic programs and missionary activity for the church. He is often best remembered for a much quoted passage from the Doctrine and Covenants: "The work of preparation and the perfection of my Saints go forward slowly, and Zionic conditions are no further away nor any closer than the spiritual condition of my people justifies."[8][9]

Notes

1. Peter A. Judd and A. Bruce Lindgren, *An Introduction to the Saints Church* (Independence, Missouri: Herald Publishing House, 1976), 29.
2. G. Leslie DeLapp, *In the World...* (Independence, Missouri: Herald Publishing House, 1973), 165.
3. DeLapp, 171.
4. Doctrine and Covenants 141:6a.
5. Doctrine and Covenants 107, 109, 110.
6. Roger D. Launius, "An Ambivalent Rejection: Baptism for the Dead and the Reorganized Church Experience," *Dialogue* vol. 23, no. 2 (Summer 1990): 61-84.
7. See Israel A. Smith transcript of message at Taravao, French Polynesia (July 29, 1950), RLDS Church Archives, Independence, Missouri.
8. Doctrine and Covenants 140:5c.
9. For further reading: Norma Derry Hiles, *Gentle Monarch: The Presidency of Israel A. Smith* (Independence, Missouri: Herald Publishing House, 1991); Roger D. Launius, *Invisible Saints: A History of Black Americans in the Reorganized Church* (Independence, Missouri: Herald Publishing House, 1988); Darlene Caswell, "Christ and Culture Reflected in RLDS Mission," in Marjorie B. Troeh and Eileen M. Terril, eds., *Restoration Studies IV* (Independence, Missouri: Herald Publishing House, 1988): 59-64; Gregory S. Savage, "Into All the World: Germany," in Maurice L. Draper and Clare D. Vlahos, eds., *Restoration Studies I* (Independence, Missouri: Herald Publishing House, 1980): 58-68; Kenneth D. Sowers, Jr., "Growing Pains," in Maurice L. Draper and Debra Combs, eds., *Restoration Studies III* (Independence, Missouri: Herald Publishing House, 1986): 54-60.

The World Church

Delegates to the 1958 General Conference met together under strangely paradoxical circumstances. To complete the work on the Auditorium, the Conference had been postponed to early October. So they gathered late but did so in the just-completed building which had, for so long, served as a symbol of their financial difficulties. With great care the Auditorium had been converted from a massive cement chamber to a beautiful and utilitarian place for the delegates to meet. Little had been spared in completing the building that had been Fred M. Smith's dream and the most tangible expression of the people's determination to withstand the onslaught of war and depression. Fred M. Smith would have been pleased with the outcome. The delegates gathered with a great sense of hope for future accomplishments.

But the delegates also met in sorrow, for they did so without the man who had led them as their prophet and president for nearly a dozen years. Israel A. Smith was killed in June 1958 in an automobile accident while on a trip to Lamoni. He had, with considerable foresight, left instructions with his counselor, F. Henry Edwards, and G. Leslie DeLapp, the presiding bishop, concerning his successor. As Israel had instructed, the letter was delivered to the Twelve on news of his death. It named his half-brother, William Wallace Smith, as the fifth president of the church, the fourth of the Reorganization.

The changes initiated by this calling emphasized the younger men of the church with Maurice Draper joining F. Henry Edwards in the First Presidency. Two new members were named to the Twelve: Charles D. Neff and Clifford A. Cole. Elbert A. Smith, beloved patriarch, was retired after many years of service. Roy A. Cheville, a University of Chicago Ph.D. and longtime professor of religion and philosophy at Graceland College, was ordained as presiding patriarch.

W. Wallace Smith was the son of Joseph Smith III and Ada Clark Smith. Born in Lamoni, Iowa, on November 18, 1900, he moved with his family to Independence, Missouri, in 1906 and lived there on Short Street. He graduated from William Chrisman High School, then attended the University of Missouri. When he left there in 1924, he began to work for a local hardware concern. General Church financial problems prevented his appointment at that time, and he lived first in St. Joseph, Missouri, and later in Portland, Oregon, where he was active in local congregations. Finally in 1947 he was called into the Council of Twelve and then, in 1950, called by Israel A. Smith into the First Presidency.

During the years that W. Wallace Smith led the church, it responded to its mission as a world church. Total membership increased from 167,000 to more than 215,000, with dozens of new jurisdictions of the church being created and maintained. In 1960, in anticipation of activity all over the world, the church moved to substitute the term "World Church" as a more fitting title than "General Church." Following President Smith's round-the-world trip, the church moved forward determined to expand its missions.

The church of the 1960s that W. Wallace Smith inherited maintained two characteristics from earlier days which were to limit its missionary activity. The first was the heritage of the Nauvoo church represented by the Latter-day Saints in Utah. That heritage caused members to assume that the Reorganization was required to make clear statements separating itself from beliefs about polygamy and secret temple rites. The second, somewhat drawing from the first, was the realization that "gathering" as it had been known in the early church was not applicable to the Reorganization, at least not as the church moved to become in reality a world church. Joseph Smith III had instructed the church on the need for persons to build up the church wherever they were. The church, as would be expected, operated on the assumption that gathering would take place at some later time. The common phrase was to "wait for Zion."

In addition to these two limiting attitudes, the Reorganization had confronted two major world wars, a worldwide depression, and considerable restructuring of the organization in less than half a century. It is easy to understand the long period of deep frustration and anxiety that hovered over the church's missionary outreach efforts. It was clear to the members of the Joint Council—the First Presidency, Twelve, and Presiding Bishopric—that the church needed to identify its objectives in light of who and what it was, not in reaction to

259

an institutional history. And that having identified a mission, the church needed to move out in a serious response to the needs of the world.

While the members were in favor of outreach, they were unaware of the influence that would be yielded by large numbers of persons coming into the church with vastly different cultural backgrounds. The impact of that influence would be quickly felt. President Smith seemed to sense this. After he had reaffirmed the principles of the Restoration movement he forewarned the Conference delegates of 1964 "...the demands of a growing church require that these principles shall be evaluated and subjected to further interpretation."[1] This was a significant watershed for the church.

A part of the interpretation of which President Smith spoke, and in some ways the beginning of it, was the initial steps of the modern missionary outreach program. The First Presidency sent Apostles Blair Jensen and Charles Neff to the Orient. The result was the first serious missionary outreach conducted among persons not already Christian. Working with Dayle Bethel and others associated there, official missions were opened in Japan, Korea, and the Ryukyu Islands. Soon the church came face to face with some of the difficulties imposed by such an outreach effort. These were best identified by Apostle Clifford Cole whose analysis is paraphrased here. What happened is that the church was required:

1. To confront the inadequacy of presenting itself on the basis of "distinctives." The non-Christian community was not interested in how the church was different from other *Christians* but what the church as Christians believed. Certainly particular RLDS beliefs were presented but in the more general Christian framework.

2. To draw the church closer to other Christian leaders and to allow members to discover the warmth, concern, and Christian love they displayed in their own activities. Having worked together the church soon began to move away from the adversary relationship to other religious groups that had been held so long. And, on the other hand, it allowed other ministerial personnel to see the church—long suspected by more orthodox organizations as being less than Christian—as fellow workers in the body of Christ.

3. To discover the great abilities of the indigenous persons to whom it witnessed and help them recognize they could do for themselves what never could be done for them. The church also discovered it had a great deal to learn from them.

4. To decentralize the administration of the church in ways never accomplished before, both because of the legal demands of some countries but also because of the need not to be seen simply as an American church.[2]

Domestically, one concern was addressed by the expanding Civil Rights movement. It was significant, as all such social questions are, because of the razor-thin edge the church constantly walks between its duty to speak prophetically to its people and the varied beliefs of the people themselves. There were strong divisions of opinion among the members on how to minister to persons of various races.

The church's official position on blacks had, since 1865, been open and supportive. But the real relationship essentially formed along the same lines of division and opinions found in any cross-section of society. President W. Wallace Smith did not favor the confrontational methods of the Civil Rights movement. F. Henry Edwards—perhaps the most outspoken member of the

261

First Presidency—considered the race question to be a social issue and thus believed it inappropriate for the First Presidency to take a stand.

The church was trying to steer its way through the conflicting and passionate turmoil of the 1960s. The Presidency urged individual members to speak and act freely. The Conference, as early as 1948, had attempted some affirmation of racial equality, but it failed after Israel Smith argued such an affirmation suggested previous unjust treatment.

In 1954 another resolution called for a committee to investigate means for taking the message of the church to blacks. It was referred to a joint quorum responsibility.[3] The 1955 beginning of the black boycott in Alabama pushed the church for a response. The resulting resolution, adopted in 1956, was weaker than many wanted, but it did affirm the church's openness to all races. It was 1963 before an official First Presidency position was made available. "Our Position On Race and Color" affirmed the rights of blacks and assured everyone that black persons were both welcome and sought as members of the church.[4]

William Russell, assistant editor of the *Herald* and a strong advocate of civil rights, took the lead in pushing the issue in church publications. The First Presidency, as editors, called for a calmer approach, feeling that there was no need for stronger action. Nor did they want to exaggerate the division that already existed in the church. A resolution, "Implementation of Racial Brotherhood," was approved, coming as it did after the assassination of Martin Luther King, Jr., and a 1968 World Conference tribute to him. The resolution called for aggressive action to share the message of the church with the black race.

During this period the number of articles and editorials concerning civil rights was limited, but even then there was considerable heat and controversy surrounding the issue. William Russell's articles, as well as some by Paul Wellington and others, received numerous letters of protest.

The Presidency's position, again provided by F. Henry Edwards, was sent to Wellington as editor of the *Herald*. President Edwards restated the church's commitment to the "principle of racial equality" but stated the church was not officially committed to the civil rights movement, or any other movement. Most definitely, Edwards determined, "it was not up to individuals on the staff to present views which were assumed to be official views."[5] Arlyn Love suggests the First Presidency was once again forced to make a decision and acted pastorally serving to protect and support the members in their many positions.

The theological implications of missionary expansion were far larger than the institution at first realized. They were larger because the church had long dealt with its theological questions by affirmations concerning its historical development. The common heritage shared by members and the importance of the story of beginnings had precluded much theological consideration. But now it was time to identify beliefs in a manner that would preserve the essential nature of the movement but remove it from explanations born in the 1830s. After all, many of the persons to be addressed were not only *not* Americans, nor a part of what we called Western civilization, they were not even Christians. The common heritage that was understood so well by Westerners was a poor basis for introduction to persons who did not understand Western culture at all.

One aspect of the emerging understanding was that there was a sense of disquietude among many members—a feeling of general unrest. Many felt the church was changing and that in the embrace of new concepts and applications the "old ways" were being discontinued and downgraded—and that with the change there was a loss of spirituality. Leaders were suspect. This suspicion was, of course, not limited to the RLDS Church. Church leaders all over the world were having to respond to the challenges that emerged when they sought to apply their beliefs and behaviors to their missionary activities in Third World nations.

At the same time, it seems that most members were supportive of this expanding missionary role. And, as is often the case in times of turmoil, there emerged a strong unity among those who supported the church's efforts to take the gospel to other lands. The worldwide vision generated considerable enthusiasm.

The Joint Council responded to the challenge and presented to the 1966 World Conference some major goals for the church to accomplish if it was to meet the needs presented by the missionary effort. These goals were (1) to clarify the church's theological position, (2) to increase the effectiveness of worship in the church, (3) to develop procedures in both evangelism and administration that would be applicable to world concepts, (4) to decentralize the administration of the church, and finally, (5) to pursue Zionic development by means of interpretative understandings meaningful to the contemporary world.

Even though the members endorsed these goals, they were harder to live with than many imagined. First of all, any new look at the theological basis of the church would be threatening to some. The primary inquiry occurred within what was known as the Basic Beliefs Committee. The work of this committee was published in 1970 as *Exploring the Faith.*

The committee, first chaired by President F. Henry Edwards and then by Clifford Cole, president of the Council of Twelve, began to shape a comprehensive statement of the faith of the church. The result was a statement ten years in the making and one which reflected the idea that historical and traditional points of view must be examined by scholarship and contemporary religious experience. As a result, the committee report no longer saw the church as a duplicate of the first-century church. Rather, it recognized the primary mission to be a fellowship of those who acknowledged Jesus Christ as their Lord.

The Word of God incarnate in Jesus Christ was understood not so much as a set of propositions but as a call to reflect Jesus Christ in all relationships. Perhaps most important was the realization that scripture as well as church history are not ends in themselves but rather means "for discovering what God intends the church to be today."[6] Apostle Clifford Cole observed the church was shifting its emphasis from RLDS distinctives to a more general concern to present the unqualified gospel of Jesus Christ and to bring persons to him.

The conclusions reflected the larger religious world in which the church lived and worshiped, as well as both classical and contemporary scholarship. The report reaffirmed a belief in divine participation in the birth and contemporary nature of the Restoration movement, but it was significant for its lack of polemics and its willingness to acknowledge a remarkable debt to the continuing Christian community. The committee reaffirmed the "real genius" of the Restoration lay not so much in recapturing the church of the past but in responding to the vital, contemporary revelation of the divine.

The discussion of how theological understandings would apply to the mission of the church was enhanced by a series of "discussion papers" prepared by members of the Religious Education Department for the Curriculum Consultation Committee. These papers, designed to be open and exploratory in nature, were, unfortunately, distributed among persons who did not understand their use and who granted them an importance they did not warrant. The resulting difficulties created a rift between the more liberal and conservative members, a concern not greatly decreased by the First Presidency's assurance of the papers' "unofficial status."

The Religious Education Department was planning a "new curriculum" for the church school and disagreement with it was lumped into the general discontent felt by some members. When this curriculum appeared, one of the most creative and world-minded the church was to produce, it was already the focus of considerable controversy. What was generally seen as the crisis of "the new curriculum" was a long time in making. If selecting a beginning date, it probably would be the publication of Garland Tickemyer's quarterlies, *The Old Testament Speaks to Our Day* (1960), which reflected the growing intellectual responsibility of the Religious Education Department. The church was beginning to feel the influence of professional schooling, even seminary training.

Much of the growing concern accumulated around educator and writer Richard Lancaster, but it was the appointment of Don Landon as director of Religious Education in 1966 and Geoffrey Spencer as director of the Church School Division that seemed to finalize the discontent. Both men were highly qualified, and the First Presidency's decision in 1967 to develop a new curriculum allowed them to start over in explaining the church to its younger members.

The central theme of the new curriculum was "to develop adequacy of expression for the beliefs of the movement designed to put discipleship above belief and to truly subject belief to the service of discipleship."[7] The curriculum itself reflected the concept of decentralization. Most of these materials were not so much detailed programs as resources upon which local leaders could develop classes. Necessary to the expanding curriculum and the work of the Curriculum Consultation Committee, eleven papers had been prepared and were delivered from 1967 to 1969 to working members of the committee and select others. They were listed as discussion—not position—papers, but if that distinction was apparent to the committee it was soon lost on many church members.

Several difficulties arose within the committee concerning points raised and what was expected of them. But the most significant problem was the leaking of the papers during 1969, in what appeared as an effort to deliberately discredit the department. More conservative church members were threatened by the material, and many used the papers as a focal point for their existing anxieties. The flames were fanned by the sale of several confidential memos and private letters, which were used as evidence that the church was in apostasy.

The 1970 World Conference was a hard one for many. Several attempts were made to reduce the budget of the Department of Religious Education but all failed. The members at large did not seem as upset as it at first

267

appeared. But much of the damage had been done, and lack of any strong institutional support made it hard for the leaders of the project. Shortly after the 1970 Conference Don Landon resigned, as did department members Verne Sparks and Wayne Ham. The curriculum, delayed by controversy, was eventually released in the 1970s. The material was unique, looked considerably different from previous materials, and approached education with new methods. The debate continued for a long time, but the curriculum was standard by the end of the 1970s.

In 1973 a statement of objectives was published by the First Presidency. It was a careful reworking of the 1966 objectives and a result of a 1972 Joint Council on church programs. The influence of the church's world thought was evident in its reflection of "the servant church" as a "repenting community, struggling to overcome its bondage to [the] human condition" and seeking a loving, nurturing, healing climate for all persons.[8]

An unexpected difficulty that arose from the church's rapid expansion into foreign cultures was the question of polygamy—historically used as the "active" difference between the Reorganization and the Utah-based Latter-day Saints—that appeared among converts in India. Unwilling to demand that certain Sora tribal men desert existing multiple families, the church held that its call was to accept polygamist persons and help them work into a Christian marriage relationship. President W. Wallace Smith addressed the 1972 World Conference instructing delegates that the Twelve were to "interpret and administer the doctrines and ordinances of the gospel in a manner appropriate to the circumstances in which they find such persons."[9] Certainly the strong "bias toward the United States reflected in the scriptures of the Restoration in relationship to images of Zion and the highly authoritarian and centralized approach to leadership, government, and authority constituted formidable barriers in the attempt of the church to become world-wide."[10] The deeper interpretation necessary to be a world church was to continue.

Responding to the advancing missionary frontier President Smith, reverting to an earlier consideration, advised that "as such secondary presidency, the council [of Twelve] should share with the First Presidency in reviewing and determining policies of church administration...."[11]

Several incidental events occurred during the decade of the 1970s that were to secure our hold on the past and point to the future. Since the church's acquisition of the Kirtland Temple in 1880, it had been interested in the preservation of historic sites. During the early years of the twentieth century the church had come into possession of the Nauvoo House, the Mansion House, the Homestead, and had developed a visitor's center at Nauvoo. In 1970 the Restoration Trail Foundation was established to oversee and preserve these sites. The group worked under the auspices of the First Presidency: the Presidency, the Presiding Bishopric, and the president of the Twelve formed the corporate body. A fifteen-member board was responsible for the sites from fund-raising to site interpretation. Kenneth Stobaugh spent more than twenty-five years preserving the church's site heritage, and William Knapp followed as historic sites director. Hundreds of volunteers worked long hours to preserve and display church history through the power of place.

The nature of the church's women's organizations had changed when the 1954 General Conference directed that the women's leader be appointed by the First Presidency with the approval of the Conference. In 1956 the same procedure was established for members of the council. Alice Burgess was named, and under her the General Council of Women was charged with updating the *Handbook for Women's Work in the Church.*

The council chose annual themes, produced study materials, and provided meeting and worship programs. Under Katherine Westwood, a newsletter (later named *Distaff*) became a major means of communication for women in the church. At the Amboy Centennial Conference in 1960 plans were announced for an institute to be held in Independence. More than 3,000 women from the United States, Canada, Australia, and New Zealand attended. In 1970 the *Distaff* became a magazine with 5,000 subscribers but was published only for a year.

In 1971 the Women's Council was transferred to the Division of Program Services and Marjorie Troeh was named Women's Ministry consultant. The 1974 Conference created the Women's Ministries Commission to be assigned to a World Church division. In October 1979 the Women's Ministries Commission was transferred to the Division of Program Planning. The significance of the Women's Ministries Commission during the next five years can hardly be overstated. The commission worked to expand the role of women in the life of the church and aided women in developing their own personal growth.

In January 1979 the First Presidency called World Church appointees and executives together to discuss the church's program in the decade of the 1980s. A series of papers was prepared and read that elaborated on the nature, identity, and mission of the church. In these discussions the authority of the church was expressed in functional terms rather than along essential grounds. And the fullness of the gospel was seen as touching the total range of human experience.

The missionary movement expanded rather rapidly. Japan and Korea were opened as the result of military personnel stationed in these two countries during the Korean War. Kisuke Sekine became familiar with the church through Priscilla Kramer, whose home was the worship center for the Saints in the area. Sekine and another interested countryman, Hiroshi Yamada, were baptized and served in their homeland as missionaries. In 1980 Sekine was called to the Council of Twelve. The first baptisms in Korea were as early as 1954, but the mission there did not expand until Apostle Charles D. Neff and several members of the Quorums of Seventy were assigned to the Orient. Through preschools, kindergartens, and clinics, the work was expanded throughout the Orient.

The work in India and in the Philippines was officially begun in 1966 although missionary activity had existed there before. Several Saints served in these locations as the beginning of the national churches carried on ministries in agricultural areas and in medical and community development.

Sanon Jolivert, a Haitian minister, found himself dissatisfied with the Pentecostal group with which he was associated and was drawn to write to the Reorganization. He had found the church listed in a compilation of world religions. Members of the Council of Twelve responded quickly and soon had established a series of meetings with Jolivert who was baptized in 1967. He brought with him many associates and their previous congregations, and by 1968 the church was officially established there. In the 1970s groups of volunteers brought improvement in health care, food production, and water care in many Haitian communities and villages. By the end of the 1980s, the Haiti Region was the church's fastest growing area, with three districts and more than 10,000 members.

In Africa the work also started with an individual who requested information about the church. In 1962 Gobert Edett of Nigeria inquired about the nature of RLDS beliefs and then began to witness what he had learned to others. The work there was halted temporarily by a bloody civil war that crippled the country. At the conclusion of the hostilities it was discovered that the mission had survived, and by 1988 nearly 4,000 Nigerian Saints worshiped in their national church. In Liberia the work began in 1974. In Kenya George Seda joined the church, and after a time at Graceland College, he returned home to start the Reorganized Church in 1977.

During the 1960s and 1970s evangelistic efforts were also undertaken in Peru, Argentina, Brazil, Mexico, Honduras, New Caledonia, Fiji, the Dominican Republic, and Taiwan. In several expanding nations the church ran into difficulties with the formal name of the church, often because of local laws about foreign ownership. Sometimes the change was required because of dissatisfaction with other existing religious groups. In Kenya the church is officially the Christian Community Fellowship of Africa; in Japan, The Church of Jesus Christ; and in Mexico the church is a national church.

One significant response to pain and poverty in some of these countries was the establishment of church-sponsored organizations to deal with such needs. The brief nature of this account precludes any discussion of the work done by many in the early days as servant ministry spread to many areas of the world. These would include the medical missionary work done in Korea and Africa and the Community One work done in the Philippines before the emergence of Outreach International. Outreach International, World Accord (formerly Canadian Saints Outreach), World Hunger, DEVCO, CORD, and other groups provided secular donors and volunteers who addressed the physical problems of people in these expanding areas. Between the church and these associated organizations, the problems of education, health care, home construction, water projects, energy sources, and food production and distribution were addressed.

A fourth goal that guided the expanding church during this period was decentralization both in terms of administration and in terms of its emphasis on fellowship. The commission system of congregational organization, which was to become a part of the Faith to Grow program, allowed small groups of persons on a local and jurisdictional level to create programs and initiate procedures. Decentralization was noted as well in the organization of missionary activities, in the selection and utilization of national ministers, and in stake and district programs.

The concept of "temple" has played an important role in the life of the church since Joseph Smith, Jr.'s first call for such construction in the 1830s. The modern church, however, was reawakened to the concept of the Temple when, in 1968, President W. Wallace Smith brought a document to the World Conference that acknowledged, "The time has come for a start to be made toward building my temple in the Center Place."[12] The church had, early in the 1830s, identified the general location, and the Saints at Kirtland had built the House of the Lord. But over the years the idea, somewhat like the concept of gathering, had waited for further instructions. Now the efforts toward preparing for the Temple began to gear up. Further instructions came through President Wallace B. Smith in Doctrine and Covenants Section 156.[13]

Yet another significant aspect of the emerging church had to do with its acknowledgment of pluralism. For the unity of the movement, its goals and desires, and its essential trust in God, was the key to its personality. It was not in some established creed or essential interpretation. The wide variety of responses, as well as some serious consideration of interpretation, were reflected in growing—and open—disagreement, tolerance, and intellectual pluralism. Not only did the *Herald* reflect this in its pages but church publications like the *University Bulletin* and unofficial, but church-related, publications such as the admittedly liberal *Courage: A Journal of History, Thought, and Action* reflected this expanding pluralism.[14]

Notes

1. Doctrine and Covenants 147:7.
2. Clifford A. Cole, "The World Church: Our Mission in the 1980s," *Commission* (September 1979): 41-46.
3. 1954 *General Conference Daily:* 94, as quoted in Arlyn R. Love, "The First Presidency's Response to the Civil Rights Movement," *JWHA Journal* 4 (1984): 43.
4. Arlyn R. Love, "The First Presidency's Response," 44.
5. F. Henry Edwards to Paul Wellington (April 29, 1965), quoted in Arlyn R. Love, "The First Presidency's Response," 41-50.
6. Barbara Higdon, "The Reorganization in the Twentieth Century," *Dialogue* vol.7, no. 1 (Spring 1972): 94-100.
7. Interview with Don Landon in William Knapp, "Professionalizing Religious Education in the Church: The New Curriculum Controversy," *JWHA Journal* 2 (1982): 50-58.
8. Geoffrey F. Spencer, "Reorganization Thought: Whence and Whither," unpublished paper delivered to the Mormon History Association, page 14.
9. Doctrine and Covenants 150:11b.
10. Geoffrey F. Spencer, 14.
11. Doctrine and Covenants 148:10b.
12. Doctrine and Covenants 149:6a.
13. Doctrine and Covenants 156:3.
14. For further reading: Jan Shipps, *Mormonism: The Story of a New Religious Tradition* (Urbana: University of Illinois Press, 1985); Alma R. Blair, "A Loss of Nerve," *Courage* vol. 1, no. 1 (September 1970): 29-36; Richard P. Howard, "Themes in Latter Day Saint History," *JWHA Journal* 2 (1982): 23; William Knapp, "Professionalizing Religious Education in the Church: The New Curriculum Controversy," *JWHA Journal* 2 (1982): 50-58; William D. Russell, "A Priestly Role for a Prophetic Church: The RLDS Church and Black Americans," *Dialogue* vol. 12, no. 2 (Summer 1979): 37-49; Alan D. Tyree, "Divine Calling in Human History," in Maurice L. Draper and Debra Combs, eds., *Restoration Studies III* (Independence, Missouri: Herald Publishing House, 1986): 86-96.

The Eighties and Beyond

The Restoration movement has made a significant impact not only on America but on the world. The larger movement, known generally as Mormonism, has gained a respectability that would have amazed some of the early converts. Members of this larger body serve in professions, government, military, education, and occupy positions of authority and influence. The Reorganization, identifying the passions of a people who felt their mission interrupted, has made great efforts to be relevant, not only as the body of Christ but to the needs of the modern world as well.

The future awaits and the Reorganization is committed to the dawning new century. Along these lines the 1978 World Conference was unprecedented and marked the promise of a continued and significant presence. W. Wallace Smith, president of the church for nearly twenty years, retired from his position of leadership. With the title "president emeritus," he stepped aside while his son Wallace B. Smith was ordained as the sixth prophet and president of the Restoration.

Two years before at the World Conference, President W. Wallace had named his son "prophet and president designate," allowing him two years in which to prepare himself for the responsibilities. After two years of serious study and preparation by his son, W. Wallace turned over to his successor a church that was larger and stronger but one that was still on the threshold of world expansion and still involved in the process of self-identification.

Born on July 29, 1929, in Independence, Missouri, Wallace B. Smith was a medical doctor with a successful practice in ophthalmology. He had served the church for years as a self-supporting minister and high priest in a wide variety of significant roles. His World Church leadership experience was limited, so he used his two years of preparation time to gain as much training as possible.

The new president assumed his duties at the age of forty-eight. Once ordained at the World Conference, he moved forward in a manner that reflected his easy but deeply concerned style. He took the church, almost immediately, into the decade of a "Faith to Grow" program. The program for the 1980s was designed to invest congregations with a new sense of purpose, of self-worth, and to extend themselves with a new emphasis on evangelism. The hope was to encourage spiritual growth and to expand membership by starting first with leadership development at the local level. The program began with a series of seminars all over the church to "forecast the social climate of the decade and ... [to] articulate a theology which would speak to the needs of our times and communicate our particular mission."[1]

The church's rapid missionary expansion, especially in Third World countries, identified the need for a solid domestic base. By 1982 a major effort had been made to identify and ordain self-sustaining members of the Quorums of Seventy and to fill the seven quorums. There was a comprehensive educational and training program developed. The hope was to create in the congregations—thus in the other jurisdictions—an increasingly capable core of well-trained and experienced persons. Not only did the church institute a priesthood review by which persons could identify their progress and work with their local officers for further implementation of their skills and abilities, but it initiated a program of priesthood education. The various quorums of the church developed strong education programs, and a variety of certification programs were established in special ministerial skills.

As a part of this, President Smith and his counselors, Howard S. Sheehy, Jr., and Alan D. Tyree, turned their attention to the development of the priesthood, as well as the members of the church, and supported the expanding educational activities of Temple School. The school, authorized by a 1974 World Conference resolution[2] as the Temple School of Zion, was given the responsibility of general theological education, ministerial training, quorum training, problem-solving seminars and workshops, production of resources for basic ministries, establishment of exploratory theology seminars, and opportunities for intercultural enrichment. Led first by Apostle William T. Higdon, then by Apostle Geoffrey Spencer, and, in 1982 by Paul M. Edwards, the Temple School Division developed a master's degree program in religious studies in conjunction with the Park College Graduate School of Religion and continuing education opportunities to thousands of members all over the world.

A set of "priesthood guidelines" developed standards as the result of the call for greater ministerial accountability provided in Doctrine and Covenants 156. They were based on the need for an informed priesthood, one that was accountable to the church and whose ministry reflected the best level of spirituality and competence that could be acquired. Recognizing that calls were a response to divine initiative, the church, nevertheless, held the position that ordination authorized one to act as an official representative of the institutional church. Though not universally accepted, the guidelines have, in the main, been well received. The First Presidency strongly recommended not only that new ordinands complete some instruction before ordination but that those who have served for several years become involved in continuing education.

Church members throughout the world sought to know what it means to be the leaven of Christ in a world of crisis. The struggles to become the church in the last decade of the twentieth century presented huge problems. But underlying all of these more immediate concerns was a committed, dedicated membership for whom the message of God is essential.

The church spoke less often of being a "chosen people" separate from the larger world. Rather, it interpreted chosenness as a mark of special responsibility. As members of a special calling, it saw that calling as part of the cooperative Christian movement. It is not a path designed to deny the Saints' but more so to fulfill the instruction to be found "...continuing in the forefront of those organizations and movements which are recognizing the worth of persons and are committed to bringing the ministry of my Son to bear on their lives."[3]

The Reorganization has relied more and more on national ministers to minimize the difficulties of inter-cultural responsibilities. The task of being a World Church produced the need to provide translated resources, economic aid, educational and training material based on cultural conditions the church barely understood. National ministers became World Church representatives in their area. Soon national ministers came together in "area conferences," and the pre-Conference meetings of international leaders became a significant means of communication and fellowship. The influence of non-American members was increasingly felt. It can be seen in the impact made by their ever-larger World Conference delegations, in the multi-cultural approaches to many hitherto American problems, and the louder and louder recommendations for the location of World Conferences somewhere other than North America.

In 1981 a worship conference was conducted to introduce the Saints to a new hymnal, *Hymns of the Saints*, a major milestone in the life of the movement. The Saints have always been a singing people. The new hymnal was the latest in a series of hymnbooks published over many years. It took nearly a decade to compile the collection. The committee under Harold Neal was composed of persons who were highly skilled in congregational music, linguistics, poetry, literature, and theology as well as divergent beliefs. The product was a hymnal reflective of the church's growth and expansion. It included 127 hymns written wholly or in part by RLDS authors and with eighty-eight tunes written, harmonized, or adapted by RLDS composers. The hymns reflected changing theological understandings, the church's involvement in other cultures, the members' interest in the environmental aspects of stewardship, a growing awareness of the need for inclusive language, and acknowledged the role of women in the church.[4]

Much happened during the 1980s. Among these events was the highly significant, thus highly controversial nature of Doctrine and Covenants 156. Two major new understandings called for attention. The first opened the way for the ordination of women. This was a difficult issue for many church members because it seemed to be a change in the pattern of God's relationship to us. And, some would argue, it was not in keeping with the scriptures as the church had always presented them. But the church at large was in support, and an emotional 1984 World Conference affirmed the role of women, moving ahead with the calling and ordination of women to priesthood. By early 1991 more than 3,000 women were serving the church in both Aaronic and Melchisedec offices. Unfortunately many persons, in response and disagreement to this practice and seeing it as the latest in a long history of "unacceptable changes" in the church, chose to separate themselves from the larger movement.

The second aspect of Section 156 that called the church into action in a dramatic manner was instruction about the building of the Temple. The call to actually begin work on the long-awaited and greatly prized Temple in Independence followed earlier guidance about preparation. The building was a part of the church's dream since 1831 when Joseph Smith, Jr., first introduced it to the Independence Saints. In modern times the church's interest was rekindled by instruction received in 1968 through President W.

Wallace Smith to renew efforts[5] and in 1980 when it became a part of the church program. In 1984, in Section 156 of the Doctrine and Covenants, the Temple concept took on more concrete dimensions as the church was instructed to move ahead actively in preparation for the Temple. By the 1988 Conference an architectural firm had been selected to work with President Smith and other leaders on the design. The call for funds went out, and it was with great pride that Bishop Norman Swails announced to the 1990 World Conference that fund-drive pledges had exceeded the goal. The full impact of what the Temple will mean to the church—how it will help define the mission and articulate the activity—is yet to be fully understood or disclosed. We are assured it will be committed to the pursuit of peace at personal, family, congregational, community, national, and international levels.

The 1980s have been a period of reaching out, of pulling back, of resource development, of reorganization of departments and divisions. This was a decade of reaching, of searching for the impact of the church on the expanding world, and of reaffirming old convictions while exploring new insights. It follows that such a period will also be a period of unrest. It is understandable that church members, with all the passion involved in personal convictions and commitments, would discover points of disagreement among themselves. This has been true right from the beginning, for many who joined the Reorganization did so out of disagreement with some of the many unification efforts of that time. It is no less true today.

The basic reality of the Restoration is to be found in the nature of continued revelation. Such belief, of course, leads to concerns about the acceptance of potential change—adjustment to the age—among leaders and members. But the questions are *how much* and *what kind* of change. And dissent is a powerful emotional conviction. The presence of organized disagreement pushes the institution to reaffirm its authority and to stand, sometimes harshly, as a rock against such encroachment. The response is often to close ranks, or to reaffirm basics, and for the sake of positioning to acknowledge views or characteristics only assumed before.

The nature of this change—sometimes seen as moving away from basics—is what lies behind much of the discontent. However, those who find in the emerging understandings further proof of God's concern for persons are more inclined to accept that which alters the old ways. On the other hand, those for whom such change threatens their understandings of the basics of the church are inclined to believe that each change is in itself increasing evidence of apostasy.

The church has grown and expanded with an increased understanding of what is expected in the contemporary age. The church can never really be the same from year to year because of its key beliefs in the presence of God. An open scriptural canon suggests there is more to be said; the church's openness is a response to that continued direction.

Within the Restoration heritage there is much disagreement. The LDS community often sees many of the Reorganization's beliefs and behaviors as rejections of basic understandings. On the other hand, the Reorganization has moved away from theological developments that it feels can be traced to misunderstandings and unacceptable activities during the Nauvoo period. Between the "Reorganites" and the "Brighamites" much is shared: history, hymns, scriptures. But in their beliefs they have moved far apart. This is not only a matter of scripture and interpretation, but the separation reflects the different postures required of the groups because of their environment and relationship to American society.

The RLDS Church grew up reflecting its midwestern emergence and as such was involved in adjustment. The American Midwest was a closed frontier; society was formed, and the church entered into an already existent condition. If it wanted to accomplish its task of bringing the gospel to the people of the land, then it had to get along with them. The emerging understandings were reflective of that assimilation with the larger Christian community. The LDS church, however, grew into maturity in the wilds of a country that was hostile, fighting first the environment and then the encroaching society and the government that followed. It was, by nature, far more aggressive and, as is often the case, found it far easier to take a stand, stick to it, and fight along those lines. As a result, the LDS movement is probably more well defined and the membership more closely related by adherence to a particular position.

Obviously there is much to be shared in terms of heritage, and so much in common so much that it recommends more joint efforts. For more than two decades the historians of various faiths within the larger movement have worked together in an effort to more openly and honestly reflect their mutual history. But the struggles to differentiate between the LDS and the RLDS are to a large extent over, no longer serving as a means to identify the Reorganization.

* * *

As I write I look outside my window and watch the activities as scurrying men and women push the earth with huge machines. The earliest indications of a building that will tower over the Independence landscape appear: a wall, a shoring tower, the ramp of the worshipers' path. On land set apart by Joseph Smith, Jr., in 1831, land which since has served as a gathering spot for wagons heading to Santa Fe-California-Oregon, a place to house a Confederate field hospital during the Battle of Railway Cut, and a parking lot for Auditorium employees, the Temple will rise. With it rise the hopes of a people.

Our short narrative history needs to end at this point. The administration of President Wallace B. Smith and the work of his counselors, the Twelve, the Presiding Bishopric, the Quorums of Seventy, the World Church divisions, field and congregational leaders, and missionaries continues as I write. The membership grows, alters, changes, emerges, and plans for congregational activities, for community responsibilities, or to their next moment of legislative involvement. All of this is still too fresh to be reported accurately or for much historical work to be done.

The next generation of members, like the next generation of historians, may tell the story differently. At least they will advance it along its chronological path. Others will write their interpretations, will document the hundreds of events and ideas only hinted at here, and will see the story differently. But for now I hope this brief account will reflect something of the story of how we came to be here at this time. Remembering that our response, even today, is a part of that expanding story, we will move forward to make our history reflective of the men and women whose lives of dedication and commitment have brought us this far.[6]

Notes

1. First Presidency Report, *1982 World Conference Bulletin.*
2. 1974 World Conference Resolution 1126.
3. Doctrine and Covenants 151:9.
4. The committee was composed of Rosalee Elser, Barbara Higdon, Roger Revell, Ammon Roberson, Aleta Runkle Page, Geoffrey Spencer, Alta Topham, Barbara Howard, Alan Tyree, and John Thumm. Peter Judd joined in 1975, and Richard Clothier and Ken Cooper were early members but quit in 1975.
5. Doctrine and Covenants 149.
6. For further reading: *Church Members Manual* (Independence, Missouri: Herald Publishing House, 1991); Richard A. Brown, *Temple Foundations: Essays on an Emerging Concept* (Independence, Missouri: Herald Publishing House, 1991); Alan D. Tyree, ed., *Exploring the Faith* (Independence, Missouri: Herald Publishing House, 1987); Douglas D. Alder and Paul M. Edwards, "Common Beginnings, Divergent Beliefs," *Dialogue* 1 (Spring 1978): 18-28; Rod Downing, "Peace and the RLDS Church—Foundations for the Future," in Marjorie B. Troeh and Eileen M. Terril, eds., *Restoration Studies IV* (Independence, Missouri: Herald Publishing House, 1988): 21-30; Paul M. Edwards, "Leadership and the Ethics of Prophecy," *Dialogue* vol. 19, no. 4 (Winter 1986): 77-84; C. Robert Mesle, "Zion and the Future of the RLDS Church," in Marjorie B. Troeh and Eileen M. Terril, eds., *Restoration Studies IV* (Independence, Missouri: Herald Publishing House, 1988): 31-39; Howard S. Sheehy, Jr., "The Church: Structure, Function, and Unity," in Maurice L. Draper and Debra Combs, eds., *Restoration Studies III* (Independence, Missouri: Herald Publishing House, 1986): 13-20.

Select Bibliography

Allan, James B., and Glen M. Leonard. *The Story of the Latter-day Saints*. Salt Lake City, Utah: Deseret Book Company, 1976.

Anderson, Mary Audentia Smith, ed. *Joseph Smith III and the Restoration*. Independence, Missouri: Herald Publishing House, 1952.

Backman, Milton V., Jr. *The Heavens Resound: A History of the Latter-day Saints in Ohio, 1830-1838*. Salt Lake City, Utah: Deseret Book Company, 1983.

Basic Beliefs Committee (Clifford A. Cole, chair). *Exploring the Faith*. Independence, Missouri: Herald Publishing House, 1970. See also, Alan D. Tyree, ed., 1987 edition.

Blair, Alma R. "The Tradition of Dissent—Jason W. Briggs." In *Restoration Studies I*, edited by Maurice L. Draper and Clare D. Vlahos. Independence, Missouri: Herald Publishing House, 1980: 146-161.

_____. "Reorganized Church of Jesus Christ of Latter Day Saints: Moderate Mormonism." In *The Restoration Movement: Essays in Mormon History*, edited by F. Mark McKiernan, Alma R. Blair, and Paul M. Edwards. Lawrence, Kansas: Coronado Press, 1973: 207-230.

_____. "Early Nauvoo Saints Misunderstood Kingdom," *Restoration Trail Forum*, vol. 3, no. 4 (March 1963): 8.

Booth, Howard J. "Recent Shifts in Restoration Thought." In *Restoration Studies I*, edited by Maurice L. Draper and Clare D. Vlahos. Independence, Missouri: Herald Publishing House, 1980: 162-175.

Briggs, Jason W. *A Word of Consolation to the Scattered Saints*. Beloit, Wisconsin: private printing, 1853.

Brock, Carolyn. *Asante Africa*. Independence, Missouri: Herald Publishing House, 1990.

Brown, Richard A. *An Illustrated History of the Stone Church*. Independence, Missouri: Herald Publishing House, 1988.

_____. *Temple Foundations: Essays on an Emerging Concept*. Independence, Missouri: Herald Publishing House, 1991.

_____. *Church Members Manual*. Independence, Missouri: Herald Publishing House, 1991.

Brunson, L. Madelon. *Bonds of Sisterhood: A History of the RLDS Women's Organization, 1842-1983.* Independence, Missouri: Herald Publishing House, 1985.

Cole, Clifford. "The World Church: Our Mission in the 1980s," *Commission* (September 1979): 41-46.

Conrad, Larry W., and Paul Shupe. "An RLDS Reformation? Construing the Task of RLDS Theology." In *Restoration Studies III,* edited by Maurice L. Draper and Debra Combs. Independence, Missouri: Herald Publishing House, 1986: 210-219.

Cross, Whitney R. *The Burned-Over District: The Social and Intellectual History of Enthusiastic Religion in Western New York; 1800-1850.* Ithaca, New York: Cornell University Press, 1950.

Davis, Inez Smith. *The Story of the Church* 9th ed. Independence, Missouri: Herald Publishing House, 1977.

DeLapp, G. Leslie. *In The World ….* Independence, Missouri: Herald Publishing House, 1973.

Deskin, Verne. "You Are Involved in Polygamy." *Courage* vol. 1, no. 2. (December 1970): 89-92.

Draper, Maurice L. *Isles & Continents.* Independence, Missouri: Herald Publishing House, 1982.

_____. "Apostolic Ministry in the Reorganization." In *Restoration Studies I,* edited by Maurice L. Draper and Clare D. Vlahos. Independence, Missouri: Herald Publishing House, 1980: 219-231.

_____. "Polygamy Among Converts in East India," *Courage* vol. 1, no. 2 (December 1970): 85-88.

_____. "Reunions." In *Restoration Studies II,* edited by Maurice L. Draper and A. Bruce Lindgren. Independence, Missouri: Herald Publishing House, 1983: 142-151.

Edwards, Paul M. "Theocratic-Democracy: Philosopher-King in the Reorganization." In *The Restoration Movement: Essays in Mormon History,* edited by F. Mark McKiernan, Alma R. Blair, and Paul M. Edwards. Lawrence, Kansas: Coronado Press, 1973: 341-357.

_____. *The Chief: An Administrative Biography of Fred M. Smith.* Independence, Missouri: Herald Publishing House, 1988.

_____. "The New Mormon History," *Saints Herald* vol. 133, no. 11 (November 1986): 12-14, 20.

_____. *Preface to Faith: A Philosophical Inquiry Into RLDS Beliefs.* Salt Lake City, Utah: Signature Books, 1984.

Faulring, Scott H., ed. *An American Prophet's Record: The Diaries and Journals of Joseph Smith.* Salt Lake City, Utah: Signature Books, 1989.

Flanders, Robert Bruce. *Nauvoo: Kingdom on the Mississippi.* Urbana, Illinois: University of Illinois Press, 1965.

_____. "The Kingdom of God in Illinois: Politics in Utopia," *Dialogue* vol. 5, no. 1 (Spring 1970): 63.

_____. "To Transform History: Early Mormon Culture and the Concept of Time and Space," *American Society of Church History* vol. 40, no. 1, (March 1971): 108-117.

Flint, B. C. *An Outline History of the Church of Christ (Temple Lot)* 2nd ed. Independence, Missouri: Board of Publications; The Church of Christ (Temple Lot), 1953.

Hale, Van. "The King Follet Discourses: Textual History and Criticism," *Sunstone* 8 (1983): 5-12.

Hansen, Klaus J. "Mormonism and American Culture: Some Tentative Hypotheses." In *The Restoration Movement: Essays in Mormon History,* edited by F. Mark McKiernan, Alma R. Blair, and Paul M. Edwards. Lawrence, Kansas: Coronado Press, 1973: 1-25.

Ham, Wayne, ed. *Publish Glad Tidings: Readings in Early Latter Day Saint Sources.* Independence, Missouri: Herald Publishing House, 1970.

Higdon, Barbara. "The Reorganization in the Twentieth Century," *Dialogue* vol. 7, no. 1, (Spring 1972): 94-100.

Hiles, Norma Derry. "Charles Derry: A Palimpsestic View," *John Whitmer Historical Association Journal* 4 (1984): 22.

_____. *Gentle Monarch: The Presidency of Israel A. Smith.* Independence, Missouri: Herald Publishing House, 1991.

Howard, Richard P. "The 'Book of Abraham' in the Light of History and Egyptology," *Courage* (Pilot Issue 1970): 33-46.

_____. "The Origins of Mormon Polygamy, And the RLDS Response," *Journal of Mormon History* 3 (1963): 14.

_____. *Reorganization with Joseph Smith III.* Independence, Missouri: Temple School, 1974.

_____. "An Analysis of Six Contemporary Accounts Touching Joseph Smith's First Vision." In *Restoration Studies I,* edited by Maurice L. Draper and Clare D. Vlahos. Independence, Missouri: Herald Publishing House, 1980: 95-117.

_____. "The Nauvoo Heritage of the Reorganized Church," *Journal of Mormon History* 16, (1990): 41-52.

291

————. "Joseph Smith, The Book of Abraham, and the Reorganized Church of the 1970's," Part I *Saints' Herald* vol. 117, no. 10 (October 1970): 28-30; Part II vol. 117, no. 11 (November 1970): 20-21, 47; Part III vol. 117, no. 12 (December 1970): 24-26.

————. *Restoration Scriptures.* Independence, Missouri: Herald Publishing House, 1969.

————. "The Changing RLDS Response to Mormon Polygamy: A Preliminary Analysis." In *Restoration Studies III*, edited by Maurice L. Draper and Debra Combs. Independence, Missouri: Herald Publishing House, 1986: 145-162.

————. "Observations on the Development of Early Church Structure in the Latter Day Saint Movement," *Church Administration: Building the Team.* Independence, Missouri: Temple School, 1982.

————. "Joseph Smith's First Vision: The RLDS Tradition," *Journal of Mormon History* 7 (1980): 23.

Hunt, Larry E. *F. M. Smith: Saint as Reformer* 2 vols. Independence, Missouri: Herald Publishing House, 1982.

————. "F.M.S.: The Formative Years of an RLDS President," *Journal of Mormon History* 4 (1977): 70.

Jensen, Andrew. *Latter-day Saints Biographical Encyclopedia* 4 vols. Salt Lake City, Utah: Andrew Jensen History Company, 1902, 1914, 1920, 1936.

Jennings, Warren. "The City in the Garden: Social Conflict in Jackson County, Missouri." In *The Restoration Movement: Essays in Mormon History*, edited by F. Mark McKiernan, Alma R. Blair, and Paul M. Edwards. Lawrence, Kansas: Coronado Press, 1973: 99-119.

Judd, Peter A. (with Clifford A. Cole). "Viewing Our History," *Distinctives Yesterday and Today.* Independence, Missouri: Herald House, 1983.

Judd, Peter A., and A. Bruce Lindgren. *An Introduction to the Saints Church.* Independence, Missouri: Herald Publishing House, 1976.

Knapp, William J. "Professionalizing Religious Education in the Church: 'The New Curriculum' Controversy," *John Whitmer Historical Association Journal* 2 (1982): 47.

Lambert, Neal E., and Richard H. Cracroft. "Literary Form and Historical Understanding: Joseph Smith's First Vision," *Journal of Mormon History* 7 (1980): 133.

Launius, Roger D. "R. C. Evans: Boy Orator of the Reorganization," *John Whitmer Historical Association Journal* 3 (1983): 42.

_____. *The Kirtland Temple: A Historical Narrative*. Independence, Missouri: Herald Publishing House, 1986.

_____. "The Reorganized Church in the Nineteenth Century: A Bibliographical Review." In *Restoration Studies IV*, edited by Marjorie B. Troeh and Eileen M. Terril. Independence, Missouri: Herald Publishing House, 1988: 171-187.

_____. *Invisible Saints: A History of Black Americans in the Reorganized Church*. Independence, Missouri: Herald Publishing House, 1988.

_____. *Joseph Smith III: Pragmatic Prophet*. Urbana, Illinois: University of Illinois Press, 1988.

_____. "Joseph Smith III and the Quest for a Centralized Administration (1860-73)." In *Restoration Studies II*, edited by Maurice L. Draper and A. Bruce Lindgren. Independence, Missouri: Herald Publishing House, 1983: 104-120.

_____. "Politicking against Polygamy: Joseph Smith III, the Reorganized Church, and the Politics of the Antipolygamy Crusade, 1860-1890," *John Whitmer Historical Association Journal* 7 (1987): 35-44.

_____. "Method and Motives: Joseph Smith III's Opposition to Polygamy, 1860-1890," *Dialogue* vol. 2, no. 4 (Winter 1987): 106.

_____. *Father Figure: Joseph Smith III and the Creation of the Reorganized Church*. Independence, Missouri: Herald Publishing House, 1990.

_____. *Zion's Camp: Expedition to Missouri, 1834*. Independence, Missouri: Herald Publishing House, 1984.

Legg, Phillip R. *Oliver Cowdery: The Elusive Second Elder of the Restoration*. Independence, Missouri: Herald Publishing House, 1989.

Lindgren, A. Bruce. "The Development of the Latter Day Saints Doctrine of Priesthood, 1829-1835," *Courage* vol. 2, no. 3 (Spring 1972): 439-443.

Love, Arlyn R. "The First Presidency's Response to the Civil Rights Movement," *John Whitmer Historical Association Journal* 4 (1984): 41-50.

McKiernan, F. Mark. "Mormonism on the Defensive: Far West, 1838-1839." In *The Restoration Movement: Essays in Mormon History*, edited by F. Mark McKiernan, Alma R.

Blair, and Paul M. Edwards. Lawrence, Kansas: Coronado Press, 1973: 121-140.

_____. *The Voice of One Crying in the Wilderness: Sidney Rigdon, Religious Reformer, 1793-1876.* Lawrence, Kansas: Coronado Press, 1971.

McKiernan, F. Mark, Alma R. Blair, and Paul M. Edwards, eds. *The Restoration Movement: Essays in Mormon History.* Lawrence, Kansas: Coronado Press, 1973.

Newell, Linda King. "Cousins in Conflict: Joseph Smith III and Joseph F. Smith," *John Whitmer Historical Association Journal* 9 (1989): 3-16.

Newell, Linda King, and Valeen Tippetts Avery. *Mormon Enigma: Emma Hale Smith, Prophet's Wife, "Elect Lady," Polygamy's Foe, 1804-1879.* New York: Doubleday and Company, 1984.

Parkin, Max H. "Kirtland, A Stronghold For The Kingdom." In *The Restoration Movement: Essays in Mormon History,* edited by F. Mark McKiernan, Alma R. Blair, and Paul M. Edwards. Lawrence, Kansas: Coronado Press, 1973: 63-98.

Quinn, D. Michael. "The Evolution of the Presiding Quorums of the LDS Church," *Journal of Mormon History* 1 (1974): 25.

Rannie, Edward. "The United Order of Enoch," *Saints' Herald* vol. 59, no. 42 (October 1912): 995.

Romig, Ronald E., and John H. Siebert. "The Genius of Zion and Kirtland and the Concept of Temples." In *Restoration Studies IV,* edited by Marjorie B. Troeh and Eileen M. Terril. Independence, Missouri: Herald Publishing House, 1988: 99-123.

Ruoff, Norman D., comp. *The Writings of President Frederick M. Smith. Volume I: Theology and Philosophy.* Independence, Missouri: Herald Publishing House, 1978.

Russell, William D. "Reorganized Mormon Church Beset by Controversy," *Christian Century* (June 18, 1970): 769-771.

Shields, Steven L. *Divergent Paths of the Restoration* 4th ed. Los Angeles, California: Restoration Research, 1990.

Shipps, Jan. *Mormonism: The Story of a New Religious Tradition.* Chicago: University of Illinois Press, 1985.

_____. "The Prophet Puzzle: Suggestions Toward a More Comprehensive Interpretation of Joseph Smith," *Journal of Mormon History* 1 (1974): 3.

Smith, Gregory. "America at 1830," *Saints Herald* vol. 133, no. 9 (September 1986): 17-19.

Smith, Joseph III. "An Address to the Saints," *The True Latter Day Saints' Herald* vol. 1, no. 11 (November 1860): 225.

Smith, Joseph III, and Heman C. Smith (vol. 1-4); and F. Henry Edwards (vol. 5-8). *The History of the Reorganized Church of Jesus Christ of Latter Day Saints.* Independence, Missouri: Herald Publishing House, 1896, 1897, 1900, 1903, 1969, 1970, 1973, 1976.

Smith, Joseph, Jr. *The King Follet Discourse.* Auckland, New Zealand: Messenger Publishing Company, n. d.

Spencer, Geoffrey F. "Revelation and the Restoration Principle." In *Restoration Studies II,* edited by Maurice L. Draper and A. Bruce Lindgren. Independence, Missouri: Herald Publishing House, 1983: 186-192.

_____. "Reorganization Thought: Whence and Whither." Unpublished paper delivered before the Mormon History Association, in possession of author.

Spillman, W. B. "Pat." *Studies in Restoration History: The Hastening Time* vols. 1-4. Independence, Missouri: Herald Publishing House, 1989-1990.

_____. "On Conceptualization of Zion," *Courage* vol. 3 (Fall 1972): 37.

Struble, Patricia. "Mite to Bishop: RLDS Women's Financial Relationship to the Church," *John Whitmer Historical Association Journal* 6 (1986): 23-32.

Toscano, Paul, and Margaret Toscano. *Strangers in Paradox: Explorations in Mormon Theology.* Salt Lake City, Utah: Signature Books, 1990.

Troeh, M. Richard, and Marjorie Troeh. *The Conferring Church.* Independence, Missouri: Herald Publishing House, 1987.

Tyree, Alan D., ed. *Exploring the Faith.* Independence, Missouri: Herald Publishing House, 1987.

Underwood, Grant. "The New England Origins of Mormonism Revisited," *Journal of Mormon History* 15 (1989):15-23.

Vlahos, Clare D. "Moderation as a Theological Principle in the Thought of Joseph Smith III," *John Whitmer Historical Association Journal* 1 (1981): 3-11.

_____. "The Challenge to Centralized Power: Zenus [sic] H. Gurley, Jr., and the Prophetic Office," *Courage* vol. 1, no. 3 (1971): 141-158.

White, O. Kendall, Jr. *Mormon Neo-Orthodoxy: A Crisis Theology.* Salt Lake City, Utah: Signature Books, 1987.

Whitmer, David. *An Address to All Believers in Christ.* Richmond, Missouri: published by the author, 1887.

Whitmer, John. "The Book of John Whitmer Kept by Commandment," RLDS Archives, Independence, Missouri. This is available in F. Mark McKiernan and Roger D. Launius, eds. *An Early Latter Day Saint History: The Book of John Whitmer Kept by Commandment.* Independence, Missouri: Herald Publishing House, 1980.

Winks, Robin W., ed. *The Historian as Detective: Essays on Evidence.* New York: Harper Colophon Books, 1968.

Young, Biloine W. "Minnesota Mormons: The Cutlerites," *Courage* vol. 3, no. 2-3 (1973): 117-137.

Primary and Private Collections:

RLDS Conference Minutes: RLDS Archives.

Minutes of the First Presidency: RLDS Archives.

Minutes of the Quorum of Twelve: RLDS Archives.

Latter Day Saints' Messenger and Advocate.

Synopsis of the Faith and Doctrines of the Church of Jesus Christ of Latter-day Saints (Plano, Illinois: RLDS Church), 1865.

Saints' *Herald,* 1860-1990.

Minutes of the Joint Council: RLDS Archives.

F. Henry Edwards Interview Tapes: RLDS Archives; Mormon History Collection; Graceland College; Paul M. Edwards, private collection.

Fred M. Smith Papers: Mormon History Collection, Graceland College.

A Book of Commandments, for the Government of the Church of Christ, Organized According to the Law, on the 6th of April 1830, 1833 (Reprint). Independence, Missouri: Herald Publishing House, 1972.

Order of Enoch Files: RLDS Archives.

Letter File: RLDS Archives.

Correspondence Between Israel A. Smith and Pauline Hancock on Baptism for the Dead. Photo reproduction in possession of author.

Times and Seasons.

Oral History Memoir of President Maurice L. Draper, 4 vols., RLDS Archives.

Appendix

Important Events in Church History

December 23, 1805—Joseph Smith, Jr., born Sharon, Vermont.

1815—Joseph Smith, Sr., and family removed to Palmyra, New York.

1820—Joseph Smith's first vision, Manchester, New York.

1823—Joseph Smith, Jr., second vision and shown plates of Book of Mormon.

1827—Joseph Smith, Jr., received plates of Book of Mormon.

February 1828—Martin Harris took transcript of characters to Prof. Anthon and Dr. Mitchell of New York.

April 7, 1829—Oliver Cowdery became scribe for Joseph Smith.

May 15, 1829—Joseph Smith and Oliver Cowdery baptized each other and received Aaronic priesthood.

June 1829—the Three Witnesses: Oliver Cowdery, Martin Harris, and David Whitmer. Served as the Three Witnesses to the Book of Mormon.

June 1829—the Eight Witnesses were shown and handled the plates.

June 1829—Book of Mormon copyrighted.

March 1830—Book of Mormon as printed by E. B. Grandin of Palmyra, completed.

April 6, 1830—church organized.

June 1, 1830—first conference of the church.

October 1830—departure of first missionaries.

January 31, 1831—missionaries reached Independence, Missouri, and started preaching to Indians.

February 1, 1831—Joseph Smith, Jr., arrived in Kirtland.

February 4, 1831—Edward Partridge appointed first bishop.

June 6, 1831—high priests first ordained.

July 1831—Colesville Branch arrived in Zion.

August 2 and 3, 1831—land of Zion, City of Zion, and Temple Lot dedicated.

August 4, 1831—first conference in Zion held at the home of Joshua Lewis.

September 12, 1831—at conference in Hiram, Ohio, William W. Phelps instructed to purchase press and type.

January 25, 1832—Joseph Smith, Jr., ordained president of high priesthood at Amherst, Ohio.

April 26, 1832—Joseph Smith, Jr., acknowledged president of high priesthood in council in Independence, Missouri.

June 1832—*The Evening and the Morning Star*, first publication of the church, printed in Independence, Missouri.

November 6, 1832—Joseph Smith III born at Kirtland, Ohio.

February 2, 1833—Joseph Smith, Jr., completed Inspired Version of Holy Scriptures.

March 18, 1833—Quorum of High Priests first organized in Kirtland.

June 1, 1833—instructions received concerning Temple in Kirtland.

June 25, 1833—a plat for city of Zion with explanation by First Presidency.

July 2, 1833—Joseph Smith, Jr., completed corrections of Inspired Version.

July 20, 1833—printing press in Independence destroyed by mob.

July 23, 1833, cornerstone of Temple at Kirtland laid.

November 7-8, 1833—exodus from Jackson County, Missouri.

December 1833—*The Evening and the Morning Star* published at Kirtland.

December 18, 1833—Joseph Smith, Sr., ordained patriarch.

February 17, 1834—first Standing High Council organized at Kirtland, Ohio.

July 3, 1834—High Council organized in Zion.

October 1834—*Messenger and Advocate* first published in Kirtland.

February 14, 1835—twelve apostles chosen for first time in Restoration.

February 28, 1835—first Quorum of Seventy organized at Kirtland.

August 17, 1835—general assembly of the church held, Book of Doctrine and Covenants adopted.

January 21, 1836—leading officers of the church anointed and blessed in Temple.

March 27, 1836—House of the Lord at Kirtland dedicated.

July 1, 1837—first foreign mission of the church sailed from New York.

July 23, 1837—England, first sermon preached in Preston.

October 1837 *Elders' Journal*, Joseph Smith, editor, first published at Kirtland.

March 14, 1838—Joseph Smith and family arrived in Far West, Missouri.

October 30, 1838—mob massacred Saints at Haun's Mill in Missouri.

October 31, 1838—Joseph Smith and others arrested during parley.

Winter 1838-1839—general exodus of Saints from Missouri.

April 22, 1839—Joseph Smith, Jr., arrived in Quincy, Illinois.

May 1, 1839—first purchase of land at Commerce, later Nauvoo, Illinois.

May 10, 1839—Joseph Smith arrived with his family at Commerce.

September 1839—most of Quorum of Twelve started for England, where they arrived early in 1840.

October 5, 1839—William Marks appointed president of the Stake of Nauvoo.

November 1839—first number of *Times and Seasons* published at Commerce, Illinois. First Nauvoo Edition of Book of Mormon published.

May 27, 1840—first number of Latter Day Saints' *Millennial Star* published in England.

December 16, 1840—charter of Nauvoo signed by Governor Carlin to take effect February 1, 1841.

January 1841—first British edition of Book of Mormon published.

January 30, 1841—Joseph Smith, Jr., elected sole trustee for church.

April 6, 1841—cornerstones laid for temple at Nauvoo pursuant to instructions on January 19, 1841.

March 15, 1842—Joseph Smith editor of *Times and Seasons*.

March 24, 1842—Ladies' Relief Society organized, Emma Smith, president.

March 21, 1843— the Young Gentlemen and Ladies' Relief Society, Nauvoo, organized.

May 23, 1843—Addison Pratt, Noah Rogers, Benj. F. Grouard, K. F. Hanks, set apart to go to Pacific Islands.

August 31, 1843—Joseph Smith moved into Nauvoo Mansion House; the following month opened it as hotel.

May 1, 1844—the three missionaries to South Sea Islands arrived at Tubuai and by 14th two of them reached Tahiti.

June 16, 1844—first convert on the Pacific Isles baptized.

June 27, 1844—assassination of Joseph Smith, Jr., and Hyrum at Carthage, Illinois.

February 1846—general exodus from Nauvoo.

1851—Book of Mormon published in Danish, and Doctrine and Covenants in Welsh.

November 18, 1851—Jason W. Briggs reported revelation, about same time a similar revelation to Zenos H. Gurley, Sr., both to the effect that the son of Joseph was his true successor.

June 12, 1852—conference at Beloit, Wisconsin.

1852—Book of Mormon published in French, German, and Italian;
also, April 6, in Welsh; Doctrine and Covenants published in Danish.

April 8, 1853—seven men ordained to Quorum of Twelve in Reorganization.

January 1860—*The True Latter Day Saints' Herald* published as monthly.

April 6, 1860—Joseph Smith III acknowledged and ordained as president of high priesthood.

February 4, 1863—Charles Derry arrived in England.

May 18, 1863—Jeremiah Jeremiah opened Wales mission.

August 11, 1863—E. C. Briggs and Alexander McCord arrived in Salt Lake City, Utah.

February 6, 1864—Zion's Hope Sunday school organized in St. Louis.

May 1, 1865—Joseph Smith III appointed editor of *Saints' Herald*. On this account he moved to Plano in January 1866.

May 1865—Sunday school movement endorsed by the First Presidency and the Twelve.

April 1866—resolutions adopted for publication of Inspired Version of the Bible.

December 1867—announced Inspired Version ready for mailing.

1867—return movement started to Jackson County, Missouri, by members of the Reorganization.

April 2, 1869—Alexander H. Smith and David H. Smith appointed to Utah.

July 1, 1869—first publication of *Zion's Hope*.

April 12, 1870—organization of the First United Order of Enoch approved by General Conference.

July 24, 1872—John Avondet opened mission in Switzerland.

June 2, 1873—John Avondet opened mission in Italy and remained until February 1874.

July 1873—branch organized in courthouse in Independence, Missouri.

December 3, 1873—Charles Wandell and Glaud Rodger arrived in Society Islands en route to Australia.

January 22, 1874—Elders Wandell and Rodger arrived in Sydney, Australia.

1874—mission opened in Germany.

November 1, 1874—the *Messenger* first published by J. W. Briggs in Salt Lake City; continued until early in 1877.

May 16, 1875—Magnus Fyrando and H. N. Hansen arrived in Denmark and visited Sweden.

July 1878—*Saints' Advocate* published for use in Utah, W. W. Blair, editor.

April 30, 1879—Emma Smith Bidamon, widow of Joseph Smith, Jr., died.

October 7, 1881—Joseph Smith and general officers left Plano for Lamoni, Iowa.

November 1, 1881—first issue of *Saints' Herald* in Lamoni.

April 6, 1882—General Conference met in Independence, Missouri, first time in fifty years.

April 6, 1883—General Conference met in Kirtland Temple, Ohio.

1884—Spaulding manuscript found in Honolulu by L. L. Rice and James H. Fairchild.

October 1884—first issue of *Sandheden's Banner*, Peter Andersen, editor.

1884—Brick Church built in Lamoni, Iowa.

January 1888—first issue of *Autumn Leaves*, edited by Marietta Walker.

April 6, 1888—cornerstone laid for Stone Church, Independence, Missouri.

September 1890—mission opened in Hawaii by Albert Haws and G. J. Waller.

January 3, 1891—*Zion's Ensign* first issued.

April 1891—General Sunday School Association organized by direction of General Conference.

April 1893—general organization of Zion's Religio Literary Society for young people.

1893—general organization of Daughters of Zion.

March 1894—decision in the U.S. Circuit Court, in the Temple Lot Suit.

September 23, 1894—missionary boat "Evanelia," bound for the South Sea Islands, dedicated.

September 17, 1895—decision of Judge Thayer in the U.S. Circuit Court of Appeal gave possession and legal title to the Temple Lot to the Church of Christ.

September 1895—Graceland College opened in Lamoni, Iowa, and classes started.

June 1898—Graceland College graduated its first class, Frederick M. Smith.

1898—Saints' Home opened in Lamoni, Iowa, for benefit of the old folk.

1898—Book of Mormon published in Hawaiian.

1901—stakes organized in Independence, Missouri, and Lamoni, Iowa.

1903—Book of Mormon published in Danish.

April 1903—George Schweich, grandson of David Whitmer, delivered to RLDS Church the Book of Mormon manuscript, John Whitmer's Manuscript History, a copy of Book of Mormon characters taken by Martin Harris to New York, a few sheets of early revelations, and a few other valuable items.

January 1907—Herald Office in Lamoni destroyed by fire, with great loss of valuable historical manuscripts.

December 15, 1909—Sanitarium dedicated and opened in Independence, Missouri.

April 18, 1910—United Order of Enoch incorporated in Independence, Missouri.

1911—new manuscript of the Book of Mormon translated by Alexander Kippe into German and published.

August 15, 1911—Children's Home opened in Lamoni, Iowa.

July 2, 1913—*Stepping Stones* first published.

September 1914—Graceland opened as junior college.

December 10, 1914—Joseph Smith III died in Independence, Missouri.

May 5, 1915—Frederick M. Smith ordained president.

April 1916—former Independence Stake divided into Independence, Kansas City, and Holden stakes.

May 1917—Far West Stake organized.

April 1920—Independence declared to be Zion, and principal headquarters of the church.

July 1920—Frederick M. Smith and T. W. Williams went to British Isles, Germany, Holland, France, Italy, and Palestine.

May 24, 1921—first issue of *Saints' Herald* in Independence, Missouri.

May 5, 1923—purchase of the Campus, Independence, Missouri.

July 29, 1923—first summer service held outdoors on the Campus.

February 2, 1926—excavation started for building of the Auditorium.

April 1926—seven presidents of Seventy reorganized.

April 1927—General Conference held in lower room of Auditorium.

October 1928—General Conference held for first time in upper assembly room of Auditorium.

April 1930—Centennial Conference of church held in Auditorium.

November 11, 1930—cornerstone laid for new building for Sanitarium.

December 18, 1930—first CBS network broadcast of *Messiah* by Messiah Choir.

January 1931—Brick Church at Lamoni, Iowa, burned.

June 1937—Youth Convention accepted name of Zion's League.

1941-1942—new Sanitarium prepared for use.

October 1942—first issue of *Guidelines*.

December 31, 1942—church debt paid and new policy of reserve established.

March 20, 1946—Frederick M. Smith died at Independence, Missouri.

April 7, 1946—Israel A. Smith ordained president of the church at Independence, Missouri.

1947—European church headquarters building purchased, Rotterdam, Holland.

January 1948—first issue of *Daily Bread*.

April 1948—first supervisor of Priesthood Education, Floyd M. McDowell appointed.

1948—Department of Ministry to College People organized.

1949—first mission in Alaska organized.

1949—Resthaven purchased for Home for Handicapped Aged Women.

April 4, 1950—W. Wallace Smith ordained counselor to President Israel A. Smith.

April 6, 1950—organization of Center, Detroit International, and Los Angeles Metropolitan stakes.

1951—new building for German Mission headquarters, Hannover.

March 1951—braille edition of Book of Mormon completed by Myrtle Fortney and Braille Corps of Denver Red Cross.

January 1954—first issue of *University Bulletin*.

February 1954—contract let to complete Auditorium foyer and entrance.

September 11-12, 1954—Washington, D.C., church opened.

November 28, 1954 (Sunday)—first baptisms in Korea by Priest Bill Whenham.

August 28, 1955—formal opening of new church building and Latin-American Mission, Weslaco, Texas.

March 23, 1956—new Resthaven building officially opened.

April 11, 1956—premier showing of "Other Sheep," first color motion picture produced by Audio-Visual Department.

June 10-23, 1956—first session, School of Restoration.

July 1956—old Saints' Home in Lamoni razed.

August 1956—first braille edition of Doctrine and Covenants completed by Edna Koontz and Bonita Gates.

September 1956—Graceland offers first four-year course in religion.

October 1956—first issue of *Stride*.

December 1, 1956—*The Hymnal* published.

July 1957—work begins on the Auditorium conference chamber.

April 13, 1958—church's first converts in India—baptized by Elder W. E. Connell.

June 9, 1958—Justin Azim James, first convert in Pakistan, baptized by Elder W. E. Connell.

June 14, 1958—President Israel A. Smith died in automobile accident.

September 21, 1958—Auditorium conference chamber dedicated.

October 5, 1958—first Conference convened in completed Auditorium chamber.

October 6, 1958—President W. Wallace Smith ordained.

November 23, 1958—the 42nd annual *Messiah* performance given—the first in completed conference chamber.

May 15, 1959—death of Elbert A. Smith.

June 1959—Brazil's first baptism and ordination, Ferdinand Frohmut.

June 24, 1959—Dutch translation of the Doctrine and Covenants.

October 8-11, 1959—Kirtland conference of high priests.

October 21, 1959—D. Blair Jensen and Charles D. Neff survey Orient.

November 1959—first baptism in Spain, George Ventura.

November 29, 1959—*Messiah* broadcast on television from Auditorium.

1960—first printing of the Spanish Book of Mormon.

1960—centennial celebration of *Saints' Herald* (1860-1960).

April 3-10, 1960—Amboy Centennial Conference.

April 1960—regional administration first instituted.

April 7, 1960—dedication of the Auditorium organ.

April 17-20, 1961—World Church Women's Institute, Independence, Missouri.

May 14, 1961—Floyd McDowell Commons dedicated, Graceland College.

January 1, 1962—New Zealand organized as separate mission.

January 1962—*Saints Herald* becomes semimonthly publication.

April 1, 1962—dedication of the Auditorium.

April 1, 1962—first issue of Australia edition of *Saints Herald.*

1962—reorganization of Center and Central Missouri stakes; organization of Blue Valley and Santa Fe stakes.

January 1963—first issue of periodical, *Restoration Witness.*

March 31-April 7, 1963—World Institute in Evangelism, Independence, Missouri.

November 19, 1963—Apostles Percy Farrow and Duane Couey survey Nigeria.

1964—Omaha-Council Bluffs and San Francisco Bay stakes organized.

January 8-10, 1965—Television and Radio Seminar, Independence, Missouri.

March 21-26, 1965—Worship and Hymnody Institute, Independence, Missouri.

October 7-10, 1965—high priests conference, Kirtland, Ohio.

November 14, 1965—Gobert Edett of Nigeria ordained an elder.

September 12, 1966—Nine-month concentrated training program for appointees opened at School of the Restoration.

September 23-24, 1966—first mission conference held in Japan.

November 10, 1966—church officially registered in Peru.

November 19, 1966—Independence Messiah Choir presented fiftieth anniversary performance.

1966—Book of Mormon published in German language.

March 6-10, 1967—first in a series of three seminars of the Joint Council of First Presidency, Council of Twelve, and Presiding Bishopric.

May 7, 1967—Frederick Madison Smith Library at Graceland dedicated.

June 6-10, 1967, first International Institute for Women's Leaders, Lamoni, Iowa.

August 26-September 1, 1967—college student conference, Lamoni, Iowa.

October 29, 1967—first in a series of Auditorium worship services by First Presidency.

November 18-19, 1967—Seminar on the Church and the Future of Higher Education, Independence, Missouri.

1967—first Older Youth Service Corps team to British Isles.

1967—missions abroad projects completed: private school in Papeete, Tahiti; community and social center in Matamoros, Mexico; medical clinic in Mosan, Korea; and school for children of the Sora tribes in Orissa State, India.

1967-1968—fifteen World Church goals institutes held in regions.

April 12, 1968—Haiti Mission officially opened.

1968—"Commission" system of Headquarters staff organization begun with assignment of several apostles to commissioner posts.

1968—beginning with January *Herald*, a series of articles on "basic beliefs" of the church published by Basic Beliefs Committee.

1968—four new stakes designated by the World Conference: Tulsa, Denver, Des Moines, and Seattle.

October 16, 1968—New Caledonia Mission officially opened.

1968—Martin Luther King Memorial Scholarship Fund established by Graceland College.

1969—*Saints' Herald* becomes a monthly family magazine and efforts are made to place the *Herald* in every home of the church through congregations.

1969—publication of *For What Purpose Assembled* marked beginning of major emphasis on the church as mission.

February 1, 1970—new administrative structure begun at Headquarters, designed to enhance decentralization.

February 20, 1970—first RLDS medical-dental health team arrives in Haiti.

April 1970—*Distaff*, monthly magazine of the Women's Department, and *Courage*, an independent, church-related, scholarly journal published.

April 7, 1970—World Conference considers higher education implications of Report of the Commission on Education.

April 7, 1970—World Conference adopts new format for Doctrine and Covenants.

September 1970—Graceland College begins course offerings at Independence Education Center.

June 1-5, 1971—joint conference of more than 450 high

priests and seventies met at Graceland College, first such event in church history.

August 8-14, 1971—first adult singles reunion convened at Graceland.

September 3-6, 1971—"Focus '71," a World Church conference for older youth, met at the Auditorium.

November 12, 1971—centenary of organization of Lamoni Church celebrated.

November 14, 1971—copy of a portrait of Joseph Smith, Jr., presented to the National Portrait Gallery of the Smithsonian Institution, Washington, D. C.

September 1972—*Commission* magazine first published by the Commission of Education to replace *Dimensions* and *Distaff.*

September 18, 1972—John Whitmer Historical Association organized.

1972—new graded curriculum for church school introduced into field jurisdictions.

February 1973—Honduras Mission officially organized.

April 29, 1973—ribbon-cutting ceremony officially opens Graceland's facility in the Independence area.

July 7, 1973—Alice Myrmida Smith Edwards, daughter of Frederick M. Smith, died.

October 21, 1973—formal opening of Flournoy House (home of the man who sold the Temple Lot property to Bishop Partridge in 1831).

January 29, 1974—Health Ministries Commission releases a four-year summary of health ministries made available by the church to peoples of eleven nations.

May 23, 1974—publication of the *First Supplement to the Hymnal.*

June 3-7, 1974—newly appointed Women's Ministry Commission convenes at Independence.

July 1, 1974—Velma Ruch becomes acting president of Graceland College.

September 14-15, 1974—a joint council of First Presidency, Council of Twelve, and Quorum of Presidents of Seventy meet to consider the church's theological position on the observation of the Sacrament of the Lord's Supper.

November 20, 1974—historical documents-on-microfilm-ex-change made between First Presidencies of the RLDS and the LDS churches.

March 14, 1975—Suzanne Selden, R.N., Australia, begins a two-year health ministry tour in Nigeria.

April 7, 1975—Park College Board of Trustees relinquish management of the college to a new twelve-member board, nine of whom comprise the Graceland College Board of Trustees.

April 12-16, 1975—first Asia-Pacific Church conference held at Hong Kong.

August 6-13, 1975—first Melchisedec training school held at Graceland College, for ministerial personnel and their wives.

September 1975—*Second Supplement to the Hymnal* published by Herald House.

January 1976—seminar on the church and higher education held at Park College.

March 1976—first International Women's Forum convenes at Independence, Missouri.

April 1976—Task Force on Aging, appointed in 1974, files initial report with the First Presidency.

April 1, 1976—History Commission organized by the First Presidency.

June 27, 1976—Governor Christopher Bond of Missouri rescinds the infamous 1838 "extermination order" of Governor L. W. Boggs, at Far West Stake Reunion.

July 12, 1976—new $17.5 million acute-care tower of the Independence Sanitarium and Hospital officially opened.

September 18-October 2, 1976—health ministries teams of volunteers extend health care to Omaha Indian tribespeople at Macy, Nebraska.

July 1, 1976—President-Designate Wallace B. Smith begins his work.

September 22, 1976—Giovanni D'Asaro baptized—the first member of the church in Rome, Italy.

November 21, 1976—St. Louis District organized into a stake.

January 1, 1977—"regional organization" extended to church jurisdictions beyond North America.

July 17, 1977—Kirtland Temple certified as a United States National Landmark.

September 30, 1977—first national conference of native American people.

April 5, 1978—W. Wallace Smith retired and Wallace B. Smith ordained president of the church.

January 1979—news edition of *Saints Herald* begins as a separate midmonth publication.

April 6, 1979—Mackay Hall, Park College, entered in the National Register of Historic Places.

August 19, 1979—Lamoni, Iowa, celebrates its centennial year.

April 9, 1980—first Oriental apostle, Kisuke Sekine, ordained at the Sesquicentennial World Conference.

September 1981—*Hymns of the Saints* published and introduced at a churchwide worship workshop.

September 26, 1984—Barbara McFarlane Higdon inaugurated as president of Graceland College.

June 1985—Herald House celebrates *Saints Herald*'s 125th year.

July 1985—*Saints Herald* midmonth and first-of-the-month editions combined to make one monthly publication.

November 17, 1985—eighty-five women ordained into Aaronic and Melchisedec priesthoods.

June 20-21, 1986—peace symposium at Kirtland Temple.

July 1, 1987—Donald J. Breckon becomes new president of Park College.

December 1-2, 1989—working conference on peace at Washington, D.C., Metropole.

April 6, 1990—groundbreaking for the Temple in Independence, Missouri.

1990-1991—Herald House publishes new editions of Inspired Version, Doctrine and Covenants, and Book of Mormon (1908 and 1966) using newest computerized technology.

1991—number of women ordained exceeds 3,000.

Presidents of the Church

Joseph Smith, Jr.—ordained January 25, 1832; killed June 27, 1844.

Joseph Smith, III—ord. April 6, 1860; died December 10, 1914.

Frederick M. Smith—ord. May 5, 1915; d. March 20, 1946.

Israel A. Smith—ord. April 7, 1946; d. June 14, 1958.

W. Wallace Smith—ord. October 6, 1958; president emeritus April 5, 1978; d. August 4, 1989.

Wallace B. Smith—ord. president designate March 31, 1976; ord. president April 5, 1978.

Counselors in the Presidency

Jesse Gauze—left the church in 1832 before being ordained.

Sidney Rigdon—ord. March 18, 1833; rejected 1844.

Frederick G. Williams—ord. March 18, 1833; rej. and released November 7, 1837.

Hyrum Smith—ord. November 7, 1837; ord. patriarch January 19, 1841; killed June 27, 1844.

William Law—ord. January 19, 1841; expelled April 18, 1844.

William Marks—ord. April 1863; d. May 22, 1872.

William W. Blair—ord. April 10, 1873; d. April 18, 1896.

David H. Smith—ord. April 10, 1873; r. April 1885.

Alexander H. Smith—ord. April 9, 1897; r. and ord. presiding patriarch April 18, 1902.

E. L. Kelley—ord. April 9, 1897; r. and ord. presiding bishop April 18, 1902.

Frederick M. Smith—ord. April 18, 1902; ord. president of the church May 5, 1915.

Richard C. Evans—ord. April 20, 1902; r. and ord. bishop April 20, 1909.

Elbert A. Smith—ord. April 20, 1909; also ord. counselor to Frederick M. Smith May 5, 1915; r. and ord. presiding patriarch April 10, 1938.

Floyd M. McDowell—ord. October. 15, 1922; resigned October 20, 1938.

Israel A. Smith—ord. April 14, 1940; r. and ord. president of church April 7, 1946; d. June 14, 1958.

L. F. P. Curry—ord. April 14, 1940; r. April 7, 1946; d. January 23, 1977.

John F. Garver—ord. April 10, 1946; d. March 3, 1949.

F. Henry Edwards—ord. April 10, 1946; ord. counselor to W. Wallace Smith October 8, 1958; r. April 19, 1966.

W. Wallace Smith—ord. April 4, 1950; ord. president of church October 6, 1958.

Maurice L. Draper—ord. October 8, 1958; r. April 6, 1978.

Duane E. Couey—ord. April 19, 1966; ord. counselor to W. Wallace Smith April 6, 1978; r. and ord. presiding patriarch March 31, 1982.

Howard S. Sheehy, Jr.—ord. April 6, 1978.

Alan D. Tyree—ord. March 31, 1982.

Quorum of Twelve Apostles

*Thomas B. Marsh—ord. April 25, 1835; expelled 1839.

David W. Patten—ord. February 15, 1835; killed October 25, 1838.

*Brigham Young—ord. February 14, 1835; rej. 1844.

Heber C. Kimball—ord. February 14, 1835; rej. 1844.

Orson Hyde—ord. February 15, 1835; rej. 1844.

William McLellin—ord. February 15, 1835; expelled 1838.

Parley P. Pratt—ord. February 21, 1835; rej. 1844.

Luke S. Johnson—ord. February 15, 1835; expelled April 13, 1838.

William B. Smith—ord. February 15, 1835; rej. 1844.

Orson Pratt—ord. April 26, 1835; rej. 1844.

John F. Boynton—ord. February 15, 1835; dropped 1838.

Lyman E. Johnson—ord. February 14, 1835; expelled 1838.

John Taylor—ord. December 19, 1838; rej. 1844.

John E. Page—ord. December 19, 1838; rej. 1844.

Wilford Woodruff—ord. April 26, 1839; rej. 1844.

George A. Smith—ord. April 26, 1839; rej. 1844.

Willard Richards—ord. April 14, 1840; rej. 1844.

Lyman Wight—ord. April 4, 1841; rej. 1844.

*Jason W. Briggs—ord. April 8, 1853; r. April 1886.

Zenos H. Gurley, Sr.—ord. April 8, 1853; d. August 28, 1871.

Daniel B. Rasey—ord. April 8, 1853; r. April 1873.

R. W. Newkirk—ord. April 8, 1853; r. April 1873.

Henry H. Deam—ord. April 8, 1853; r. October 1864.

John Cunningham—ord. April 8, 1853; r. October 1854.

George White—ord. April 8, 1853; r. October 18, 1863.

David Newkirk—ord. April 1855; r. April 7, 1865.

Samuel Powers—ord. April 1855; d. February 16, 1873.

William W. Blair—ord. October 7, 1858; reassigned as counselor to Joseph Smith III April 1873.

James Blakeslee—ord. October 6, 1860; d. December 18, 1866.

Edmund C. Briggs—ord. October 6, 1860; r. and ord. evangelist April 18, 1902.

John Shippy—ord. October 6, 1860; cut off April 1868; later rebaptized and ord. elder.

Josiah Ells—ord. April 1865; d. October 15, 1885.

Charles Derry—ord. April 1865; resigned April 1870.

John H. Lake—ord. April 10, 1873; r. and ord. evangelist April 1902.

Thomas W. Smith—ord. April 10, 1873; d. May 27, 1894.

*Alexander H. Smith—ord. April 10, 1873; r. and ord. counselor to Joseph Smith III and as presiding patriarch April 1897.

*William H. Kelley—ord. April 10, 1873; r. April 19, 1913.

Joseph R. Lambert—ord. April 10, 1873; r. and ord. evangelist April 1902.

Zenas H. Gurley, Jr.—ord. April 9, 1874; r. April 1886.

James Caffall—ord. September 5, 1873; r. April 1902.

James W. Gillen—ord. April 13, 1887; r. 1900.

Heman C. Smith—ord. March 30, 1888; r. April 1909; elected church historian April 16, 1897.

Joseph Luff—ord. April 13, 1887; r. and appointed church physician April 1909.

*Gomer T. Griffiths—ord. April 13, 1887; r. and ord. evangelist October 1922.

I. N. White—ord. April 12, 1897; r. and ord. evangelist April 14, 1913.

John W. Wight—ord. April 12, 1897; r. April 1913.

Richard C. Evans—ord. April 12, 1897; r. and ord. counselor to Joseph Smith III April 20, 1902.

Peter Andersen—ord. April 7, 1901; r. April 1920.

Frederick A. Smith—ord. April 19, 1902; r. and ord. presiding patriarch April 20, 1913.

Francis M. Sheehy—ord. April 20, 1902; r. April 1920.

Ulysses W. Greene—ord. April 20, 1902; r. and ord. evangelist October 1922.

Cornelius A. Butterworth—ord. April 23, 1902; r. October 18, 1922.

John W. Rushton—ord. April 20, 1902; r. April 1947.

James F. Curtis—ord. April 20, 1909; r. and ord. evangelist April 9, 1938.

Robert C. Russell—ord. April 20, 1909; r. and ord. evangelist October 18, 1922.

James E. Kelley—ord. April 19, 1913; d. June 4, 1917.

William Aylor—ord. April 19, 1913; resigned October 18, 1922.

*Paul M. Hanson—ord. April 19, 1913; r. October 8, 1958.

*James A. Gillen—ord. May 19, 1913; resigned April 13, 1934.

Myron A. McConley—ord. April 8, 1920; r. and ord. evangelist October 5, 1948.

Thomas W. Williams—ord. April 8, 1920; r. April 1925.

John F. Garver—ord. October 13, 1922; r. and ord. counselor to Israel A. Smith April 10, 1946.

D. T. Williams—ord. October 13, 1922; r. and ord. evangelist October 8, 1958.

F. Henry Edwards—ord. October 13, 1922; r. and ord. counselor to Israel A. Smith April 10, 1946.

Edmund J. Gleazer, Sr.—ord. October 13, 1922; r. and ord. evangelist October 8, 1958.

Roy S. Budd—ord. October 13, 1922; r. October 1936.

Clyde F. Ellis—ord. September 30, 1923; d. June 21, 1945.

George G. Lewis—ord. April 15, 1932; d. September 14, 1948.

C. George Mesley—ord. April 10, 1938; resigned April 10, 1954.

Arthur A. Oakman—ord. April 10, 1938; r. and ord. evangelist April 6, 1964.

*Charles R. Hield—ord. June 19, 1938; r. April 6, 1964.

D. Blair Jensen—ord. April 10, 1946; r. April 18, 1966.

W. Wallace Smith—ord. April 8, 1947; r. and ord. counselor to Israel A. Smith April 4, 1950.

Roscoe E. Davey—ord. April 8, 1947; r. and ord. evangelist April 6, 1964.

Maurice L. Draper—ord. April 8, 1947; r. and ord. counselor to W. Wallace Smith October 8, 1958.

Reed M. Holmes—ord. October 5, 1948; r. and ord. presiding patriarch April 3, 1974.

Percy E. Farrow—ord. October 5, 1948; r. April 18, 1966.

Donald O. Chesworth—ord. April 4, 1950; r. April 14, 1972.

Donald V. Lents—ord. August 29, 1954; r. April 9, 1980.

*Charles D. Neff—ord. October 8, 1958; r. April 3, 1984.

*Clifford A. Cole—ord. October 8, 1958; r. April 9, 1980.

Duane E. Couey—ord. April 5, 1960; r. and ord. counselor to W. Wallace Smith April 19, 1966; ord. counselor to President Wallace B. Smith April 6, 1978; r. and ord. presiding patriarch March 31, 1982.

Cecil R. Ettinger—ord. April 5, 1960; r. April 3, 1974.

Russell F. Ralston—ord. April 7, 1964; r. April 2, 1976.

William E. Timms—ord. April 7, 1964; r. April 6, 1978.

Alan D. Tyree—ord. April 19, 1966; r. and ord. counselor to Wallace B. Smith March 31, 1982.

Earl T. Higdon—ord. April 19, 1966; r. April 3, 1974.

Aleah G. Koury—ord. April 19, 1966; r. April 9, 1980.

Howard S. Sheehy, Jr.—ord. April 5, 1968; r. and ord. counselor to Wallace B. Smith April 6, 1978.

J. C. Stuart—ord. April 15, 1972; r. March 31, 1982.

*Paul W. Booth—ord. April 4, 1974.

*William T. Higdon—ord. April 4, 1974.

Lloyd B. Hurshman—ord. April 4, 1974; r. April 14, 1988.

C. Eugene Austin, Sr.—ord. April 2, 1976.

Roy H. Schaefer—ord. April 6, 1978; r. April 14, 1988.

317

Phillip M. Caswell—ord. April 6, 1978.
Kisuke Sekine—ord. April 9, 1980.
Everett S. Graffeo—ord. April 9, 1980.
Kenneth N. Robinson—ord. April 9, 1980.
Joe A. Serig—ord. March 31, 1982.
James C. Cable—ord. March 31, 1982.
**Geoffrey F. Spencer—ord. April 6, 1984.
A. Alex Kahtava—ord. April 15, 1988.
John P. Kirkpatrick—ord. April 15, 1988.

---

*Served as president of the Quorum of Twelve
**Current president of the Quorum of Twelve

Presiding Bishops

Edward Partridge—ord. February 1831; d. May 27, 1840.

George Miller (successor to Partridge as presiding bishop)—ord. November 19, 1841; rej. 1844.

I. L. Rogers—ord. April 7, 1860; resigned April 1882 (was first bishop of the Reorganization).

George A. Blakeslee—ord. April 1882; d. September 20, 1890.

E. L. Kelley—ord. April 10, 1891; r. April 1916.

Benjamin R. McGuire—ord. April 16, 1916; r. April 19, 1925.

A. Carmichael—ord. April 19, 1925; r. April 15, 1932.

L.F.P. Curry—ord. April 17, 1932 (acting since February 1931); served as counselor to Frederick M. Smith in addition to duties as presiding bishop (1938-1940); r. as presiding bishop and ord. counselor to Frederick M. Smith April 14, 1940.

G. Leslie DeLapp—ord. April 14, 1940; r. April 18, 1966.

Walter N. Johnson—ord. April 19, 1966; r. April 15, 1972.

Francis E. Hansen—ord. April 15, 1972; r. April 14, 1988; ord. evangelist April 15, 1988.

Gene M. Hummel—ord. April 15, 1988.

Counselors to Presiding Bishops

Isaac Morley—ord. June 3, 1831; r. (at death of Partridge) 1840.

John Corrill—ord. June 3, 1831; r. August 1, 1837.

Titus Billings—ord. August 1, 1837; r. (at death of Partridge) 1840.

William Aldrich—ord. April 1866; r. April 1873.

Philo Howard—never ordained but appointed April 1866; d. January 25, 1869.

Elijah Banta—ord. April 1873; resigned October 1874; ord. April 1882; resigned April 1891 (at death of Blakeslee).

David Dancer—ord. April 1873; resigned April 1882 (at resignation of I.L. Rogers).

Henry Stebbins—ord. April 1875; resigned April 1882 (at resignation of I.L. Rogers).

E. L. Kelley—ord. April 13, 1882; r. and ord. presiding bishop April 10, 1891.

George H. Hilliard—ord. April 1891; d. October 8, 1912.

Edwin A. Blakeslee—ord. April 1891; resigned April 1916.

James F. Keir—ord. April 1916; r. April 1925.

Israel A. Smith—ord. April 1920; r. April 1925.

Mark H. Siegfried—ord. April 19, 1925; r. February 1931.

John A. Becker—ord. April 13, 1926; r. February 1931.

G. Leslie DeLapp—ord. April 17, 1932 (active from February 1931); r. and ord. presiding bishop April 14, 1940.

N. Ray Carmichael—ord. April 8, 1934; r. April 14, 1940.

Clarence A. Skinner—ord. April 14, 1940; resigned April 9, 1946.

Henry L. Livingston—ord. April 14, 1940; r. April 18, 1966.

Walter N. Johnson—ord. April 14, 1946; r. and ord. presiding bishop April 19, 1966.

Francis E. Hansen—ord. April 19, 1966; r. and ord. presiding bishop April 15, 1972.

Harold W. Cackler—ord. April 19, 1966; r. April 6, 1978.

Gene M. Hummel—ord. April 14, 1972; r. and ord. presiding bishop April 15, 1988.

Ray E. McClaran—ord. April 6, 1978.

Norman E. Swails—ord. April 14, 1988.

Presiding Patriarchs
(Presiding Evangelists)

Joseph Smith, Sr.—ord. December 18, 1833; d. September 14, 1840.

Hyrum Smith—ord. January 19, 1841; killed June 27, 1844.

Alexander H. Smith—ord. April 9, 1897; d. August 12, 1909.

Joseph R. Lambert—ord. April 17, 1910; r. April 20, 1913.

Frederick A. Smith—ord. April 20, 1913; r. and named emeritus April 10, 1938; d. June 25, 1954.

Elbert A. Smith—ord. April 10, 1938, r. October 8, 1958.

Roy A. Cheville—ord. October 8, 1958, r. and named emeritus April 3, 1974.

Reed M. Holmes—ord. April 4, 1974; r. March 31, 1982.

Duane E. Couey—ord. March 31, 1982.

Presidents of High Priests Quorum

Don Carlos Smith—ord. February 15, 1836; d. August 7, 1841.

C. C. Rich—ord. high priest in Missouri August 10, 1837; expelled 1839.

George Miller—ord. fall 1841; rej. 1844.

Isaac Sheen—ord. April 9, 1850; d. April 1874.

Charles Derry—ord. April 1874; resigned April 19, 1901.

Frederick G. Pitt—ord. April 19, 1901; ord. evangelist April 17, 1910.

Joseph A. Tanner—ord. April 17, 1910; r. October 1928.

John F. Sheehy—chosen pro tem October 1928; r. April 1932 (not ordained).

Ward A. Hougas—ord. April 15, 1932; r. October 12, 1958.

Garland E. Tickemyer—ord. October 12, 1958; resigned April 12, 1972.

Roy H. Schaefer—appointed president pro tem April 13, 1972; r. April 4, 1974.

Geoffrey F. Spencer—ord. April 4, 1974; r. and ord. apostle April 6, 1984.

Paul M. Edwards—ord. April 6, 1984.

Presidents of Seventy

Hazen Aldrich—ord. March 1, 1835; r. and ord. high priest April 6, 1837.

Joseph W. Young—ord. March 1, 1835; rej. 1844.

Levi W. Hancock—ord. February 28, 1835; rej. 1844.

Leonard Rich—ord. February 28, 1835; r. and ord. high priest April 6, 1837.

Zebedee Coltrin—ord. March 1, 1835; r. and ord. high priest April 6, 1837.

Lyman Sherman—ord. March 1, 1835; r. and ord. high priest April 6, 1837.

Sylvester Smith—ord. March 1, 1835; r. and ord. high priest April 6, 1837.

John Gould—ord. April 6, 1837; r. and ord. high priest September 3.

James Foster—ord. April 6, 1837; d. December 21, 1841.

Daniel S. Miles—ord. April 6, 1837; rej. 1844; d. 1845.

Josiah Butterfield—ord. April 6, 1837; rej. 1844; d. 1844.

Salmon Gee—ord. April 6, 1837; dropped March 6, 1838.

John Gaylord—ord. April 6, 1837; expelled January 13, 1838.

Henry Harriman—ord. February 6, 1838; rej. 1844.

Zera Pulsipher—ord. March 6, 1838; rej. 1844.

Archibald M. Wilsey—ord. April 6, 1860; r. and ord. high priest April 6, 1873.

William D. Morton—ord. April 6, 1860; r. and ord. high priest April 1873.

George Rarick—ord. April 7, 1860; r. and ord. high priest April 10, 1873.

Crowell G. Lamphear—ord. April 6, 1860; r. and ord. high priest April 1879.

E. C. Briggs—ord. July 1, 1852; r. and ord. apostle October 12, 1860.

James Blakeslee—ord. April 6, 1860; r. and ord. apostle October 1860.

John A. McIntosh—ord. July 3, 1860; r. and ord. high priest October 8, 1869.

Edmund C. Brand—ord. September 12, 1875; d. October 12, 1890.

Duncan Campbell—ord. April 1873; r. and ord. high priest May 1901.

Charles W. Wandell—ord. August 22, 1873; d. March 14, 1875.

Glaud Rodger—ord. April 18, 1880; d. August 3, 1884.

John S. Patterson—ord. April 11, 1885; expelled April 1887.

James W. Gillen—ord. April 14, 1885; r. and ord. apostle April 13, 1887.

Heman C. Smith—ord. April 14, 1885; r. and ord. apostle March 30, 1888.

Columbus Scott—ord. April 14, 1885; resigned April 1915.

John T. Davies—ord. April 14, 1885; r. and ord. high priest April 19, 1900.

I. N. White—ord. April 14, 1888; r. and ord. apostle April 12, 1897.

John C. Foss—ord. April 14, 1888; superannuated April 18, 1905.

Robert J. Anthony—ord. April 1, 1889; d. May 9, 1899.

James McKiernan—ord. April 10, 1891; resigned April 8, 1916.

Francis M. Sheehy—ord. April 14, 1897; r. and ord. apostle April 16, 1902.

Hyrum O. Smith—ord. April 20, 1900; r. and ord. high priest April 16, 1913.

James F. Mintun—ord. April 20, 1900; r. and ord. high priest April 13, 1917.

Warren E. Peak—ord. April 20, 1900; r. and ord. high priest April 13, 1917.

Romanan Wight—ord. April 1902; resigned April 1909.

T. C. Kelley—ord. April 18, 1906; r. and ord. high priest April 1926.

John A. Davis—ord. April 20, 1909; r. and ord. high priest November 20, 1921.

Elmer E. Long—ord. April 7, 1916; returned to quorum membership April 7, 1926.

Arthur B. Phillips—ord. April 8, 1913; r. and ord. a bishop December 2, 1923.

James T. Riley—ord. April 1916; returned to quorum membership April 8, 1926.

James W. Davis—ord. April 13, 1918; resigned April 1942.

Edward A. Curtis—ord. April 1920; r. 1932.

Raleigh L. Fulk—ord. October 7, 1923.

Eli Bronson—ord. April 1926; r. April 1932.

Roscoe E. Davey—ord. April 1926; r. and ord. apostle April 8, 1947.

Guy P. Levitt—ord. April 1926; resigned May 1937.

Ernest Y. Hunker—ord. April 15, 1932; r. and ord. evangelist April 1952; d. March 22, 1966.

Harold I. Velt—ord. April 15, 1934; r. and ord. evangelist December 30, 1951.

Zenos Z. Renfroe—ord. April 10, 1938; selected senior president April 1952; r. April 8, 1960.

Percy E. Farrow—ord. April 12, 1942; r. and ord. apostle October 5, 1948.

Glen H. Johnson—ord. April 9, 1947; r. April 7, 1964.

George A. Njeim—ord. April 13, 1947; r. April 6, 1970.

James C. Daugherty—ord. April 8, 1948; r. and ord. high priest April 4, 1968; d. June 22, 1974.

Russell F. Ralston—ord. April 6, 1950; selected senior president April 1960; r. and ord. apostle April 1964.

Sylvester R. Coleman—ord. April 8, 1954; r. and ord. high priest December 12, 1965.

Harry L. Doty—ord. April 8, 1954; selected senior president April 1964; r. and ord. evangelist 1976.

C. Houston Hobart—ord. April 10, 1960; r. April 10, 1980.

Luther S. Troyer—ord. April 8, 1964; r. and ord. evanglist April 12, 1972.

Harry W. Black—ord. April 9, 1964; selected senior president April 1, 1976; r. 1986.

Louis C. Zonker—ord. April 21, 1966; resigned and ord. evangelist March 1977.

Wayne E. Simmons—ord. April 5, 1968; r. May 1973.

T. Ed Barlow—ord. April 12, 1970; d. November 20, 1979.

A. Alexander Kahtava—ord. April 4, 1974; r. and ord. apostle April 15, 1988.

Victor B. Hatch, Jr.—ord. April 1, 1976; r. April 15, 1988.

Kenneth E. Stobaugh—ord. April 1, 1976; r. and ord. high priest April 11, 1986.

Clayton H. Condit—ord. April 10, 1980.

Gary B. Beebe—ord. April 10, 1980; r. and ord. high priest April 1984.

Ray J. Burdekin—ord. March 31, 1982.

Joe B. Bayless—ord. March 31, 1982; selected senior president April 1988.

Don H. Compier, ord. April 11, 1986, res. 1988.

Richard W. Hawks—ord. April 16, 1986.

David R. Brock—ord. April 16, 1988.

Stephen M. Veazey—ord. April 16, 1988.

Stephen A. Koehler—ord. April 6, 1988.

General Church Women's Leaders

Advisory Board, Daughters of Zion

Anna Stedman—senior member, 1893

Marietta Walker—senior member, 1894-1895

Cassie B. Kelley—chairperson, 1896

Bertha A. Greer—chairperson, 1897

Mary E. Hulmes—president, 1898-1904

Emma E. Smith—president, 1905-1910

Advisory Board, Women's Auxiliary for Social Service

Emma E. Smit— president, 1911-1913

Evaline Burgess—president, 1914-1916

Lula M. Sandy—president, 1917

Grace Krahl—president, 1918-1919

Ruth L. Cobb—director general, 1920-1921

Dora Pankey Gliners—superintendent, 1922-1924

Blanche Edwards—superintendent, 1925-1927

Dona C. Haden—1928

Lenoir Woodstock—1930-1934

General Council of Women

Pauline James Arnson—director, 1934-1955
Alice Burgess—leader, 1955-1958
Kathryn Westwood—leader, 1958-1970
Marjorie Troeh—women's ministry consultant, 1970-1974

Women's Ministry

Marjorie Troeh—commissioner, 1974-1982
Ardis Everett—acting and commissioner, 1982-1985
Carol Anway—acting commissioner, 1985-1990
Gail E. Mengel—commissioner, 1990-

Index*

---

*Does not include references in Appendix

Lamoni, Iowa, 173ff., 188, 231ff., 236, 242.
Lancaster, Richard, 266.
Landon, Donald, 266.
Latter Day Saints' Messenger and Advocate, 67, 124.
Law, William, 109, 160, 162.
Law, Wilson, 109.
Law of Consecration, 69ff., 89.
Lectures on Faith, 68.
Letter of Instruction left by Joseph Smith III, 201.
Liberty, Missouri, 84, 91.
Liberty Jail, 91.
Luff, Joseph, 183, 239.
Lyman, Amasa, 91.

McConley, Myron A., 212.
McDowell, Floyd M., 213.
McGuire, Benjamin M., 200, 248.
McLellin, William, 88.
McRae, Alexander, 91.
Mack, Lucy, 28.
Mack, Solomon, 28.
Manchester, New York, 36, 38, 39, 45, 49.
Mansion House (Nauvoo), 99.
Marks, William, 92, 99, 119, 132ff., 241.
Marriage, celestial, 107ff.
Marsh, Thomas B., 76, 92.
Masonry, 100.
Meder, Moses A., 175.
Mentor, Ohio, 50, 52.
Messenger, The, 155.
Messenger and Advocate (Rigdon's), 124.
Metropoles, 253.
Mexico, 254, 272.
Millennial Star, 105.
Miller, George, 71.
Montrose, Iowa, 92.
Mormon Battalion, 102.
Moroni, 35ff.
Mulholland, James, 34, 35.
Murdock, John, 51.

Nauvoo, Illinois, 35, 46, 68, 92, 95ff., 133.
Nauvoo Charter, 96ff., 114.
Nauvoo Expositor, 109ff., 113.
Nauvoo House, 40, 100.
Nauvoo Legion, 98, 110, 113.
Nauvoo Temple (see Temple, Nauvoo).
Neff, Charles D., 258, 260, 271.
Nelson, William, 147.
New Caledonia, 272.